The Hidden Price of
GREATNESS

The Hidden

GREAT

Ray Beeson &

Price of

NESS

Ranelda Mack Hunsicker

Overcomers Ministries
Ventura, California

Formerly Published by:
Tyndale House Publishers, Inc. WHEATON, ILLINOIS

Formerly published by Tyndale House Publishers, Inc. with ISBN 0-8423-1380-X

Library of Congress Cataloging-in-Publication Data

Beeson, Ray.
  The hidden price of greatness / Ray Beeson and Ranelda Mack
Hunsicker.
      p.   cm.
  Includes bibliographical references.
  ISBN 0-9748269-0-1
  1. Christian biography.   I. Hunsicker, Ranelda Mack, date.
II. Title.
BR1700.2.B44   1991
270'.092'2—dc20
[B]   91-25605

Material from *The Letters of Francis Schaeffer,* edited by Lane T. Dennis,
copyright © 1985, used by permission of Good News Publishers/
Crossway Books, Wheaton, Illinois 60187.

Material from *Light in My Darkest Night,* by Catherine Marshall,
copyright © 1989 by Leonard E. LeSourd, published by Chosen Books,
Fleming H. Revell Company, Old Tappan, N.J. Used by permission.

Unless otherwise noted, Scripture quotations are from the *Holy Bible,*
New International Version. Copyright © 1973, 1978, 1984 International
Bible Society. Used by permission of Zondervan Bible Publishers.
Scripture quotations marked NASB are from the *New American
Standard Bible,* copyright © 1960, 1962, 1963, 1968, 1971, 1972, 1973,
1975, 1977 by The Lockman Foundation. Used by permission.

97   96   95   94   93
8   7   6   5   4   3

Ray Beeson
dedicates this book to his parents,
Bob and Agnes Beeson.
In believing in me,
you have added strength to my life.

Ranelda Mack Hunsicker
dedicates this book to her parents,
Dr. Frank J. and Inez Mack.
Your gentle strength under pressure
taught me first and best
what Jesus meant when he said,
"Whoever wants to become great among you
must be your servant."

Ray Beeson

In 1983 Ray Beeson founded Overcomers Ministries as a teaching ministry with an emphasis on spiritual warfare and prayer. Ray's full-time ministry began with Dick Eastman at the International Prayer Corp in 1975. Later, he taught Eastman's seminar "The Change The World School of Prayer" as part of the World Literature Crusade ministry, traveling throughout much of the United States and parts of Canada.

Ray graduated from Central Washington State College in 1967 with a Bachelor's Degree in Mathematics/Education, and in 1973 with a Master's Degree in Secondary School Administration. He went on to teach public school mathematics in Washington State for the next eight years.

His ministry has also involved youth pasturing and writing. His books include *The Real Battle* (Tyndale, 1988), *That I May Know Him* (Fleming Revell, 1990), *The Hidden Price of Greatness* co-authored with Ranelda Hunsicker (Tyndale, 1991), *Spiritual Warfare and Your Children* co-authored with Kathi Mills (Thomas Nelson, 1993), *Create In Me a Clean Heart* (Thomas Nelson, 1995), *Strategic Spiritual Warfare* co-authored with Patricia Hulsey (Thomas Nelson, 1995) and *In Memory of Joseph Greycloud* (Overcomers Ministries, 1997).

Currently Ray is concentrating on three primary subjects in his teaching and writing: Spiritual warfare, prayer, and the life of Jesus.

Ranelda Mack Hunsicker

For Ranelda, life is a quest, and her delight is taking people with her on the journey...through writing, presenting workshops, and leading small groups. She has a passion for finding out the "how and why" of things, probing life's mysteries, and tracing God's guiding hand in it all.

Before devoting her energies completely to writing, she taught at the elementary and high school levels in public and private schools. She has served in the church as a Sunday school teacher, children's church director, and workshop speaker. Her writing credits include *Teachers in Focus, Guideposts, Decision, The Christian Reader, Sunday Digest,* and other inspirational magazines. In addition to her freelance writing projects, Ranelda enjoyed seven years as a staffwriter for *Insight for Living*, the radio ministry of Chuck Swindoll.

Ranelda's published book projects are:
- *David Brainerd* (Bethany House *Men of Faith* series, 1999), a biography of the colonial missionary to Native Americans whose journal is still a devotional classic.
- *How to Grow a Young Reader*, co-authored with Kathryn Lindskoog (Shaw Publishers, 1999); a lively exploration of children's literature for parents and teachers with annotated reading lists;
- *In God We Trust: Stories of Faith in American History* (co-authored with Tim Crater; Chariot, 1997); fifty narratives for young readers about men and women who played important roles in our nation's development;
- *The Hidden Price of Greatness* (co-authored with Ray Beeson; Tyndale, 1991; foreword by Sherwood Wirt; condensed version published and distributed by the Billy Graham Evangelistic Assoc.), an inspiring look at how suffering shaped the lives of nineteen outstanding Christians;
- *Secrets: Unlocking the Mystery of Intimacy with God* (Aglow, 1991).

CONTENTS

ACKNOWLEDGMENTS

From Ray Beeson:

Many projects are completed only because of team effort. This is the case with *The Hidden Price of Greatness*. I had the privilege of playing quarterback on the team. Each time I passed the ball, however, it was caught by Ranelda. Repeatedly her ability to communicate with style and simplicity helped score touchdowns. In many instances, she formulated the plays as well as carrying the ball. Although my heart is deeply imbedded in every line of the work, this is truly Ranelda's book.

There were several other important team members. My wife, Linda, provided support and encouragement for me. Research from Dave Guzik, Lance Ralston, Norm Green, and Carl Dreves strengthened our strategy. For each effort, small or great, thank you.

Another group of people to whom I owe much are those who struggled on in pain. They remained faithful to the Lord and thus added courage to my life. Many of them are represented in the biographies of this book; many are not. I am thankful for all their stories. In my deepest trials I know now I am not alone.

From Ranelda Mack Hunsicker:

My greatest thanks goes to the many Christian biographers and historians who cared enough to record the tears and triumphs of others and to the transparent believers who shared their struggles to walk as Christ walked.

Thanks also to my husband, Don, who ate TV dinners while I did research, read and responded to every page I wrote, and didn't complain about driving to Ventura or paying the phone bill. For better and for worse he has proved the greatness of love.

I am also indebted to my critique group—Carol Houdek and Linette and Paul Thomas—who worked through this book with me, to my pastor Gordon Slyter who introduced me to Ray Beeson, to my dear friend Kathryn Lindskoog who provided valuable insights and encouragement, and to Harold Ivan Smith who asked the right question: "Where are the real heroes in an age of celebrities?"

FOREWORD

Having published a number of books about great Christians of the past and present, I thought I knew them pretty well, but this volume by Ray Beeson and Ranelda Mack Hunsicker tops them all. I am delighted to be able to introduce the reader to this well-researched investigation into the "Price of Greatness" that was exacted from the lives of some of God's choice servants.

Behind the fame which has come down to us in the 1990s we see depicted here lives that were full of challenges, obstacles, and defeats, as well as glorious victories and accomplishments. As we sit with our cups of coffee and read about the trials and disappointments, the agony and the ecstasy that was part of their everyday living, we wonder whether we, in their sandals, could have measured up.

Not only does this thoughtful book describe the way these men and women served the Lord, it seeks to draw from their life-styles and accomplishments guidance for us who are committed to serving the Lord Jesus Christ in this generation. You will glean much information from these pages, but you will also learn how to apply the principles of effective Christian living to yourself in today's environment. I commend this book warmly and hope its influence will go far and wide throughout the fellowship of believers who make up the Body of Christ.

Sherwood Eliot Wirt

INTRODUCTION

In the pages of this book, you will meet Christians who learned to use pain as a tool for growth. Out of their weakness, they became strong. Jesus Christ warned his followers that anyone desiring to become great in God's kingdom must be willing to share his suffering. Seneca, the Roman philosopher and statesman, said, "It is a rough road that leads to the heights of greatness."

Unfortunately, Christians often distort God's purpose in pain. In an effort to display the abundant life Jesus promised, some paint unrealistic pictures of the prosperity, health, and comfort available to those who follow Christ. Others pursue the opposite extreme, glorifying pain and unwittingly attributing evil to a good God.

We desperately need a clear understanding of the role that pain plays in character formation and the perfecting of faith. Jesus never called us to become masochists. God takes no pleasure in our pain. However, he takes great pleasure in our development. Suffering is never the goal; it is the road.

In an effort to profit from the pain in our lives, we began searching Scripture and the history of the church for a clear perspective on the subject. What we discovered is a mighty cloud of witnesses, all testifying that Christian suffering is essential to holiness and effective witness. Across centuries, cultures, and circumstances, the evidence agrees.

Missionary and author Lettie Cowman captures the heart of what we learned in these words:

> *Grief has always been the lot of greatness.*
> *It is an open secret.*

It's time we freed ourselves from the prevalent idea that the power of God in a human life should lift it above all trials and conflicts. Suffering saints are not second-class Christians. The fact is, God's power produces conflict, struggle, *and* growth.

This book showcases portraits of ordinary people who *became* extraordinary as they walked down life's hard roads. Adversity worked in them determination to triumph. These heroes of faith demonstrate the power of the New Testament message that through Christ we are more than conquerors.

In each chapter you will find: (1) a true story of God's transforming power at work in human pain, (2) a summary of the prizes won by those who paid the price, and (3) an opportunity to apply healing principles to your own hurts. Obviously, pain can't be divided into neat categories. It cuts across boundaries, wounding us spiritually, physically, mentally, and relationally. But it may dominate in a particular area, and so we have clustered the chapters into sections to aid you in finding immediate help for your deepest point of need.

The scenes shared from the lives of famous Christians have been slightly dramatized in order to more accurately convey their emotional impact. However, much care has been taken in maintaining complete integrity of historical fact. In order to make your reading experience more personal and less academic, we have not footnoted our sources. An extensive bibliography of our sources substantiates our research.

We encourage you to use the biographical timelines and bibliographic notes at the end of the book to continue exploring the dimensions of Christian character found in the lives of God's people.

As you read *The Hidden Price of Greatness*, our deepest prayer is that you will be better enabled to "live a life worthy of the Lord . . . bearing fruit in every good work, growing in the knowledge of

God, being strengthened with all power according to his glorious might so that you may have great endurance and patience" (Col. 1:10-12). May you increasingly realize the greatness God has planned for you.

Ray Beeson
Ranelda Mack Hunsicker

Section One

•••••••••••••••

PEOPLE
PAIN

CHAPTER 1
From Prodigal to Pillar

Augustine and his friends strolled down one of Milan's busy streets. Preoccupied with a speech he was mentally rehearsing, Augustine almost collided with a jubilant beggar. "Look at that poor fellow," he said with amusement when the man passed by them. "Have you ever seen anyone so pitifully happy?"

They laughed at the beggar, who had obviously reaped a bountiful day of begging. He joked with passersby, his stomach full and his mind momentarily free from care.

As Augustine watched him, his amusement turned to despair. The man's happiness stung his sense of justice. "Meanwhile, for all my labors and intricate maneuvers, happiness eludes me," Augustine muttered.

"What ails Milan's great public orator?" quipped one of the young men who walked beside him. "Worried about your speech in honor of the emperor?"

"Only about the number of lies that fill it!" Augustine retorted. The others laughed, but he felt ill. Surely life was more than this joyless performance for the court. If only he had the simple pleasures of that beggar, or, better yet, of Bishop Ambrose.

Could it be that after all the years of rejecting his mother's faith, he was to find truth in the doctrines of Christ and the

3

church? Each day he leaned more that way, sickened by his own life, the decadence of the Roman Empire, and the emptiness of the philosophies he studied.

One thing blocked him. *What was the source of evil? Where was its root?* No one could adequately explain that. Augustine had long struggled with this dark mystery at work in the world and in his own heart. It had left him exhausted, and still he saw no answer.

Augustine and his friend Alypius sat in their small home reading. There was nothing sweeter to the two men than poring over their books in one another's company. But lately the atmosphere had become heavy with the agony of Augustine's inner struggle.

Laying Paul's *Epistles* on the small table beside him, Augustine said, "I'm certain the path to man's salvation is found only in Christ and the Holy Scriptures."

"Then why not become a Christian and put this war of yours to rest?"

"Because, as I have told you before—"

"Yes, yes, I know," Alypius cut in. "A man of your passions was not meant for a life of chastity."

"Do not mock me, friend. I am firmly caught in the toil of sexual pleasure, a slave to my own lust."

"Come, Augustine, let us sit in the garden. Perhaps its coolness will subdue your fevered brain. This summer heat is merciless."

Augustine reached for the *Epistles* and walked with Alypius into the garden beside their home. He chose a tree near the one his friend took refuge under and sat down to read. Before long his agitation drove him to his feet. Leaving the book behind, he walked to a quiet corner of the garden and flung himself beneath a fig tree.

Hot tears coursed down his cheeks at the thought of his

wretched condition. *Is there any vile thing I have not done? Robbery. Fornication. Lying.* A thousand sins of the flesh that had broken his mother's heart.

Why not make an end of my ugly sins now? Why am I always saying "tomorrow"? The great storm broke within him, and he knew as never before his own powerlessness.

As he wept, the sing-song voice of a child came from the house nearby. Again and again the words came: "Take up, read! Take up, read!"

What game could the child be playing? Augustine wondered. He cast about in his mind for a chant like the one he heard, but remembered none. *Could it be a divine command to open the Scripture again? Will God at last give me an answer? Yes!*

Augustine rushed back to the place where Alypius was sitting, where he had abandoned Paul's *Epistles.* He opened the book and quickly read the first thing his eyes focused on. The words of Paul's letter to the Romans shot like an arrow into his heart:

> . . . not in orgies and drunkenness, not in sexual immorality and debauchery, not in dissension and jealousy.
> Rather, clothe yourselves with the Lord Jesus Christ.
> (13:13-14)

A light of confidence poured into his heart. All of his doubts fled. He marked the passage with his finger and closed the book. "Alypius, it is done. I am a Christian." Augustine marveled at the perfect calm he felt. "Let us go inside and tell Mother. She will be overjoyed."

From that day in the summer of 386, he put on the new clothes of Christ and took off the old tattered clothes of Augustine. He was nearly thirty-three years old, and for most of his life he had been a constant grief to his mother, Monica. She had watched him almost ruin his marvelous gifts in immorality and cultic beliefs. And every day she had prayed. Augustine's father, an ill-tempered pagan, took no interest in his son's prodigal lifestyle. At a time of particularly deep distress, Monica asked her bishop to talk with Augustine about his spiritual condition. The bishop told her such efforts were futile as long as Augustine remained unteachable. "Leave him alone for a time," he advised. "Only pray to God for him; he will of himself, by reading, discover what that error is, and how great its impiety."

Unconvinced, Monica continued begging the bishop to intervene. His response was much like the exasperated priest Eli's reaction to Hannah's agonized cry for a son. "Go thy way, and God bless thee," the bishop told Monica, "for it is not possible that the son of these tears should perish."

Monica's tears indeed watered a rich harvest. Though Augustine had many struggles and failures after he became a Christian, he never turned aside from his commitment to become a faithful disciple of Christ. With the same passion he had used in pursuing the world's pleasures, he began pursuing the Word of God and prayer.

On the eve of Easter 387, Monica saw her prodigal son and his illegitimate son baptized. It was the only thing on earth she had desired, and not long after that she died. Her funeral was not a time of mourning because Augustine knew she had died happy, content in the knowledge of his firm faith in Christ. Augustine returned to his birthplace in North Africa to spend the rest of his life in Christian service. There in the city of Tagaste he established the first monastic community in North Africa. He no longer had ambitions for success and fame, preferring a private life of spiritual devotion. About four years after his conversion he reluctantly became a priest. In another four years he became coadjutor bishop and by the age of forty-two was serving as bishop of Hippo. He continued in that office until his death at age seventy-six.

During those years Augustine wrote more than seventy

books, two of which—*Confessions* and *City of God*—remain part of great literature today. He preached almost every day, had an open-door policy regarding those who desired his counsel, corresponded with Christians throughout the Roman Empire, and contended forcefully with heretics.

Augustine laid firm foundation stones of theological teaching on the grace and sovereignty of God, justification by faith, the place of works in the Christian life, and secular versus spiritual kingdoms. His work strengthened the church to endure through the fall of the Roman Empire and the Dark Ages.

What We Can Learn from the Life of Augustine

We can scarcely imagine a less likely candidate for church leadership than Aurelius Augustine. Fascinated by sin from an early age and intent on fulfilling his desires, he was every parent's worst nightmare. The influence of a predominantly Christian society and the nurture of a devout mother seemed lost on the proud young man.

But God . . . These two marvelous words rewrote the story. It isn't what Augustine did that changed the course of his life and history; it is what God did.

> But because of his great love for us, God, who is rich in mercy, made us alive with Christ even when we were dead in transgressions. . . . And God raised us up with Christ and seated us with him in the heavenly realms in Christ Jesus, in order that in the coming ages he might show the incomparable riches of his grace, expressed in his kindness to us in Christ Jesus. (Eph. 2:4-7)

Even though Augustine had a rebellious life-style (was "dead" in his transgressions), God made him alive again and raised him

7

up with Christ. Augustine became a living testament to the grace of God. In studying his life and rich contribution to the church, we marvel at the transformation. We also wonder, Why did God do it like that? Why did he allow Augustine to waste years in sin and, no doubt, influence others to do likewise? Why did he wait so long to answer Monica's prayers? And why did he select a former prodigal as trustee of so many precious spiritual insights?

Human reason wouldn't do it that way. We prefer quick fixes, easy answers, and clear-cut, cause-and-effect explanations. But God is a God of surprises. He is a God who allows us to be deeply hurt that we may be more deeply healed. He is a God with time to wait for grace to take root in our hearts and minds (2 Pet. 3:9). He is a God who, as pastor Jack Hayford says, works in the dark.

The Lord's patient working in the life of Augustine provides us with an excellent example of agony giving way to ecstasy. For prodigals and those who love them, here is hope and healing.

◆ *The road to salvation may be long and painful.* It isn't that God kept Augustine on hold. Quite the contrary. Augustine's stubborn will blocked him from accepting the Lord's forgiveness and redirection. As a youth, he delighted in sin. His wayward actions gave him a heady sense of power. He didn't need or want his mother's God; he was his own man.

As he matured, his flippant attitude mellowed into callous rejection of the church and the Bible. He was too sophisticated for the crude simplicity of Christian doctrine. Most of all, he had a deep addiction to many things the Scriptures condemned. Ruled by ambition, philosophy, astrology, and sexual passion, his journey led away from the gospel and into cultic religion.

As an ardent devotee of Manichaeism, Augustine thought he had found in it the solution to his puzzlement with evil and suffering. (It taught a religious dualism where all matter was evil and only the spirit world pure.) In this cult he could satisfy his craving for insight into eternal things without giving up his attachment to the world. He formed strong friendships with other Manichees and devoted himself to advancing his career in rhetoric.

Augustine's story could easily end here. Many people die in a spiritually blind condition just like his, victims of their own lusts. But God kept drawing him to truth no matter how circuitous the path. Gradually Augustine became disillusioned with the Manichees' answers to life. He also experienced terrible dissatisfaction with his career. Moving, changing jobs, taking a new mistress, and experimenting with various belief systems didn't cure the sickness he suffered.

What was happening? One by one, God was removing the excuses and doubts from Augustine's brilliant mind and divided heart. He was drawing Augustine to truth without releasing him from his corrupt self so that the devastating contrast between God's light and his own darkness would shatter his pride and rebellion. God didn't want part of Augustine; he wanted all of him.

The world is full of people like Augustine who want truth on their own terms. They rage against heaven or against the church, unaware that their lack of faith in the Creator holds them in ignorance and bondage. And all the while God speaks to them from what we might think of as rather unlikely sources of divine revelation—philosophy, psychology, science, literature. He uses every available hook to draw them toward himself. As contemporary writer Richard Foster comments in his analysis of Augustine's search, "We, today, in our preoccupation with the crisis of conversion, often forget the importance of the pilgrimage that precedes and follows conversion." The restless journey of the heart in search of God is not in vain, but it exacts a high cost to the searcher and to those who wait for his safe arrival in the arms of the Savior.

◆ *The rewards of Christian parenting aren't always evident.* Of all the pains in life, there are few that cut as deeply as watching our children go wrong. From the first lisped "No!" of the toddler to the full-blown rebellion of the teen, parents' hearts can be sliced to ribbons.

It's easy to wonder if God has abandoned us and our kids in the midst of the battle. "God, whatever happened to that beautiful little baby we brought into the world?" we ask. "What happened to that sweet little child that was so eager to please and took delight in happy times together at home? Lord, what went wrong?"

In our distress and fear we quote Proverbs 22:6: "Train a child in the way he should go, and when he is old he will not turn from it." We wave it at the devil and the world, proclaiming our confidence that Christian children may wander but will *always* return safely to the Savior. Some believers contend that God has guaranteed us the salvation of our entire families. But is this actually what the Bible promises?

Consider the sons of Israel's King David. Scripture tells us David was a man who loved God with his whole heart. Yes, he committed some grave moral sins that had to be punished, but did they justify the spiritual breakdown of his whole family line? What about the outstanding example he had been most of their lives? There are no easy answers. We are simply told that Absalom died in rebellion after having murdered one of his brothers for an incestuous act; Adonijah committed treason, which resulted in death; and Solomon allowed infatuation with women and idols to separate him from God as he grew older.

Does this mean that all we can do is hope our kids come to Christ and cringe in terror that they won't? Certainly not! Monica, the mother of Augustine, could have blamed her son's condition on her husband and given up. Instead, she persisted in pursuing him as did the Holy Spirit. She knew she wasn't wrestling with flesh and blood but against spiritual forces that held Augustine in bondage. She prayed, witnessed to him, and lived her faith. She eventually won his father to Christ on his deathbed. Then she followed Augustine to Milan, Italy, certain that God was breaking down his resistance and eager to be on hand to offer whatever spiritual aid she could.

Christian psychologist Dr. James Dobson reminds hurting parents that intercessory prayer is the most effective weapon in combating Satan's attack on their children. "God's answer to our requests will not remove the freedom of choice from our children," he writes, "but he will grant them clarity and understanding in charting their own course. They will be given every opportunity to make the right decisions regarding matters of eternal significance."

♦ *God works through both mercy and severity.* He alone is the perfect parent, equally just and kind. That's why he can't accept some of the artful camouflage we stick over sin. He doesn't give up on us, but he doesn't put up with our rationalization and self-will either.

The apostle Paul's letter to the church at Rome is perhaps our clearest statement of the truth of God's grace. Tucked away in it is the following verse: "Consider therefore the kindness and sternness of God: sternness to those who fell, but kindness to you, provided that you continue in his kindness" (Rom. 11:22). In other words, the Lord specializes in "tough love."

Augustine didn't need someone to pat him on the back and assure him of God's forgiveness when he wasn't willing to repent. He also didn't need to be clubbed over the head with a Bible and threatened with hellfire. What he needed was someone who could set forth clearly the way of salvation and who would not be intimidated by his intellect or driven away by his life-style. He found that someone in his mother's friend, Bishop Ambrose.

Perhaps Monica couldn't effectively respond to her son's

highly trained philosophical mind, or maybe he just couldn't hear truth from a parent. That's why we must enlist every godly resource person available to us, and we must be willing for our loved ones to come to Christ in their own way. Dr. Dobson continues his thoughts on praying parents by saying, "The Lord will place key individuals in the paths of the ones for whom we pray—people of influence who can nudge them in the right direction."

In Bishop Ambrose, Augustine discovered a spiritual mentor. He later wrote in *Confessions*, "My heart warmed to him, not at first as a teacher of the truth, which I had quite despaired of finding in your church, but simply as a man who showed me kindness. I listened attentively when he preached to the people.

"Ambrose, with the utmost soundness, taught salvation. But salvation is far from sinners such as I was at the time. Yet, though I did not know it, I was drawing gradually nearer."

What a convicting force Bishop Ambrose's sincere praise of Monica must have been to her prodigal son! These two valiant Christians made a powerful evangelism team. "It was because my salvation was at stake that [my mother] loved Ambrose greatly," Augustine wrote. "And he loved her because of her fervent life of devotion. . . . Sometimes when he saw me he would break out in praise of her and congratulate me on having such a mother—not knowing what a son she had!"

◆ *Dying to sin isn't easy.* After Augustine became convinced of the gospel, he still could not commit to follow Christ. He hung suspended in that miserable state of knowing the truth and refusing to obey it.

"When I vacillated about my decision to serve the Lord my God, it was I who willed and I who willed not, and nobody else," he commented later. "I was fighting against myself. . . .

"I was quite sure that it was better for me to give myself up to your love than to surrender to my own lust. But while I wanted to follow the first course and was convinced that it was right, I was still a slave to the pleasures of the second. . . ."

Sometimes well-meaning people cause seekers serious spiritual damage when they encourage them to come to Christ for his forgiveness before their wills have bowed to his. All of us need to rediscover the cost of commitment—repentance and redirection of life. Otherwise, we birth pseudobelievers who make no attempt to put away their old lives of sin. Not only does this stunt their spiritual development, it provides a deadly obstacle to other seekers who question the lack of Christian character they see.

The Christian life begins in simple confession, but it is cultivated and enriched by arduous discipline. Augustine discovered this when, after surrendering his life to Jesus Christ, the old temptations to sin returned with a fury. This battle didn't mean his conversion was counterfeit or that God had rejected him. It simply meant that the new Augustine had to learn to ignore the old Augustine. Habit is a powerful force in our lives. If we spend years practicing sin, though our cleansing is instantaneous, the reconstruction of our patterns of action usually takes time. It is as we die daily to the past and its tyranny over us that we experience the power of the Resurrection to overthrow sin (Rom. 6:11-14). Augustine's motto may prove helpful in this struggle: "To my God, a heart of flame; to my fellow men, a heart of love; to myself, a heart of steel."

◆ *The pain of the past is not the measure of the future.* Augustine tasted the dregs of sin's cup before he came to Christ. Yet the grace of God eventually made him a pillar in the church. His transformation should be a tremendous encouragement to sin-scarred people. He discovered a remarkable spiritual principle: "We make a ladder of our vices, if we trample those same vices underfoot." In other words, there is no pit of sin too deep to climb out of with the Lord's help.

Unfortunately, many believers spend more time looking back at their past than looking up the ladder to heaven. The nineteenth century Scottish minister Alexander MacLaren warned Christians:

> You cannot think too much, too [negatively], of your own sins, but you may think too exclusively of them, and if you do, they will drive you to madness of despair.
>
> My dear friend, there is no remorse which is deep enough for the smallest transgression; but there is no transgression which is so great but that forgiveness for it may come.

As Augustine said, "Beware of despairing about yourself: you are commanded to put your trust in God, and not in yourself." The same can be said of children. They are ours, but, more important, they are God's. He knows how to transform their temperaments, loyalties, and interests as a parent never can. The same passions and strong will that led Augustine into sin, when mastered by Christ, became his greatest assets. In everything God is working for our greatest good and his glory.

Steps to Spiritual Greatness
- Repent of your past life.
- Reject the temptation to remain rooted in your past.
- Respond to God's grace by maximizing your potential.
- Repair your relationships with others as much as it depends on you.
- Restructure your life through discipline and accountability to other Christians.

> Being confident of this, that he who began a good work in you will carry it on to completion until the day of Christ Jesus. (Phil. 1:6)

CHAPTER 2
A House Divided

The Wesleys' little brood sat silent and still under Mother Susanna's watchful eye. From twelve-year-old Samuel down to five-year-old Hetty, they all knew family prayer time must be honored. No matter how much they longed for the supper to follow, they dared not show disrespect for the Scripture and prayers.

Father Samuel's voice droned on in supplication for King William of Orange. At last he was done, and the children could add their soft chorus of amens. But there was no amen from Susanna. She lifted her head and met her husband's questioning gaze.

"Why do you not say amen and thus honor your king and obey Scripture?" Samuel asked.

The children knew supper would be cold in more ways than one. Their parents had crossed swords—again.

"Because he is not my king," Susanna answered, her face set in determination. "He is a usurper. The throne belongs to the House of Stuart, not William of Orange."

"Sukey, if that be the case," Samuel told her, "we must part, for if we have two kings, we must have two beds."

Susanna countered, "Since I'm willing to let you quietly enjoy your opinions, you ought not to deprive me of my little liberty of conscience."

The atmosphere of the Epworth rectory was charged with

electricity as its strong-willed master and mistress faced off in battle. Susanna had not intended to quarrel with Samuel. But she had never been one to mask her convictions or compromise them to another's authority.

Later that evening Samuel called her into his study and knelt before her. He closed his eyes and began to pray. "O God, I pray that Thou wouldst send down divine vengeance on me and my offspring if ever again I touch this woman or come into bed with her before she entreats both Thee and me for pardon."

He looked up, expecting an apology. But Susanna held her ground, and Samuel left for London. *Will this be the end of our marriage?* she wondered.

There was much to keep Susanna busy while Samuel was away at the Church of England Convocation. The budget had been stretched to the limit to provide Samuel with money for his London trip. Susanna struggled to feed and care for their five children. Meanwhile, her body grew heavy with her fourteenth baby. (Eight of the Wesleys' children had already died.)

She couldn't turn to the people in their town of Epworth for comfort or aid. They already resented Samuel's presence as curate of the parish: his city ways, his education, his lack of common sense, his royalist sympathies, his harsh disciplines, his High Church formality. They had laughed when his barn fell down and clucked their tongues when his wife had to manage the parish farm lands. She dared not add to their antagonism.

Susanna stole a few minutes to write a close friend about her problem. "I am more easy in the thoughts of parting because I think we are not likely to live happily together." *Are we the same two people who couldn't endure the separation of Samuel's naval chaplaincy before we married? Now it seems we cannot endure one another's nearness.*

Many days of uncertainty passed. The London Convocation ended. Then King William III died, and Anne, daughter of

James II, became queen. Susanna rejoiced in the restoration of a Jacobite to England's throne. Samuel decided to return home since the political problem was resolved. Susanna soon gave birth to a baby daughter, who was named Anne in honor of the new queen.

A measure of peace returned to the Wesley home, and their fifteenth child was conceived. (That child was John Wesley, founder of the Methodist church.)

This 1702 crisis was not the first or last clash between Susanna and Samuel. They struggled on together in the Epworth parish, barely surviving financially. Their nineteenth and final child was born in 1709 only one month after their home burned down. They lost everything they owned and nearly lost little John as well. In spite of all these hardships, they remained true to their marriage vows, their deep religious convictions, and the welfare of their children.

Susanna's skill in raising the ten children who survived infancy and in managing the family business makes her a classic model of Christian motherhood. What few people realize is that her gifts had to shine through the clouded window of her marriage. She loved her husband deeply and always tried to give him her best, but he was not her match—except in stubbornness! Still, she cultivated respect for him in the areas where she could and taught her children to love and honor him.

She used her strong leadership talents in raising well-educated and disciplined children. The two remembered today are John and Charles Wesley, the founders of Methodism. Susanna's godly life and witness affected the community as well as her family. As many as two hundred worshipers attended her kitchen services at the rectory during her husband's repeated lengthy absences. In the years just before Susanna's death, she lived with her son John at the Foundry, early home of Methodism. There her teaching was highly prized and her influence pervasive. Though a devoted Anglican, she was largely responsible for the development of Methodism. Her rigorous spiritual disciplines taught in the home and her insistence on self-evaluation and repentance provided the core of John Wesley's teachings.

Grief, poverty, illness, and back-breaking work filled Susanna's life. She was left penniless and homeless when Samuel died. Her favorite son, Samuel, Jr., who was her only reliable source of income, died before she did. But at his death, Susanna could say with assurance, "None know what they can bear till they are tried. . . . Surely the manifestation of His presence and favour is more than an adequate support under any suffering whatever."

What We Can Learn from the Life of Susanna Wesley

In all loving relationships, there is a dynamic tension between individuality and submission. Husband and wife, parent and child, pastor and parishioner, Creator and creature—these are all areas where we feel the tug of wills. Usually love produces an almost involuntary cooperation. We *want* to please those we care about.

It seems sometimes that everything would be fine in our relationships if it weren't for the pressure points. Like a speck of grit in the eye or a pebble in a shoe, conflict usually comes along that annoys us. These trouble spots divide into the categories of pride, power, and performance. We have trouble yielding in areas that strongly connect with our identity and cherished beliefs (pride), our control over circumstances (power), and our ability to act effectively (performance).

When these areas suffer, we often try to reinforce our sagging morale by increasing our demands upon others and venting our frustrations emotionally. Spouses and children are handy targets for scoring ego points.

Samuel and Susanna were smart enough to know that it wasn't worth breaking up a marriage over the issue of who should be king of England. So what was that fight really all about? We can't be sure, but we can presume that Samuel's failure as a pastor and family provider probably ground his self-esteem into powder. He may have felt that his home was the only place where his opinions and authority were honored, and the temptation to test his wife's respect for him may have prompted his forceful blessing on the king she despised.

So there Susanna stood faced with a choice between disobeying her husband and violating her own conscience and belief. The power struggle was on.

In a marriage this kind of power struggle is hard to turn off. Intelligence and strong opinion fuel the confrontation. Before either adversary realizes it, the hairline crack in the relationship turns into a chasm. We have a name for that pit—irreconcilable differences. If either spouse is emotionally unstable, as Samuel appears to have been, those differences become more profound. Any appeal to logic or objective discussion is out. So are compromise and concession. Attempt at further communication provokes cold withdrawal or hot retaliation. And in such family fights, there are *no* winners.

Some Christians say the way to resolve tensions is for the wife to relinquish any opinions or actions that cause discord. They point to Ephesians 5:22, confident that this biblical command for wifely submission settles all matters of marital conflict. Other Christians protest that God obviously gifts women with fine minds, management skills, and leadership ability, gifts he would not bestow if he hadn't intended them to be used freely. Meanwhile, Christians in both camps go on fighting—and divorcing!

What can we do to ease the tension between submission and individual expression? Evidently Susanna Wesley found a way because she welcomed Samuel back and remained a loving and devoted (though still opinionated!) wife until his death. It's unfortunate her son John didn't ask her to compile a list of her marriage methods like the one he obtained of her child-rearing methods. (He married an emotionally unstable and impossible woman who finally left him.)

Although there are no official "Susanna Wesley Marriage

Methods," we can study her marriage and identify some helpful techniques. These represent a successful blend of loving submission and personal freedom that can enhance any close relationship. They won't eliminate the pain of a difficult marriage, but they can ease the hurt and bring healing.

◆ *Maintain personal piety rather than nurse grievances. Piety* is a word that has fallen out of use in our day; too often it has fallen out of practice as well. Susanna made her devotion and obedience to God central. Although she was a woman of great natural beauty, she focused her energy on becoming a woman of deep inner beauty (1 Pet. 3:1-2, 4).

Susanna's advice to her oldest son—advice she daily followed—reveals the firm course she charted:

> Get as deep an impression on your mind as is possible of the constant presence of the great and holy God. He is about our beds and about our paths and spies out all our ways. Whenever you are tempted to the commission of any sin, or the omission of any duty, pause and say to yourself, "What am I about to do? God sees me."

That one last thought alone, held firmly in the heart and mind, would end many family disagreements.

◆ *Remain faithful in well-doing even when weary.* Susanna used her gifts most frequently to strengthen her family. Rather than succumb to despair, she determined to raise a houseful of well-behaved, spiritually sensitive children. She didn't point at their father and write off their futures; she just rolled up her sleeves and went to work.

Her example of staying busy at home would have pleased the apostle Paul (Titus 2:4-5). No one in Epworth could use the preacher's wife as an excuse to criticize Christianity. She home-schooled her children, oversaw the house and fields, and still made time to pray three times a day. Proverbs 12:4 says, "A wife of noble character is her husband's crown." Samuel Wesley may have been poverty-stricken, but with a wife like Susanna he should have felt like a king.

◆ *Cultivate an attitude of loving loyalty.* Susanna honored Samuel's strengths and forgave his faults, year after difficult year. It grieved her to see his talents wasted on the ungrateful and ignorant people of Epworth. She wrote her brother regarding the tragedy of Samuel's career:

> And did I not know that Almighty Wisdom hath views and ends, in fixing the bounds of our habitation, which are out of our ken [understanding], I should think it a thousand pities that a man of his brightness, and rare endowments of learning and useful knowledge, in relation to the church of God, should be confined to an obscure corner of the country, where his talents are buried, and he determined to a way of life for which he is not so well suited as I could wish. . . .

At times Samuel was a difficult man to live with, but he was also a man worthy of considerable admiration. A true intellectual, he never slacked in scholarly study and writing. He was sophisticated and energetic, deeply committed to God and the church. Besides all that, he loved his family; he just wasn't quite sure what to do with them sometimes. Susanna had her moments of desperation, but they never destroyed her respect for Samuel. She did her best to nourish, encourage, and bless him as Scripture commands (Eph. 5:22-33).

◆ *Diminish pain through creative expression.* In addition to her rigorous home duties, this talented lady took on other projects that brought fulfillment to her life. She wrote three religious textbooks for children. Her home became a center of encouragement and spiritual ministry in the community. Though her

world was small and its walls may have seemed high, she flour-
ished in its confines and bore much fruit.

During Samuel's long absences for several annual Church of
England convocations in London, Susanna looked for ways to
meet the needs of the parish. Her evening family altar gradually
turned into a well attended community service. She was a gifted
woman who complemented her minister husband just as Priscilla stood by her husband, Aquila (Acts 18; Rom. 16:3; 1 Cor.
16:19). But unfortunately, Samuel wanted none of it. He wrote
her from London with instructions to stop the home meetings.

◆ *Confront important issues rather than lose personal integrity.* Susanna could not have been the quality Christian wife and mother
she was without strong force of character. Samuel's criticism of her
growing kitchen congregation provoked her to write:

> If you do, after all, think fit to dissolve this assembly, do
> not tell me that you desire me to do it, for that will not
> satisfy my conscience; but send me your positive com-
> mand, in such full and express terms as may absolve me
> from all guilt and punishment, for neglecting this oppor-
> tunity of doing good, when you and I shall appear before
> the great and awful tribunal of our Lord Jesus Christ.

She knew God had laid the people of Epworth on her heart and
had caused the warm response she had received. She knew she was
called to submit to her husband, but she also knew souls were at
stake. She was careful not to honor one great truth at the expense
of another. She confronted Samuel's sense of priority and prevailed.
He didn't forbid her ministry and on his return to Epworth found
the community's hostility toward him completely gone.

Telling her husband what she truly believed was costly. It was
also an act of loving respect. In Proverbs 24:26 we find that "an
honest answer is like a kiss on the lips." More husbands and

wives need to practice that kind of kissing. It is a wonderful way to increase intimacy and understanding.

♦ *Rule out retreat.* In a letter about her ongoing poverty due to Samuel's poor money management, Susanna made it clear she would not solve her problem by leaving him. "Where he lives, I will live, and where he dies, I will die and there will I be buried. God do so unto me and more also if aught but death part him from me." She had carved these words from the Book of Ruth into her heart.

When there is no option but to make a marriage work, it is amazing what miracles can occur. But tentative hearts and minds generate options for relief rather than renewal, escape rather than submission to the will of God. Such thoughts sent Samuel running from his family to London. Susanna didn't chase him, but she didn't bar the door when he returned. Love kept a light in the window and a welcome mat at the door.

Life for the Wesleys was never easy. But it was worthwhile. Susanna's unwavering devotion to her Lord and her family later produced the powerful evangelistic team of John and Charles Wesley. And to her own life came a wonderfully refined character.

Did she think what she endured was worth it? Here is her answer:

> Though man is born to trouble, yet I believe there is scarce a man to be found upon earth but, take the whole course of his life, hath more mercies than afflictions, and much more pleasure than pain. All my sufferings, by the admirable management of Omnipotent Goodness, have concurred to promote my spiritual and eternal good. . . . Glory be to Thee, O Lord!

There are limited records of Samuel Wesley's feelings for his family, but one incident stands out. When he was sent away to debtor's prison, he went without any money to buy food while there. (Prisoners were responsible for their own provisions.) Susanna worried so about this that she sent him her wedding ring to sell so he could get food. Samuel sent it back. Evidently he thought a wife who could offer that kind of unconditional love was worth keeping.

Men and women have more in common than they have differences. We all have wills to choose, minds to think and reason, emotions to feel and respond, spirits that reach out to God. Repressing any of these gifts is not the road to fulfillment. Proper direction is. The sincere love of God poured into our lives supplies that direction.

Steps to Spiritual Greatness

- ◆ Commit. Strengthen your resolve to make your marriage work.
- ◆ Cherish. Treat your spouse and children like the precious treasures from God that they are.
- ◆ Confront. Deal with the realities of your life, discuss them as honestly as possible, and plan for improvement.
- ◆ Compliment. Congratulate each other on achievements, especially those that bless the family.
- ◆ Consecrate. Surrender your family to God in prayer, and recognize his supreme lordship.

Be imitators of God, therefore, as dearly loved children and live a life of love, just as Christ loved us and gave himself up for us as a fragrant offering and sacrifice to God. (Eph. 5:1-2)

CHAPTER 3
A Sea with No Shore

Francis Schaeffer gazed up at the Swiss Alps towering above the town of Champréy. He felt small and tired and empty. How long had he been fighting this battle for purity in the church? Twenty years. It seemed like forever. He was only thirty-nine, but he was weary of the war. All the meaning had gone out of life, and he couldn't seem to get it back.

The years had been so full: Accepting Christ at eighteen; off to college, then seminary; struggling with the flood of liberal theology that had swept through the Presbyterian church; staking his life and his ministry on the absolute historical truth and divine inspiration of the Bible.

He had followed Carl McIntire in his attack against compromising Christians, liberals, and Roman Catholics because he believed he was doing what God wanted. The separatist movement had seemed so right. How could a fight for purity in the church be wrong?

And fight he had. So much so that he and McIntire had been called the "apostles of discord." Schaeffer looked back over their years together. After becoming the first ordained pastor in McIntire's Bible Presbyterian Church denomination, he had helped establish the American Council of Churches. They stood uncompromisingly for the truth against the Federal

Council of Churches and the newly formed National Association of Evangelicals. He and his family were in Switzerland now to extend and strengthen the separatist movement internationally.

The winter chill filled his heart as he walked outside Champrey, thinking about what it all meant. Soon it would be 1951. He had been in Switzerland almost three years. Long enough and far enough away from the American scene to get a different perspective on the conflict. Long enough to ask questions.

Is it possible we've all fought so long we don't know how to do anything else? he wondered. Now that they'd hurled every dart they could find at the liberal machines, was there nothing left for them but hurling darts at one another? The casualty rate in their ranks was incredible. Somehow there had to be more to Christianity than this heartless holy war.

Later, with his wife, Edith, in the old chalet where they lived, he struggled to put his feelings into words. "For the sake of honesty I have to go all the way back to my agnosticism and think through the whole matter." Hard words, but they had to be said. He had to find a greater reality in his faith or else abandon it.

All through that long winter Schaeffer searched for real Christianity. He tramped the trails about Champrey and hiked in the mountains on clear days. When it rained, he paced back and forth in the hayloft of their chalet and constantly prayed.

The more he tried to talk to God about the emptiness he saw in the church and in his own heart, the more discouraged he became. He was increasingly convinced that the separatist movement could not receive God's blessing. It was filled with anger and pride rather than love. *But where was the answer?*

Schaeffer searched the Scriptures. He retraced the path of his conversion. Still he found no joy or peace.

Then at Easter he traveled to Geneva to speak at a conference led by Hugh E. Alexander, a man ignited by the fire of the Welsh Revival. There he found people who took spiritual warfare seriously but did it with a song and a smile. They had the reality he'd been seeking! *What was their secret?*

At that conference Schaeffer learned about the guidance and empowerment of the Holy Spirit and about identifying with Christ's death and resurrection. More than that, he experienced it. After returning home, he wrote a friend, "I really feel lighter than I have for years."

Hard decisions lay ahead if he was to separate himself from the pitched battle that his Christian brothers seemed intent on waging. But of one thing he was certain: He didn't intend to lose his newfound joy. He would do whatever was necessary to keep hold of this new relationship with God.

Any more battles Francis Schaeffer fought would have to be by God's rules and with his blessing. "God willing, I will push and politick no more. . . . The mountains are too high, history is too long, and eternity is longer."

Out of that agonizing winter of 1951 was born the heart of L'Abri Fellowship and the twenty-five books and two film series produced by Francis Schaeffer. Out of that winter was born a giant for God.

For the next several years the Schaeffers' lives were tinged with grief over the severe conflicts within their fledgling denomination. Francis Schaeffer, the trusted friend and right-hand man of Carl McIntire, became another of the man's targets for criticism and slander. Schaeffer refused to defend himself, believing that Christians should not engage in self-vindication.

The Schaeffers also experienced other crises, including eviction from Champrey, their two-year-old son's bout with polio, and a daughter's illness with rheumatic fever. They knew the white heat of the furnace of affliction. But because of the personal resurrection of faith Francis Schaeffer had experienced, he was able to stand strong and fight valiantly against the true enemy, Satan.

In 1955 the Schaeffers began L'Abri Fellowship—a youth ministry—in Huemoz, Switzerland, and severed their old ties. Their hearts had grown too large with the love of God and the vision of a lost world to remain embroiled in religious squabbles.

In 1971 Schaeffer wrote *True Spirituality* and shared the secrets he'd learned in the crucible of the 1950s. There he wrote, "Lovelessness is a sea which knows no shore, for it is what God is not. . . . In the midst of being right, if self is exalted, my fellowship with God can be destroyed."

At his death in 1984, Francis Schaeffer was acclaimed as an evangelical thinker who had left his mark on the church. His bitter experience with the separatist movement had a great impact on the nature of that mark. In all his books, he taught that Bible-believing Christians must not put up walls between one another. The only valid wall was between those who accepted the Bible as the absolute Word of God and those who did not. Even with the latter group, he insisted that an attitude of love must be maintained and the door of dialogue kept open.

In keeping with that position, Schaeffer remained quiet about his denominational membership so that he could minister more effectively to all Christians. He avoided using sectarian terms. In his book *The Church before the Watching World*, he wrote, "We must practice an observable and real oneness—before God, before the elect angels, before the demonic hosts, before the watching liberals and before the watching world."

Because of his major shift in attitude from that of his early ministry, Francis Schaeffer will be remembered as an important shaper of twentieth-century evangelicalism. He was a leading figure in the mobilization of the evangelical church for cultural, intellectual, and political confrontation with the kingdom of darkness.

What We Can Learn from
the Life of Francis Schaeffer

Observers of the early Christian church commented, "See how they love one another!" Too often since, the world has looked at Christians and said, "See how they hate one another!" The famous poet and cynic Lord Byron wrote, "Christians have burnt each other, quite persuaded that all the Apostles would have done as they did."

A careful look at Scripture reveals that even the first-century church experienced inner turmoil and conflict. There were complaints in Jerusalem about what was done with church money. Peter and Paul disagreed about how to treat Gentile converts. Missionary partners Paul and Barnabas split up over whom to take along as an assistant. The Corinthian church divided into warring factions under the banners of their favorite preachers.

Certainly this is not the answer to Jesus' prayer, "That all of them may be one, Father, just as you are in me and I am in you" (John 17:21). So why is it this way in the church? James sums up the problem well: "What causes fights and quarrels among you? Don't they come from your desires that battle within you?" (James 4:1).

What desires drive us to crush our brothers and sisters in Christ? For some the motivation is greed, ambition, or envy. For others it is the burning desire to be right in an ultimate, authoritative sense, the unbending determination to have the final word.

Of course, we don't recognize these sins as our motives. We say we want purity and holiness in the church, more spiritual leadership, a return to biblical authority. We may even begin our fight with clean hands and hearts, but then the twin tempters, Pride and Power, rush to help us win. Before we realize it, we torch part of the body of Christ without much remorse.

The fires we set may seem small compared to the bonfires that claimed early martyrs' lives. They may be only the tiny flames of gossip and insinuation. But a little fire burning long enough can destroy a mighty forest. A little criticism and strife can destroy lives and splinter fellowship. Those same flames that we light also burn the love of God out of our hearts.

Francis Schaeffer became the victim of this terrible spiritual disease. Fortunately, he identified the problem and let God do surgery on his motives and actions. His experience points up several kinds of sorrow we may feel as a result of conflict with other Christians.

◆ *Sorrow comes when we try to do God's pruning for him.* The church can be compared to a grapevine. Jesus is the vine, the Father is the vine dresser, the Holy Spirit is the lifeblood, and we are the branches (John 15:1-8). With that image in mind, consider how impossible it is for one branch to attempt pruning of another. Our spiritual vitality suffers from the poison of bitterness and unforgiven wrongs. This spiritual anemia saps our ability to live as we know Christ desires. The fruit of the Spirit withers and the wine of joy runs dry. We may keep going through the motions, but the life is gone.

Any doubt we might have about the serious damage Christian division brings in our personal relationship with Jesus is settled by the apostle John. In his epistle to the church, he writes: "We know that we have passed from death to life, because we love our brothers. Anyone who does not love remains in death" (1 John 3:14). Our salvation remains, but our daily experience of Christ's presence and power soon disappears. The more our love for other believers declines, the more Satan reigns.

◆ *Sorrow should fill our hearts when we grieve the Holy Spirit by dividing the body of Christ (Eph. 4:30).* He is the one who unites us in love, and his heart is broken by our divisions. Paul supplied the Ephesian church with a helpful checklist of actions that grieve the Holy Spirit: lying, deceit, unresolved anger, theft, bitterness, rage, brawling, slander, greed, immorality, and every form of malice (4:17–5:21). When we engage in these divisive practices, we dishonor the Spirit of Christ who lives in us. The Holy Spirit bears witness that we have received God's forgiveness and commands us to show the same compassion for one another. We preserve the unity of the Spirit as we work to live in peace (Eph. 4:2-6).

◆ *When we recognize our failure to express the character of Christ, godly sorrow results.* This kind of sorrow brings us face to face with the chasm between our behavior and God's purpose for us. It is impossible to get a clear vision of Calvary love without also experiencing conviction of our lack of love.

Love should be at the heart of church discipline. Members are mutually accountable for attitudes and actions that grieve the Spirit and damage Christ's body. Such disciplinary action causes pain, but it can be redemptive for everyone involved when restoration results. It provides an excellent opportunity to rediscover God's unconditional love and forgiveness, as well as an occasion to display love for one another (2 Cor. 2:1-10).

This godly sorrow, or true repentance, never leads to death (2 Cor. 7:10). In a letter to a friend who had also been a casualty of the separatist movement, Schaeffer said, "I believe that the pain you have felt, and I have felt, is . . . the pain of birth in a day of blessing, as the whole body is made more ready for the Bridegroom's coming. Surely the birth pains mean little if such a result is born through our dear Lord's grace."

◆ *Our own sorrow is multiplied by compassion for others who are experiencing the wounds of church combat.* While Francis Schaeffer remained immersed in the conflict, he had little awareness of how many of God's children were suffering from his and others' actions. But after he dealt with his lack of love, his perceptions changed. No longer could Christian brothers and sisters be reduced to expendable pawns in a theological chess game.

All around us are believers who have been wounded by the criticism and unkindness of other Christians. Once we have cleansed our hearts of malice, we are urged to come alongside them and minister healing. We are also called on to speak out in a loving and honest way about the source of their pain. This may not make us popular, but it puts us squarely in the footsteps of Jesus. Francis Schaeffer wrote many painful letters attempting to open the eyes of those who had learned to excuse their cruelty "for the good of the cause."

◆ *One of the deepest sorrows comes as we watch the work of God suffer because of conflict in the church.* Jesus prayed for believers to be one so that the world might believe in him. The startling truth behind that prayer is that when we are not one we give the world a reason *not* to believe.

In his book *The Church at the End of the 20th Century,* Schaeffer wrote, "We cannot expect the world to believe that the Father sent the Son, that Jesus' claims are true, and that Christianity is true, unless the world sees some reality of the oneness of true Christians." He continued, "Anything that an individual Christian or Christian group does that fails to show the simultaneous balance of the holiness of God and the love of God presents to a watching world not a demonstration . . . but a caricature of the God who exists."

Francis Schaeffer experienced such deep conviction regarding the centrality of love to effective Christian living that he came to regard loveless Christianity as counterfeit living. In his life is echoed the message of the apostle Paul who wrote, "If I . . . can fathom all mysteries and all knowledge . . . if I give all I possess to the poor and surrender my body to the flames, but have not love, I gain nothing" (1 Cor. 13:2-3).

Jesus stands before a large portion of the church today as He did in the book of Revelation and says,

I know your deeds, your hard work and your perseverance. I know that you cannot tolerate wicked men, that
you have tested those who claim to be apostles but are
not, and have found them false. You have persevered and
have endured hardships for my name, and have not
grown weary. Yet I hold this against you: You have forsaken your first love. Remember the height from which
you have fallen! Repent and do the things you did at
first. (2:2-5)

Steps to Spiritual Greatness

- Forbear. Be as patient with slow growth and immaturity
  in other Christians as God is with yours.
- Forgive. Release those who have failed (including yourself). Through Christ, all debts are paid in full.
- Forget. Ask God to help you erase the memories of past
  wrongs so that fellowship may be renewed.
- Fill up. Allow the Holy Spirit to fill you with love.
- Fight on. Instead of attacking flesh and blood, do battle
  with the real enemy, Satan.

Aim for perfection . . . be of one mind, live in peace. And
the God of love and peace will be with you. . . . May the
grace of the Lord Jesus Christ, and the love of God, and
the fellowship of the Holy Spirit be with you all. (2 Cor.
13:11, 14)

Section Two

◆◆◆◆◆◆◆◆◆◆◆◆◆

MENTAL ANGUISH

CHAPTER 4
In Search of Sanity

Alexander Cruden fingered the pages of his newly published *Complete Concordance of the Old and New Testaments.* The rich paper and meticulous print did justice to his painstaking work in compiling the text. Yet he felt empty.

The project had been his entire life for over a year. Now it was finished, and the future lay before him, uncharted and lonely. The *Concordance* had been in print less than a month, but already his dreams of success had been snuffed out by the death of Queen Caroline.

Cruden reeled from the shock. Gone was his royal patroness. Gone her promised gift of 100 pounds for his work on the *Concordance.* Gone his title as Queen's Bookseller. From the heights of achievement and hope of prosperity, he plunged to the depths of despair. What was he to do?

Alone in his bookshop, deserted from neglect during the lengthy writing project, Cruden found his thoughts filled more and more with the face of his widowed friend Mrs. Pain. Surely she must be lonely after the recent death of her husband. And he knew she admired him. She even called him her "chaplain" and had him lead in Scripture reading and prayer in her home each Sunday evening. He'd been like a family member for the past fifteen years.

Through the long, lonely winter of 1737, Cruden mused on how he and Mrs. Pain could meet each other's needs. He could provide her with companionship and spiritual leadership. She could give him a comfortable home and freedom from financial concerns. He decided it was divinely destined.

Cruden found his initial advances warmly received. Quickly gaining confidence, he poured out his affection for his lady love in an elegant letter. However, to his surprise, Mrs. Pain began to avoid him.

Annoyed and confused, Cruden sat down at his desk and wrote another letter, this time in a different tone. "I will dine with you on the 18th of March and intend to get a plain answer. . . ."

Cruden arrived for dinner and found a quite unexpected scene. Mrs. Pain was flanked by two gentlemen friends. *Why has she invited them tonight? Is this her way of refusing me?* he wondered. Dinner passed with no opportunity for any privacy. Then Mrs. Pain rose abruptly from the table and said, "Gentlemen, you must excuse me. I've spilled something on my gown and shall have to go change."

Cruden frowned. *Some strange business is afoot,* he thought. He joined the other gentlemen in the parlor to wait for Mrs. Pain. As the hands of the clock moved forward without her return, he became increasingly angry. *Why should the woman want to make a fool of me? Especially after receiving me so willingly in the past.* It was beyond tolerating.

Cruden paced the floor and then announced that he was leaving. As he walked back to his lodgings, the darkness filled him with thoughts of how he might still triumph over Mrs. Pain. At last he hit upon a plan. He would sit in the front seat of her gallery at church and take part in worship with a vigor that would show everyone she had not got the best of him.

On Sunday his plan went off exactly as he'd imagined. *No, better!* he thought. All eyes in the church had turned to him as he'd stood and shouted out the responsive reading. It was a dramatic moment they were not likely to soon forget. And why shouldn't he be bold? God was on his side. Divine purpose would not bow to a fickle female. Mrs. Pain would soon see her error.

The next day Cruden had a visit from a Mr. Wightman. He recalled having seen the man once before but had no idea why he would be calling. Wightman talked with Cruden awhile and persuaded him—he wasn't sure how—to stay home from the bookshop and rest for a day or two. He said it would do him no end of good. It would restore his vigor.

Cruden agreed. He had been working feverishly for well over a year. Perhaps he did need a rest.

As he sat in his room leafing through some papers the following morning, he heard a great commotion on the steps. Then the door of his room flew open and in stomped the neighboring blacksmith brandishing a club. Behind him Cruden's landlord and landlady shouted, "He's a lunatic! Watch out!"

Cruden agreed. The blacksmith must be mad. But as he struggled to escape the man's onslaught, he realized the word *lunatic* was meant for him.

His landlord and landlady persisted in demanding that Cruden be taken to the madhouse. Someone had filled their ears with lies, convincing them he was dangerous. *Could it have been one of the men from Mrs. Pain's dinner?* Cruden wondered.

Fury flowed through him like liquid fire. He grabbed the blacksmith's stick and drove his enemies from the room. He chased them down the stairs, but, while he fought off the blacksmith, the landlord enlisted men from the street to come in and overpower him.

Cruden revived to find himself in his bed and a surgeon tending his cuts. "I want Dr. Hulse," Cruden insisted, "and the Constable." The surgeon left, but no one else came except a now contrite landlady with a tray of food. He lay in bed for two days, too weak to do anything but read his Bible.

Then a messenger brought an invitation from Mr. Wightman.

He wanted Cruden to visit him at his house in Spring Gardens. Desperate to escape his present situation and hopeful that Wightman might assist him in getting justice, Cruden hurriedly dressed and climbed into the waiting coach.

The light hurt his eyes, so the gracious driver pulled the blinds down. Cruden collapsed on the seat from exhaustion. After some time passed and they did not arrive at Mr. Wightman's, he became curious and looked out the coach window.

"This is not the way to Spring Gardens!" he shouted to the driver. "We are on Ludgate Hill, and this is the road to the madhouse! Stop! You cannot do this to me. I am not mad!"

But the driver refused to listen and drove Cruden to the door of the private madhouse at Bethnal Green.

"How great is my affliction!" Cruden moaned. "This is the way to put an end to all my usefulness in the world and expose me to the highest degree. Oh, what shall I do? God help me!" He struggled to see the hand of Providence in his desperate situation. His voice racked with pain, he cried, "I desire to submit to the will of God."

Today the name of Alexander Cruden is synonymous with one of the world's most popular Bible concordances. Ever since its publication in 1737, it has been a favorite of Bible scholars. Dwight Moody told his followers that the only tools they needed to study God's Word were a Bible and *Cruden's Concordance*. What few know is that its author struggled much of his life with mental instability.

Cruden's first mental breakdown came at the age of nineteen. A young woman in his hometown of Aberdeen refused his love and then was found to be pregnant by her brother. Wild with grief, Cruden had to be restrained in the local jail for two weeks. As soon as he recovered, he fled Aberdeen and never returned until late in life. From then on, he seems to have lost his grip on reality and his ability to relate to people.

He established himself in a moderately successful career as a proofreader and bookseller, but he never found a woman to share his life. Cruden's crowning achievement in compiling the concordance was soon followed by the ten-week stay at Bethnal Green asylum. His sister arranged his third trip to a mental asylum when he was fifty-four. The stay was brief and never repeated.

Though highly gifted in a few areas, Cruden exhibited odd and irrational behavior in others. He pestered employers, potential sweethearts, and politicians. On numerous occasions he asked the king to knight him for his concordance's service to the kingdom. He also requested an official title as national corrector, a court-appointed guardian of the country's morality. Much of his time in public was spent reproving those who swore or engaged in Sabbath-breaking activities.

During the long and lonely years of misunderstanding, Cruden struggled to make his case known to the public. He poured out his complaint at the injustice he had suffered, sought recompense in the court, and struggled to advance his career. He never received the restitution or honor he sought. Instead, he convinced most people that the rumors of his insanity were probably true.

Cruden's devotion to God remained resolute through his experiences, and his personal piety deepened as his years increased. He constantly grieved over the sacrilegious attitude of the British. Late in life he started a one-man prison ministry and was known for his acts of charity. His mind seems to have become more stable as he lost himself in the needs of others. The quaint seventy-one-year-old corrector died on his knees in prayer.

What We Can Learn from
the Life of Alexander Cruden

Every talent has its price tag. Alexander Cruden had a remarkable ability for performing highly technical and detailed work with incredible precision. As a result, he gained distinction as author of an excellent concordance. But the price of that honor was loneliness and peculiarity. A man who spent his life chasing each word of the Bible from cover to cover (without the aid of a computer!) was a man who lived in a very different world than those about him.

Cruden felt passionately about the rightness of things. He edited and improved his concordance several times and apologized that it was not as perfect as he wished. In the same way, he longed to correct the lives of those about him. Sin and spiritual apathy annoyed him like a page full of misspelled words.

If Cruden were alive today, undoubtedly he would be active in some moral reform effort. Critical, confrontational, and uncompromising, he embodied the traits of most radical reformers. Such people sacrifice cultural conformity for the sake of their causes, and they sometimes crack under the pressure of society's demands. The marvel is that when Cruden's mind cracked, the light of God shone through.

There are many "Crudens" in the church today. They may be lonely leaders or eccentric overachievers. Others are bumbling misfits at the edge of social activities. Are they stupid? Certainly not. Are they evil? No! Are they hurting? Yes! If we come close enough to touch their pain, we may by surprised by how much God will teach us through their lives.

♦ *Equating social grace with spiritual grace wounds many sincere Christians.* The church has always been tempted to honor the beautiful and gracious people in its midst. That is why James, in his epistle, warned against giving the best seats to the most affluent and attractive. We look at the outside image of men and women, judging them by their physical appearance, health, intelligence, and wealth.

God, on the other hand, looks at the heart. He weighs it to see if it holds his grace and goodness. He tests its integrity. And often he passes over the "beautiful people" in favor of what appears to be a crude lump of clay.

We aren't comfortable with some of God's choices in gifting his children. We would prefer that God use only those we admire and enjoy. But the Bible reminds us that just as every part of the physical body is essential, every member of Christ's body, the church, is indispensable.

> The eye cannot say to the hand, "I don't need you!" And the head cannot say to the feet, "I don't need you!" On the contrary, those parts of the body that seem to be weaker are indispensable, and the parts that we think are less honorable we treat with special honor. And the parts that are unpresentable are treated with special modesty, while our presentable parts need no special treatment. (1 Cor. 12:21-24)

Perhaps a look at Jesus' parable of the seed can provide a clearer insight into the varieties of Christian productivity (Matt. 13:1-8). Some seed fell on stony ground and some on bad soil; it produced no harvest. The seed that fell on good ground always yielded fruit. But what we may miss is that Jesus said some of that *good* ground only produced thirty or sixty times what was sown. He makes no judgment regarding the degree of productivity. Neither should we.

We need to make room in the church for eccentric, disturbed, and socially inept people to cultivate and use their gifts and abilities. We might find some of their accomplishments quite amazing. A person like Cruden suffering from mental and emotional instability may have a narrow field of ministry, but he is no less valuable than any other faithful servant of Christ. Such a person should be welcomed and affirmed by the family of God for what he or she has to offer. In a warm and accepting fellowship these individuals have the best chance for maximum development and healing.

Too often, however, the only room in the church for the unconventional or abnormal is a side room, out of the way of the movers and shakers. It takes time and special attention to nurture these "unpresentable parts" of the body, time too many of us aren't willing to take. Yet the Lord commands us to comfort, support, and encourage the feebleminded, the fearful, and the distressed, and to affirm one another's gifts in whatever form they take.

♦ *The single-minded usually suffer criticism and misunderstanding.* We're apt to be fearful of or annoyed by those who exhibit their passionate concern too freely. We're often quick to judge them as unbalanced, extreme, and obsessive. Before we reject them, we need to remember that many of our Bible heroes could (and did!) wear those labels.

God uses brilliant and attractive people like the prophet Daniel and Queen Esther. He also chooses servants like Jeremiah and John the Baptist whose appearance and behavior send shock waves through society. We need a new view of the kingdom of God and the diversity of its wonders. We need to realize that nonconformity is yeast for the bread of life. Instead of looking for the standard cultural marks of success and normalcy, we should be looking for the stamp of Christlikeness.

Unfortunately, fear of those who are different often drives people to persecute sincere seekers and believers. Those who suffer such unjust treatment can take comfort that Jesus also endured shunning and violent rebuke. At one point in his ministry, his family came to take him home because they said he was out of his mind.

Cruden's biographer, Alexander Chalmers, said of him, "Yet, just because he was so unlike themselves, he sometimes struck home. Ever since the days of St. Paul, the great missionaries have not feared being called madmen by the sane men who live in grooves. Indeed they may truly be mad. But this madness of theirs gives the spirit a wider range than can ever be dreamt of by groove-dwellers. . . ."

◆ *Poor spiritual discernment produces great pain in others.* We all struggle to distinguish the difference between what is peculiar and what is evil. Throughout church history there have been epidemics of interest in the devil and demons. These revivals in recognition of Satan's power over human behavior are essential to accurate understanding of the spiritual battle we face. At the same time, they present temptations to label every unusual action or idea as the work of a demon.

How can we distinguish between mental imbalance or illness and actual demonic influence? Mercifully, God has given us several tools:

1. Scripture. Measuring our ideas and actions by the Word of God reveals danger zones where correction and deliverance may be needed.
2. The gift of discerning of spirits. The Holy Spirit supernaturally reveals evil spirits at work.
3. Speech and behavior. The fruit of people's lives gives evidence of their hearts' intention and motivation.

When probed with these tools, Alexander Cruden's life does not reveal evil intent. He had many areas of weakness, but his heart was right with God. He loved the Bible, relied daily on times of prayer and meditation, and showed loving concern for others. In spite of his traumatic experience as a young adult, he sought out and maintained employment. He handled his business affairs responsibly enough to provide a refuge for his needy sister and others. At his death, he left a generous endowment to a Christian university and another to provide Christian literature to the poor.

◆ *Immaturity and self-will may cause pain.* Not all the hurts we experience can be blamed on someone else. Although Cruden cared for others, he retained a noticeable degree of self-centered behavior and egotism. He wanted to impress people with his achievements and went to ridiculous lengths in his effort to do so. God didn't write him off because of this, but he allowed life to buffet him like a schoolmaster's paddle.

We don't know how much Cruden's traumatic first love affair damaged his emotional and social development. There may have been other painful experiences that affected him much earlier. Whatever the cause, his emotions were unstable and his behavior could be quite erratic. He was rigid and rule-oriented in his personal life and theology. Bible trivia and Christian legalism seem to have fascinated him at the expense of learning spiritual principles for life and health. He equated his will as a child of God with that of God himself, unable to accept that his divine sonship didn't do away with his fallen nature.

Cruden's continuing struggle with mental instability and social rejection served a constructive purpose in stripping him of his self-will and bowing him to the will of God. The pain he endured was not good and on occasion was probably caused by malicious people. But, because he turned to the Lord in his distress, he slowly grew to be a more mature and stable individual. At the time of his last confinement in an asylum he said, "God by His secret power and wisdom [can] make it issue for His own glory and [my] good."

Following that crisis, Cruden became involved in prison ministry at Newgate, a particularly horrible prison near his home. There he found people with worse problems than he had had. He became involved in some of their lives, and in the process his own life stabilized. There is healing in directing our attentions other-ward. As Philip Yancey has aptly said, "God created us incomplete, not as a cruel trick to edge us toward self-pity, but as an opportunity to edge us toward others with similar needs."

◆ *Relief comes through trusting God with our mental health.* It isn't in struggling to stay sane that we experience peace. Instead, it is in releasing our minds to Christ's safekeeping. Because of the stigma attached to mental illness, we cringe at the thought of going through that furnace of affliction. We can actually tremble so much at the thought of insanity that we lose our senses.

Most Christians agree that a person can know and serve God with a physical illness or handicap. But it takes more courage to admit that a person can know and serve him in a state of unreason. Today the church bases its faith so entirely on human logic and mental assent to right creeds that it stumbles at God's special workings in the lives of those with muddled minds. But history and current experience prove that a bit of abnormality is no barrier to the presence and power of God.

While he was chained to his bed in the asylum, Cruden filled his time with prayer and meditation on God's Word. He would imagine scenes from Bible stories on the bare wall opposite his bed. The people of the Bible so inspired him that they became more real to him than his situation. One day during his confinement, he wrote in his journal, "[I] passed a great part of my time in the exercises of Devotion, having such uncommon Peace and Serenity in Mind, that Bethnal Green was in some respects rather a Palace than a Prison."

Mental distress doesn't mean God has forsaken us. He is there in the prison of the mind, whispering messages of comfort and healing. In the words of a minister from Elizabeth Goudge's novel *The Scent of Water,* "If you lose your reason, you lose it into the hands of God. It's safe there, you know. It's the only place where anything is safe."

Steps to Spiritual Greatness

- Relax. You cannot master life in your own strength.
- Restore. Fill your thoughts with beautiful things from God's Word.
- Respond. Let God and others touch you with their love.
- Respect your limitations. Christianity isn't a performance contest.
- Relinquish. Trust your life—past, present, and future—to the One who made you.

Let not the wise man boast of his wisdom or the strong man boast of his strength or the rich man boast of his riches, but let him who boasts boast about this: that he understands and knows me, that I am the Lord, who exercises kindness, justice and righteousness on earth, for in these I delight. (Jer. 9:23-24)

CHAPTER 5
Fainthearted Soldiers

The stout young preacher Charles Spurgeon stared out the carriage window at the throngs that jammed the streets leading to Surrey Music Hall. None of the large crowds he'd spoken to in the past prepared him for the magnitude of this response. Was it the gospel that drew them or curiosity that a twenty-two-year-old preacher dared use such a place as the magnificent hall for his pulpit?

Regardless of what brought them, he was determined to give them God's Word and see souls won to Christ. If only he had the comfort of Susannah by his side. But she had a new ministry these days that claimed all her time—twin sons, another of God's double portions that made the young preacher marvel.

Spurgeon arrived at the music hall to find the park surrounding it filled with thousands of people who couldn't get inside the building. The vast auditorium with its three galleries and 10,000 seats was completely filled. As he walked onto the stage and looked out at the vast sea of faces, he felt completely unnerved.

I must follow right manfully in my Master's steps, he reminded himself. It was God alone who had brought him to this place of prominence so early in life. Somehow God would make him equal to it. What a day for the gospel! Never before had a place of worldly amusement yielded itself so nobly to the purpose of God.

The building was light and airy in spite of the crowd. He knew his voice would carry perfectly. After all, the place had been designed for great concert music. Tonight it would ring with the music of heaven. Of that he felt confident.

The service began on time. There were words of greeting, a prayer, a hymn. Spurgeon repeatedly fought to steady his nerves as he waited to preach. The Scripture was read and another hymn was sung. Then he took the pulpit and asked the people to join him in prayer.

"Fire! Fire!" a voice cried out above the prayer. "The galleries are giving way. The place is falling!" Spurgeon raised his head and began searching the audience for the source of the problem. Was some troublemaker seeking to disrupt the meeting or was the building really burning? He could not tell. Shadows hid much of the balconies and the back of the hall from his vision.

People rushed for the doors. They stumbled, fell, piled on top of one another. The stair balustrade cracked and gave way from the mad crush of bodies.

But Spurgeon could not see the rail breaking and could not hear the screams as people toppled off the stairs at the far end of the huge hall. His workers assured him there was no fire, that all was well. He fought to calm the crowd with his strong voice.

Gradually it became apparent there was no fire, so many of the people returned to their seats. Those who had been standing outside rushed in to claim the empty seats. Cries went up for Spurgeon to go on with his message.

"My intended text for this evening is found in the third chapter of Proverbs, the thirty-third verse. . . ." Spurgeon waited for the noise of the excited crowd to subside. He urged those milling about to return to their seats. Just as it seemed he could go on, a fresh commotion erupted.

How can I preach in such an atmosphere? he thought. His nerves tensed to the breaking point. He called for another hymn to be sung. Perhaps the music would quiet the crowd.

As he clung to the pulpit, struggling to regain his composure, he realized there was no way he could go on. He asked the people to leave in a quiet and orderly manner. Then he escaped to a side room and collapsed on the floor. He revived only to discover that seven people had died in the panic and almost thirty had been taken to the hospital.

The immensely popular Baptist preacher, who had been acclaimed as the greatest minister since Whitefield, had to be carried out of majestic Surrey Music Hall. His deacons first took him home to Susannah's comforting arms, but they soon realized that the birth of the twins had left her too weak to deal with her husband's deep depression. So they took him to a trusted friend's house where he could recuperate and escape visitors.

Plunged into a pit of anguish, he sought comfort from God. None came. Tears and doubts filled his waking thoughts and nightmares filled his sleep. He opened his Bible in search of strength; it only deepened his grief. His prayers seemed to bounce off a sky of brass.

Spurgeon paced hour after hour in his friend's garden. Numb with pain, his lips formed the questions that would not release him from torment. *Are the flowers weeping with me?* he wondered as he looked at their dew-laden petals.

Those who loved him tried to protect him from the slander of the press. When he asked his friends about the reports in the papers, their silence told him all he needed to know. But what did it matter how the press criticized him?

"My thoughts are a case of knives, cutting my heart in pieces," he cried in agony. It seemed no relief would come, that he would surely lose his sanity.

In the second week after the incident, while Spurgeon walked in the small garden, a verse from the Bible came forcefully into his mind. "Wherefore God also hath highly exalted him, and given him a name which is above every name" (Phil 2:9, KJV). The words bathed his soul and restored his faith.

The name of Jesus became a strong tower of safety. Song burst from him, and the chains about his mind broke in pieces. He was free. Dropping to his knees, Spurgeon poured his praise out to God. The garden around him was suddenly Eden, a holy place filled with the presence of his Master.

"Oh, Lord, it matters not what ever becomes of Spurgeon and his name, so long as the name of Jesus is exalted and praised." No scorn, tumult, or war could keep him from proclaiming that name. He was a man again, God's man.

On November 2, 1856, just two weeks after the disaster at the Surrey Music Hall, Spurgeon was back in the pulpit. He preached on the text that had ended his depression—Philippians 2:9—and offered his forgiveness to those whose mischief had caused the terrible panic. He also made it clear that he still intended to preach in the great music hall. The London press's charges that in attempting to preach in a place of amusement Spurgeon was "entering into a cowardly truce and alliance with the world" left him undaunted.

And preach he did! On Sunday morning, November 23, 1856, Spurgeon proclaimed the gospel in the music hall. He continued to do so every week until December 1859.

Thirty years later, London's *Daily Telegraph*—one of his worst critics at the time of the accident—heaped praise on Spurgeon. Ironically, it pointed back to that awful night of panic in the Surrey Music Hall as the primary catalyst to his fame. Because of that night, "society went out of its way to hear the young preacher. . . ."

Charles Spurgeon was plagued the rest of his ministry by depression, discouragement, illness, and fatigue. He didn't always experience the miraculous release he received following the music hall disaster. Added to his own difficulties, he had the sorrow of seeing his wife, Susannah, become a semi-invalid at thirty-six. He admitted to frequently finding his strength unequal to his zeal. But he never let go the promise that God's grace was sufficient for him.

Over the years he began to notice that periods of depression always preceded fresh visitations of God's power in his ministry. Commenting on his frequent afflictions, he said, "I would give anything to be perfectly healthy, but if I had to go over my time again, I could not get on without those sickbeds and those bitter pains and those weary, sleepless nights. Oh, the blessedness that comes to us through suffering!"

Death claimed Spurgeon at age fifty-seven. By then he had published more than thirty-five hundred sermons, written 135 books, and pastored London Metropolitan Tabernacle for thirty-eight years. During that time, his congregation grew to more than fourteen thousand members.

What We Can Learn from
the Life of Charles Spurgeon

Most of us want, as cartoon character Charlie Brown put it, a life of "ups and upper ups." It just never feels good to feel down. But there aren't enough dollars, pleasures, or achievements to keep away the low tides of life. Charles Spurgeon experienced this and once commented, "The strong are not always vigorous, the wise not always ready, the brave not always courageous, and the joyous not always happy." Christians go through times of despair—whether they're willing to admit it or not.

Throughout his life Spurgeon was honest about his frequent discouragement and depression. He tried to prepare less-experienced Christians for dark moments. He assured them that Christ, the Man of Sorrows, knew how they felt when their hearts were breaking, that the Savior would bend to catch his children's falling tears.

Trials taught Spurgeon much about the ways of God and about the human condition. In describing his despair following the music hall tragedy in a lecture he later gave to young ministers, the following key principles emerged:

◆ *Those who trust and serve God are not exempt from dejection.* The Bible is filled with stories of people who became discouraged, people God made great in spite of their limitations, handicaps, and failures.

Turning the pages of Scripture, we discover: Jeremiah, the prophet who couldn't quit crying (Jer. 9:1); Jonah, the evangelist who pouted when people repented (Jon. 4); David, the warrior king who tried to run away (1 Sam. 27); and Peter, the two-faced apostle (Gal. 2:11-12). The secret of their greatness is revealed in a brief statement about Elijah, found in James 5:17: "Elijah was a man just like us. He prayed earnestly. . . ."

Prayer is the antidote for every hopeless situation. Even when grief strikes us speechless, the Holy Spirit goes on interceding for us until relief comes. For this very reason, he is called the Comforter.

◆ *Our suffering teaches us compassion for others.* After God touched Spurgeon and restored his courage, he was not the same man. He had strength to offer forgiveness to his enemies. He had a deeper desire to reach those who lived in the grip of depression. He could offer comfort to the grieving out of the fountain of comfort that had been opened to him.

The searing memory of pain often moves us to minister to others. Jesus' story of the man who was attacked by thieves and left on the road to die describes three different responses to pain. There are those who never get close enough to human suffering to see its face. Then there are those who come close enough to see the situation but refuse to get personally involved. But, thank God, there are a few who, in the face of suffering, stop to bind up wounds and minister healing. It is significant that Jesus chose a Samaritan to represent the healers. The most reviled group in Israel—Samaritans—knew pain firsthand.

◆ *The same characteristics that make us sensitive servants of Christ may make us more keenly aware of the multitude of sorrows in life.* God often chooses people for special service because of their awareness of their own limitations. He knows they are most likely to remain dependent on his strength and guidance. However, these same people are also apt to become too introspective and collapse under a burden of false guilt. Because they are conscientious and caring, they worry.

They may also take on far more responsibility than is healthy. There is the tug between commitments to family and outside ministry, the need for time alone with God and the practical demands of daily living. In the month preceding Spurgeon's music hall experience, he had become a father for the first time, moved his family into a new home, fought some major theological battles, lost his usual pulpit at Exeter Hall, and undergone severe criticism in the London press. No wonder he was ready to collapse!

Spurgeon later recommended that such care-worn Christians imitate Jesus, who took a nap in the middle of a terrible storm at sea. "Having left everything with His Father, our Lord did the very wisest thing possible. He did just what the hour demanded." It is good to remember that the same one who called us to get into the boat is also able to take charge of the storm that rocks it. We will find ourselves unable to face tomorrow's demands if we do not rest today.

◆ *Our pain may actually prepare us for the particular mission God has planned for us.* Could Joseph have become the trusted overseer of all Egypt's wealth if he hadn't endured rejection, imprisonment, and slavery? Each trial brought him one step closer to the throne. In looking back over his years of suffering, he said to those who had wronged him, "You intended to harm me, but God intended it for good to accomplish what is now being done, the saving of many lives" (Gen. 50:20).

God places us in the school of obedience that best fits us for future usefulness. The apostle Peter, who knew well the sting of disappointment, failure, and despair, wrote: "Though now for a little while you may have had to suffer grief in all kinds of trials. These have come so that your faith—of greater worth than gold, which perishes even though refined by fire—may be proved genuine" (1 Pet. 1:6-7).

◆ *Sorrow is inevitable in the lives of those who share God's grief over sin and evil.* Spurgeon's greatest disappointment was that the power of darkness had won over the power of light that evening at Surrey Music Hall.

George Fox, founder of the Quaker movement, said, "I prayed to God that He would baptize my heart into the sense of all conditions, so that I might be able to enter into the needs and sorrows of all." He considered this baptism of suffering essential to authentic Christian ministry. Florence Nightingale said, "My mind is absorbed with the sufferings of man." Such minds must often feel the awesome weight of a world in bondage to Satan. As Jesus sat looking out over the city of Jerusalem, he wept.

Those who set out to free Satan's captives invite attack. It isn't difficult to know who prompted someone in the gallery to yell, "Fire!" and thus start the tragic panic in the music hall just before Spurgeon preached. The enemy can always find someone whose will is set against God to use as an agent of evil. History is filled with accounts of God's people suffering from such attacks. It is also filled with reports of their healings and subsequent victories. God never abandons wounded soldiers.

◆ *Great success is almost always mixed with heartache so that we will not glory in our achievements.* For a preacher in his early twenties, Spurgeon had achieved remarkable success. He could easily have succumbed to pride. The cup of suffering he sipped acted as a strong antidote to any delusions of grandeur. Pain acted as a stern reminder that he had not been blessed in order to bring honor to his own name.

In times of trial, our ambitions, honors, and plans crumble to dust. We come out of such experiences saying, "I consider everything a loss compared to the surpassing greatness of knowing Christ Jesus my Lord" (Phil. 3:8).

◆ *Dark times drive us to new levels of trust in God and release greater dimensions of his power in our lives.* Experts on creativity report that the "Aha!" of discovery is preceded by the agony of failure. We ask all our questions, try all our theories, and still find ourselves without solutions. This emptying makes room for new insights. The same process occurs on a spiritual level. Pain cuts through our theology, our complacency, our self-sufficiency. It leaves us with quiet, humble hearts that can hear the voice of God.

These principles could seem as trite and useless as sticking a Band-Aid over a severed artery. What makes them ring with meaning is the life that backs them up. When Spurgeon talked about pain in the Christian's life, he gave personal testimony. For that same reason we can look to Christ with confidence; he is well acquainted with every grief we experience (Heb. 4:15-16).

The apostle Paul reported his sorrow to his friends in the church at Corinth. He said, "When we came into Macedonia, this body of ours had no rest, but we were harassed at every turn—conflicts on the outside, fears within. But God, who comforts the downcast, comforted us" (2 Cor. 7:5-6). God will do no less for us today.

Steps to Spiritual Greatness

- Pause. Take time to examine your motives and actions. Is your heart heavy with any burdens of sin? Let the Lord renew you in his grace.
- Pray. Pour out to God all that you feel about your circumstances, yourself, and others. Then be still in his presence and hear what he will say.
- Prioritize. Allow for necessary rest and relaxation. Respect the limits of your time and strength.
- Praise. Look for God's hand of blessing in your life. What are his gifts in the midst of your pain?
- Persevere. No matter what your emotions say, do not give up!

And the God of all grace, who called you to his eternal glory in Christ, after you have suffered a little while, will himself restore you and make you strong, firm and steadfast. (1 Pet. 5:10)

CHAPTER 6
The Ultimate Shame

Helen Roseveare's heart pounded almost as hard as the fists slamming against her bungalow door. As a white missionary doctor in the middle of revolution-torn Congo (now Zaire), she had come to expect house searches. *But at this time of night? Ridiculous!* She reached for her glasses and then slipped her housecoat over her gown. The noise at the door mounted.

"Open up for the Armée Populaire. Open up or we smash down the door!"

What could the rebel Simba soldiers want at this hour? Her panic rose, but she forced herself to take the lighted hurricane lamp and walk down the narrow hallway to the front door. Hugh and Francis, her Congolese medical assistants and bodyguards, stood on alert beside it.

She had scarcely pulled back the door bolts when six drunk Simba soldiers forced their way into the house. Their anger spewed out in vile language and insults.

"Where's your husband?" asked a young lieutenant, who was obviously enjoying his command of the night raid.

"I haven't got a husband. I'm a missionary. This is a hospital and school," Helen replied.

For the next hour the soldiers pillaged the place. The loot they gathered grew into a large pile in the living room. Finally they ordered Francis and Hugh to carry their plunder to the car.

Just when she thought they would surely leave, Helen heard the lieutenant calling her to come down the hall. *What does he want now?* she wondered. She walked toward her bedroom where the officer stood.

"Go in there and get undressed," he said.

"No!" she yelled. Then she ran. She went flying through the living room, almost knocking Hugh down. "Go, Hugh! Run!" she shouted and rushed past him into the night.

Her bare feet slipped on the muddy ground and tree branches reached out like arms to grab her. Already she could hear the soldiers closing in on her. In desperation she crawled under a small hedge and curled up in a ball of terror.

Helen silently cried out to God. *My God, where are you now? Where is your peace now? Where victory?*

Soon strong hands pulled her to her feet. The odor of liquor and sweat sickened her. *My God, my God, why have you forgotten me, forsaken me?* her tortured heart screamed.

The lieutenant hit her hard across the face. Then the soldier who had discovered her took his turn. His rubber truncheon broke three of Helen's teeth and her glasses. She felt blood run down her face and soak the front of her gown.

The end will come soon, Helen thought, certain the Simbas would kill her. She begged it to come, but it did not. One of the men retrieved her broken glasses and told her to put them on so she could see to walk back to the house.

Led as a lamb to the slaughter. The words came clearly into Helen's mind. With them came the presence of Christ. He had tasted this agony too. He had been beaten, cursed, crucified. How could he suffer so willingly? Helen only wanted to run, to resist what seemed her inevitable fate.

Helen, they're not fighting you: these blows, all this wickedness, is against me, she sensed Christ saying as she walked back to the house. *All I ask of you is the loan of your body. Will you share with*

me one hour in my sufferings for these who need my love through you?
It seemed impossible.

When they reached the veranda, the lieutenant backed Helen
against the wall and threatened her with his pistol. Suddenly
Hugh leaped between them. "Leave her alone!" he shouted.

The Simbas unleashed their fury. They beat Hugh until
Helen was certain he must be dead. The sound of their trun-
cheons and boots against his flesh made her vomit.

Then the lieutenant ordered his men into the jeep and turned
to Helen. "We're taking you back to town. You're under arrest.
Go in and put your clothes on."

She walked down the hall to her bedroom. The lieutenant
followed closely. She had scarcely slipped out of her gown when
he was on her. Too exhausted to fight, Helen screamed again
and again as the man invaded her body. Pain engulfed her whole
being. Yet peace was there too—the perfect peace of Christ.

Soon it was over. The lieutenant told Helen to dress in a
good, clean dress since she now belonged to him. Then he
walked her out to the truck and told her to get into the cab
beside him for the drive. *To prison? To death? Or to something
worse?* Helen wondered.

Helen and the other white missionaries of the area were
rounded up and imprisoned with the resident nuns in a Roman
Catholic convent. Soon the wives and children of murdered
Belgian planters were added to their number. Their collective
pain surged at flood stage. Still, moments of relief came with
good news, like that of Hugh's miraculous survival, and time
spent playing with the children.

A few days after her arrival, the Mother Superior came to
Helen with an urgent request. One of the pretty young Italian
nuns had been brutally and repeatedly raped the preceding
week. The Mother Superior's efforts to comfort her seemed
futile. "I think she is on the edge of madness," she told Helen.

"I fear she is turning toward insanity because she cannot attain death."

Helen agreed to talk with the young nun as soon as it could be arranged without arousing the guards' suspicion.

Later, standing side by side at the laundry tubs, Helen and the shattered Sister Dominique began a halting conversation.

"You must tell me what happened," Helen said. "Tell me about yourself."

Sister Dominique told how she had gladly forsaken all for the love of Christ and his church. Then she said, "There is no point in my living any more. I have no purity left. I have betrayed my trust."

"That is simply not true," Helen replied. "If you belong to Christ, if you know of Christ living in you, no one can touch your *inner* purity. Don't you understand that?"

The girl continued whispering, "I have no purity," while tears coursed down her cheeks.

"You have not lost your purity," Helen insisted in her sternest voice. "If anything, you have *gained* purity in the eyes of God. Jesus Christ suffered for us. Now you have suffered for others."

"You don't understand. You can't understand. Unless it has happened to you, how can you—"

"But it has," Helen answered. "It has happened to me."

Helen Roseveare's nightmare in the Congo lasted several more weeks. After enduring abuse, threats, and another rape, Helen was finally rescued by mercenary soldiers. She went home to England, numb with pain and certain she would never return to the Congo.

Gradually her invisible wounds healed. Letters came from dearly loved Congolese coworkers. Numbness gave way to tears and tears to hope. She finally dared ask God, "Do you want me back in Congo?"

In early 1966 Helen came back to Congo to work with Dr.

Carl Becker and establish a nursing school. She devoted her energies to producing nurses who could pass government exams and provide excellent care to patients. Her twenty years of service in the heart of Africa ended when, due to her strict discipline, a student strike forced her resignation in 1973. She left behind a dream come true—an accredited nursing school in Nyankunde, five medical centers, more than fifty rural hospitals, and a flying medical service.

Once again Helen felt pain so deep she thought she could not bear it. But that pain was turned into another powerful tool for ministry as she shared her experience with other wounded missionaries. Since leaving Congo, Helen has pursued a speaking and writing ministry aimed at educating a new generation of foreign missionaries about the cost of true commitment to Christ.

What We Can Learn from the Life of Helen Roseveare

The violent land of Congo and the torment Helen Roseveare endured there seem far away. For the average American Christian, it's easy to say, "That could never happen to me." Not only is it easy to distance ourselves from the scene of Helen's suffering, it is also tempting to distance ourselves from Helen and the God who allowed her pain. Helen's experience may provoke questions about whether she missed God's will by refusing to leave a revolution-torn country. How could God's loving purpose for her life include brutal beatings and rape?

Before considering the how and why of Helen's experience, perhaps we need to consider our own vulnerability to such pain. In early 1989, then U.S. Surgeon General C. Everett Koop said, "In the United States as many as 15 million women have been beaten, raped, or suffered other forms of physical and sexual assault, with the number rising by one million a year." An increasing number of men are sexually assaulted as well. Experts estimate that a rape occurs every six minutes somewhere in America.

Statistics like that put Helen Roseveare's experience too close for comfort. Our cans of Mace, self-defense training, and glib remarks about guardian angels become totally inadequate when confronted with the terror that stalks our streets and sometimes invades our homes. Life anywhere in the world is risky business. Unless we find our sense of security and well-being in the presence of a loving heavenly Father, we will succumb to either panic, rage, or denial.

That place of trust is where Helen Roseveare invites us. Her journey from victim to survivor to conqueror was no easy trip. The cries of anguish from her heart echo in the experiences of all who suffer violent crime. Let's listen to those cries and God's loving response.

◆ *Where are you, God?* Helen's anguished cry, "My God, my God, why have you forgotten me, forsaken me?" is echoed by millions of other victims. "Why don't you do something to stop this?" God only has one answer: His Son upon the cross. Suffering is not from God, but he doesn't avoid it either.

One of the most healing truths a victim can learn is that God in Christ fully identified with human pain. The words breathed into Helen's heart that night in the Congo—"as a lamb to the slaughter"—take Jesus out of the stained glass window and put him back where he rightfully belongs in the midst of our agony. "He was despised and rejected by men, a man of sorrows, and familiar with suffering. Like one from whom men hide their faces he was despised" (Isa. 53:3).

Perhaps we struggle so hard with the injustice of human suffering because we don't fully comprehend how completely God identifies with the shame and agony we experience. The cross has become an abstract religious symbol in our culture. It's easy to forget that Jesus endured the most degrading form of execution his world had to offer. Preceding his crucifixion, he was abused physically, mentally, and emotionally. As he prayed in Gethsemane, he faced the supreme temptation to say no to obedient sacrifice.

Because Jesus said yes to the cross, those who suffer shame and violation can be assured of his presence in their pain and his healing for all their wounds. We have a God who became "like his brothers in every way, in order that he might become a merciful and faithful high priest. . . . Because he himself suffered when he was tempted, he is able to help those who are being tempted" (Heb. 2:17-18).

And victims are tempted to self-pity and suicide, to obsession with revenge, to loss of faith and denial of God's existence. For some, God becomes the ultimate source of blame, the divine enemy. For others, like Helen Roseveare, God becomes the ultimate intimate companion. For all victims, God is either closer or farther away.

♦ *Why me?* Helen Roseveare didn't deserve what happened to her. Most crime victims don't. Some of the most loving, selfless people become prey for the wicked and violent. Their willingness to meet human need makes them more vulnerable.

Psalm 73 gives a stinging description of how it feels to suffer unjustly while the wicked prosper. Asaph, the psalm's writer, was tempted to say, "Surely in vain have I kept my heart pure; in vain have I washed my hands in innocence" (v. 13). Helen must have felt that too. For years she had begged and bargained with God for a husband and ministry partner. After finally coming to complete relinquishment of her desires regarding marriage, she experienced rape. Was this her reward for denying her natural human desires and obeying God's call to missions?

No wonder Helen hoped her attackers would kill her. Violent crimes strip away dignity and respect as the will of another is forced on the victim. Some people mistakenly think of rape as a sexual act; it is anything but that. Rape is a show of brute force, a passion for domination and control. The underlying motive is not pleasure but power.

Knowing that, it isn't hard to understand why crime victims often feel helpless. Their wills have been broken, even if only momentarily, and the lost sense of self-respect is profound. For an independent and strong-willed person like Helen, this aspect is especially painful. The "Why me, God" can turn into a bitter attack on his faithfulness or, more frequently, a merciless campaign of self-accusation.

In helping her understand the why of her attack, God brought her thoughts back to Jesus. "Helen, they're not fighting you: These blows, all this wickedness, is against me." Every act of evil we endure is really an act of rebellion against the light and love of Christ. We have only been allowed to stand in his place briefly, receiving a few of his wounds. Self-esteem returns when we are able to hear his reassuring, "Well done, good and faithful servant."

With God's help Helen began to see her painful experience in Congo as a privilege. Yes, *privilege;* the word is hers. "He didn't take away pain or cruelty or humiliation," she says. "No, it was all there, but now it was altogether different. It was with him, for him, in him. He was actually offering me the inestimable privilege of sharing in some little way in the fellowship of his sufferings."

◆ *Does anyone care or understand?* While the reassurance of God's presence in our pain brings healing, we still long for people around us to share our sorrow. Victims often find themselves alone. They feel victimized again by a criminal justice system that fails to deal effectively with their enemies, by friends and family who hurt too much to help or simply don't know how, and by Christians who pass out candy-coated, quick-fix answers.

Some victims and their families try to act as if nothing has happened. Unfortunately, churches sometimes take this attitude, encouraging people to "forget the past and look to the future." Is it possible that such advice is more the result of fear than of faith? Are we afraid that if we look deeply in the face of suffering we will no longer believe in a loving God? We need not fear. If he is not bigger than our pain, he is not God.

Throughout Scripture God encourages us to pour out our hearts to him. He says he desires truth in the inner parts, the hidden places of our lives (Ps. 51:6). It takes tremendous courage to face the anger, bitterness, unforgiveness, despair, and shame that victimization produces. Helen discovered what all victims quickly learn: some people can't handle that kind of honesty. The eyes of some of her missionary friends registered compassion and concern. But others looked at her in horror, overcome with revulsion at what she had experienced.

Mercifully, a few people understood and showed their caring in practical ways. Helen's devastating experience actually endeared her to the hearts of many of the African people. They knew what she had suffered for them, and they responded to that sacrifice with love. Part of her healing came through their sharing of her grief. One of her young Congolese medical assistants wrote her to say how ashamed he was of what his countrymen had done to her. He begged her forgiveness for himself and his country. Certain she would never return after such hateful treatment, he asked that she try to remember the many people in the Congo who still loved her.

When Helen returned to Congo to the little house where she had been raped, she found it in total shambles except for the guest room. That room had been made as beautiful and welcoming as the local African women could make it in tribute to their precious doctor.

◆ *Will I ever feel whole again?* Rape and other violent crimes leave their victims physically and emotionally disoriented. There is a feeling that life has come undone; all the normal sense of control and security is gone. Shock produces numbness, as if the union between mind and body were severed. These feelings begin during the attack but may continue for some time after the event. Victims frequently have trouble expressing emotion and perform daily tasks like robots.

For several months after returning to her family home in England, Helen's bruised emotions remained locked inside. Then during a particularly moving Palm Sunday service, the dam broke. She began sobbing aloud in the church and cried continuously for the next two days. After that she could face the painful job of rebuilding her life.

Fortunately, Helen had already firmly fixed her identity in Christ before this trauma occurred. Repeated relinquishment of her "rights" to the will of God formed a safety net of grace to catch her fall. The person whose self-esteem is rooted in the actions of God rather than in self-effort will become a quick healer.

Compare Helen's reaction with that of the young Italian nun to whom she ministered. The nun's sense of identity came from *her* devotion to Christ, *her* purity. Helen lovingly pointed out to her that our real purity belongs to him and cannot be touched by anyone. It's important to note that she allowed the young woman to vent her feelings, listened with sincere concern, and then responded gently but firmly with truth.

We must face both sides of the truth—the darkness and the light—in order to experience true freedom. In the case of rape, there are some very real and practical issues to confront, such as possible disease or pregnancy, awakened sexual desire, flash-backs, and threat of repeated violations through unsafe living conditions. Some of these matters may require a person to seek the help of trained professionals. Life may never be the same, but, through personal growth and divine healing, it can actually become richer.

Recovery doesn't come through erasing the experience. It results when we are able to realize that, no matter how devastating the experience, it is only one small piece of our lives. Helen writes:

> I had to learn to live with memory in an understood perspective: I had to learn to accept it as part of the whole before I could possibly face going back to the same place, the same work, the same companions. . . . I needed to remember honestly . . . all that God had enabled us to achieve in his service.

Helen Roseveare made the pilgrimage from victim to overcomer. But she didn't make it alone. In looking back on her rape, she says, "It was an unbelievable experience. [God] was so utterly there, so totally understanding. His comfort was so complete—and suddenly I knew, I really *knew* that his love was unutterably sufficient."

Healing and transformation came as she experienced the reality of Isaiah 54:4-5:

> Do not be afraid; you will not suffer shame. Do not fear disgrace; you will not be humiliated. You will forget the shame of your youth and remember no more the reproach. . . . For your Maker is your husband—the Lord Almighty is his name.

Steps to Spiritual Greatness
- Pour out. Learn to be completely honest with God. Tell him everything you think and feel.
- Partner. Find friends and professionals who will help you recover. It is all right to need help.

- Persist. Be patient with the healing process.
- Pardon. Forgive those who have wronged you. (This does not mean they will be released from the penalty of their actions.)
- Prospect. Explore new life possibilities. Celebrate your survival!

The Lord stood at my side and gave me strength. . . .
And I was delivered from the lion's mouth. The Lord
will rescue me from every evil attack and will bring me
safely to his heavenly kingdom. To him be glory for ever
and ever. Amen. (2 Tim. 4:17-18)

Section Three

•••••••••••••••

BROKEN BODIES

CHAPTER 7
Crucified with Christ

"I am seized by a great contempt for the world," Blaise Pascal wrote to his sister Jacqueline. He was certain that confession would bring rejoicing at the Port Royal convent where she had taken vows.

Am I fallen from the faith as Jacqueline believes? Perhaps so, he thought wearily. The pleasures of Paris that had occupied him for the past few years revolted him now, yet he could find no road leading back to God. The elegant court of Louis XIV and the stimulating friends he had acquired did nothing to fill the void in his life.

His faith in God was not gone, but his fellowship had evaporated like mist in the heat of his intellectual passions. His scientific and mathematical achievements commanded the awe of France. His wit and humor made him a welcome guest in the most elite circles of society. He should have been happy, but he felt like a worm, a monster, a chaos of contradictions.

For months he experienced torment, losing himself briefly in conversation or research only to have the darkness of his soul return in every moment of still silence. Added to that were growing financial problems. He could feel his health giving way from the strain.

Pascal searched the great philosophers' writings for comfort and found none. He turned to the Bible, but it only made him weep with remorse for his horrible attachment to the world and the spiritual apathy that kept him from deliverance.

He decided to visit Port Royal. Perhaps Jacqueline could help him.

"I want to quit my occupation with the world," he told her. "My conscience drives me to cut myself off from all its follies and beguilements. But I feel abandoned by God. He does not draw me to himself, and I cannot come alone."

Jacqueline left him to his misery. His agony seemed more than he could endure. Then late on the twenty-third of November 1654 everything changed. Pascal's house on Rue des Francs-Bourgeois in Saint-Michel welcomed a special guest—God.

"FIRE," he scribbled in ecstasy on the paper before him. "God of Abraham, God of Isaac, God of Jacob, not of the philosophers and scholars." His heart took hold of what his mind could never grasp.

"Certitude, certitude, feeling, joy, peace. God of Jesus Christ." For the next two hours glory filled his entire being. The shame of his separation from his Lord was replaced by total conviction of grace. At the end of the two-hour ecstasy he wrote, "Renunciation, total and sweet." The long war was over.

"Oh, Lord, let what remains to me of life be a continual penitence to wipe out the offenses I have committed," he prayed. He could scarcely wait to go to Port Royal with this great glad news and to begin his new life of devotion.

Pascal lay on his bed, racked with pain from head to toe. He fingered his coat lapel where the hidden parchment testimony of his glorious encounter with God was carefully hidden. Four years old now, the words still burned in him. Why had he devoted himself again to geometry? Why had he allowed such a useless pursuit to dominate his life at the expense of the eternal?

"No more!" he vowed. He took up his pen and poured out his heart to God.

> Lord, you gave me health to serve you, and I have made an utterly profane use of it. You now send me sickness to correct me. . . . Lord, I confess that I have esteemed health as good, not because it is an easy means to serve you usefully . . . but because by its favor I could abandon myself with less restraint to the abundance of life's charms, and better enjoy their deadly pleasure.

Pascal cried out for God's correction. "Grant that in this illness I may consider myself as in a kind of death, separated from the world, stripped clean of all the objects of my attachments, alone in your presence. . . ."

A final barrier had been breached. He would not look back this time. All that he had, all that he was, all the devotion of his heart and mind would belong to God alone.

For the last four years of his life, Blaise Pascal kept that commitment with a fierce abandonment that demands respect. He poured himself into work on a comprehensive apology for the Christian faith. He fearlessly defended the doctrine of salvation through grace. He gave all he had to the needy and filled his heart and mind with God's Word.

At his death in 1662, Pascal's brief life of thirty-nine years overflowed with accomplishments. In our modern secular society Pascal is best remembered as a genius in mathematics, physics, and literature. He is considered the father of integral calculus. The namesake of this remarkable seventeenth-century intellectual is a sophisticated computer language that processes numerical and textual data. While that may be a fitting tribute to his marvelous mind, it ignores the heart of the man. Only in the emotion-packed pages of the *Pensées* (a compilation of the notes for the Christian apology he did not live to write) do we discover what mattered most to Pascal—his pursuit of God.

In his final years Pascal offered his life to God as a living sacrifice. His intellectual pride, his fascination with the world, his impatience and intolerance became mortal enemies, more to be feared than the disease that consumed his body. While some of his ascetic practices were misguided, Pascal courageously explored the nature of faith and grace, leaving a powerful testament of a heart on fire with God.

What We Can Learn from the Life of Blaise Pascal

In his short life Pascal suffered excruciating pain. He experienced spiritual and mental distress, but both were eclipsed by the horror of his physical distress. Pain was Pascal's daily companion by the age of eighteen. At twenty-four he experienced a temporary paralysis that lasted several months. His autopsy revealed advanced intestinal tuberculosis and a massive brain hemorrhage. His ability to transcend profound pain in meaningful activity is a tribute to the grace of God at work in his life. When Pascal's name is mentioned, achievement and genius come to mind rather than suffering and incapacity.

The apostle Paul stated as fact that "no one ever hated his own body" (Eph. 5:29). If a man ever had reason to, Pascal did. He was blessed with a mind that needed constant challenge and stimulation, but that mind was trapped in a weak body constantly subject to illness and disease. Bursts of research and activity gave way to periods of incapacity. Every project he started was in danger of being left unfinished due to his ill health and the threat of death.

Like modern sufferers, Pascal tried several means to distract himself from his pain. He used his intellect to probe the mysteries of life until his health demanded relief from the stress.

Then he attempted to humor his body by giving it leisure and delight, indulgence and diversion. While the body profited from this approach, his inner landscape became a wasteland. Finally, he turned to a rigorous pursuit of spirituality, praying to transcend the physical world.

In these pursuits he discovered that "man is a being filled with error. This error is natural and, without grace, ineffaceable." If he was to enjoy triumph in or over pain, it would be through God's grace alone. We can profit by Pascal's mistakes and follow in his footsteps toward the Lord's arms of mercy.

♦ *The road of pride in one's accomplishments leads to pain.* In terms of intellect and accomplishment, Pascal had many reasons for pride. A child prodigy in math, he enjoyed frequent praise for his mental gifts. By age sixteen he had published his first essay, based on his study of the cone and projective geometry. At nineteen he invented a calculating machine, a forerunner of the modern computer. His scientific and mathematical research amazed Europe's leading intellectuals. His questing mind probed the vacuum, the nature of air and fluids, the laws of probability, and the triangle.

When his attention turned to spiritual matters, it was first his mind rather than his heart that embraced the doctrine of grace. He eagerly committed himself to the cause of Jansenism (an evangelical movement in the Roman Catholic church). His study of human nature led him to a logical deduction that grace alone could produce salvation, as Jansenism taught. He set out at once to convert others through reason and wit. His biting defense of the Jansenists against the Jesuits awed readers with its style and effectiveness. His letters were translated into many languages and remained much loved for more than two hundred years. Whatever he put his mind to prospered.

In the midst of this acclaim and success, Pascal became increasingly aware of his bondage to pride and conceit. He could not resist the passion to excel even when he knew the terrible cost to his physical well-being. He understood the words of Ecclesiastes: "Of making many books there is no end, and much study wearies the body" (12:12). And, "with much wisdom comes much sorrow; the more knowledge, the more grief" (1:18).

In our remarkable "information age," many of us experience that same grief. In a quest for knowledge and achievement, we sacrifice health and relationships. Like Pascal, we reach our goals only to find the taste of ashes in our mouth. Our frustration is compounded by efforts to deny our God-given abilities rather than dedicate them to their Giver for his glory.

In describing her brother, Pascal's sister could easily be describing the modern fast-track achiever: "Those who did not know him were at first surprised when they heard him in conversation because he always seemed to be taking charge, with a sort of domination." A friend commented that Pascal seemed constantly angry, as if he wanted to swear. It's not hard to discover the source of that anger—superiority, self-absorption, and physical exhaustion.

◆ *The path of pleasure leads to death.* When Pascal's fragile health collapsed, doctors ordered him to take the pleasure cure, to lay aside his research and enjoy society. He disliked the prescription, but he determined to follow it in hopes of regaining his health. However, we should not imagine him reveling in the depths of Parisian immorality. Pascal's idea of self-indulgence was a life of theater-going, intellectual sparring, gentlemanly gambling, and society parties. This mild-mannered prodigal, so used to rigorous discipline of mind and body, allowed himself to enjoy life's pleasures and wasted hours.

His physical health definitely improved during this period of decreased demand. But his awareness of God's presence and his pursuit of eternal things declined rapidly. The problem was not with rest and relaxation; Pascal was in desperate need of both. His mistake was setting aside spiritual nourishment while he stuffed himself with the husks of worldly pleasure. In looking back on these years, he sorrowed that he had crucified the Lord afresh by ignoring him.

Pascal's attitude toward spiritual things during his worldly years is revealed in his reaction to his sister Jacqueline's desire to enter the Jansenist convent. He argued with her insistence on giving the rest of her life to austere religious devotion. He particularly opposed her request to give her portion of the family inheritance to the convent.

With piercing insight into her brother's personality, Jacqueline said, "If you do not possess the strength to follow me, at least do not hold me back. Do not show yourself ungrateful to God for the grace He has given to a person whom you love." She recognized that Pascal was jealous of her clear focus on eternal matters. Like a man trapped in quicksand, he fought to be free only to sink deeper into the things of the world.

How many times have we experienced that same struggle? Whenever we attempt to serve two masters, we invite misery. Like the rich young ruler who came to Jesus seeking salvation, we turn away sorrowful because we cannot let go of what is in our hands. It is not comfort or money or acclaim or title that corrupts us; it is our love of these things that chokes out the love of Christ.

◆ *The way of perfection leads to the cross.* Having truly tasted the delight of God's favor, Pascal could not content himself without it. The depth of his remorse for his spiritual coldness is a searing indictment of today's careless, carnal Christian. After experiencing cleansing and restoration in his fellowship, Pascal set out to rid his life of everything but God.

The Jansenist doctrine, like that of many pietistic and holiness groups since, taught complete relinquishment of all secular pursuits, pleasures, and interests. Pascal tried to follow that narrow path, but his fascination with science and mathematics kept distracting him. With every distraction came a fresh load of unnecessary guilt.

Pascal didn't believe his works would save him, but he saw God's grace as a gift so profound that it demanded a commitment to holy living. "No compromise" could easily have been his motto. He took seriously Scripture's commands to mortify (put to death) the earthly nature. If Jesus said it was better to lose an eye or a hand than to allow either to lead one into sin, who was Pascal to hold back from the surgery? Like many Christians today, in his effort to obey revealed truth, he went a step too far and fell into error.

As his illness and resulting disability progressed, he dismissed his servants, refused to take pleasure in food, and stripped his sickroom of any adornments. Throughout the horrors of his illness and the torture of seventeenth-century medical treatment, he expressed no discomfort. Most of his estate, including his books, he gave to the poor. Those who visited found him animated with spiritual joy and humble as a child.

Pascal's remaining energy of mind and body were poured into hundreds of notes for what he envisioned as a comprehensive apology for the Christian faith. The miraculous healing of his niece's incurable eye fistula convinced him more than ever of the power of God and of the love that sends that power into our broken world. The notes he scribbled as he searched the Scriptures and prayed pulsed with spiritual passion.

Still he was not satisfied with his devotion and purity. Pascal was as determined to excel in holiness as he had been in any other pursuit. So he began to wear a belt studded with sharp points under his clothing. Whenever he experienced a prideful thought or pleasure or felt his attention drift from Christ, he bore down on the belt with his elbow until the spikes dug into his flesh.

Such masochistic behavior offends our modern sensibilities. But how many times have we inflicted similar, though more subtle, pains on ourselves? How many Christians practice various forms of self-hatred in the name of discipleship? The needs of the body are ignored, the life of the mind despised, and the natural affections for family and friends denied—all in the name of Christ.

The apostle Paul attacked these deadly attitudes in his letter to the Galatian Christians. He shamed their move from faith to works. "After beginning with the Spirit, are you now trying to attain your goal by human effort?" he asked (3:3). In a moment of supreme vexation with those who insisted on circumcision as essential to right relationship with God, Paul wrote, "As for those agitators, I wish they would go the whole way and emasculate themselves!" (5:12).

Paul of all people could have understood the battle Pascal faced. He, too, had a brilliant mind. He excelled as a leader. He had incredible spiritual insight. His reasons for pride abounded. But he knew that God alone could position the pricks and thorns of life in such a way as to deal with his arrogant zeal and his religious conceit. We can't purify ourselves any more than we can provide grace for our eternal salvation.

So how can we grow in grace and godly character? Paul summed up the road to righteousness in one simple but profound statement: "Love your neighbor as yourself." True faith works by love—love of God, love of others, love of our own flawed selves. That three-part love flows only from the cross of Jesus Christ and is activated in our lives by submission to the Holy Spirit. In his power we can say, "I have been crucified with Christ and I no longer live, but Christ lives in me. The life I live in the body, I live by faith in the Son of God, who loved me and gave himself for me" (Gal. 2:20).

Achieving a balance between the freedom of grace and the call to self-discipline is no easy matter. After years of struggle, the great reformationist Martin Luther wisely advised Christians:

> Everyone can use his own discretion as to fasting and watching, for everyone knows how much he must do to master his body. Those, however, who think they become pious through works have no regard for fasting but only for the works and, imagining that they are pious when they do much in that direction, sometimes break their heads over it and ruin their bodies.

In his misguided effort to please God, Pascal advocated self-hatred. He would have done well to ponder a proverb from another wise man: "Hatred stirs up dissension, but love covers over all wrongs" (Prov. 10:12). Self-hatred serves only to stir up internal dissension; it calls attention to the very sin it tries to eradicate. But the merciful love of Christ covers a multitude of human errors. Because of that covering love, Paul could write, "There is now no condemnation for those who are in Christ Jesus" (Rom. 8:1).

God in his majestic covering love looked beyond Pascal's preoccupation with self and received his passionately devoted heart. Through grace the sickroom became a cathedral of praise, and the bed of pain became an altar of consecration. The testimony of Pascal is that the Lord reveals himself most clearly through our weakness, not our perfection. Was his suffering wasted? Let him answer:

> It is a good thing to be wearied and spent by the useless search for the true good, so that one may hold out one's arms to the liberator.

Steps to Spiritual Greatness

- Trust that health is not a measure of heaven's favor.
- Test your understanding of truth against the whole counsel of Scripture.
- Trade your preoccupation with pain for a deeper understanding of Christ's suffering.
- Teach others the lessons you learn through pain.
- Triumph over pain by excelling in some meaningful endeavor.
- Tame the temptation to glory in anything (including illness or health) except the work of Christ.

Since, then, you have been raised with Christ, set your hearts on things above, where Christ is seated at the right hand of God. Set your minds on things above, not on earthly things. For you died, and your life is now hidden with Christ in God. . . . And whatever you do, whether in word or deed, do it all in the name of the Lord Jesus, giving thanks to God the Father through him. (Col. 3:1-3, 17)

CHAPTER 8
Eyes of the Heart

Fanny Crosby's shoulders bent more than usual as she faced another day in the dreary Manhattan apartment. Since her precious baby had died, time had hung on her like a lead weight. *What can't be cured can be endured.* She repeated the phrase her grandmother had lived by and taught her early in life. But it didn't ease the ache in her heart.

All she had wanted was to be a wife and mother like any other young woman. Her heart was so hungry for love. She enjoyed teaching, but it wasn't enough. Neither was being the school's famed "blind poetess." Who wanted to spend a lifetime being made over by people who had no idea what you really felt or thought? Marriage to Van and escape from the city had seemed the ideal solution six years ago.

Memories of the little home she and Van had made in the village of Maspeth rushed back. Life had seemed perfect, especially after the baby came. But now. . . . Now they were back in New York City, but for what? She still had Van, but he could not sweeten the bitter taste of sorrow. It had been over three years since the baby had died, yet the wound still throbbed.

She grieved over the horrible war caused by the South's insurrection too. Her anger boiled at the thought of all the lives wasted in the past three years of fighting. Words to a stinging battle song against the evil traitors bubbled into her mind. *Vanity and vexation!*

What shall I do with the rest of my life? At forty-three it was ridiculous to think of another child. She didn't want to go back to teaching at the Institution. But her charity work at the John Street Methodist Church and her poetry writing left her unfulfilled.

Desperate for direction and inspiration, Fanny visited one church and then another. She knew her help must come from God, but she also knew she must search out his plan for her. On a visit to the Dutch Reformed church, Pastor Stryker suggested she meet a musician friend of his named William B. Bradbury.

Bradbury! Fanny immediately agreed. She was eager to know this man who had written so many of the great revival songs of the past few years. And Pastor Stryker said Bradbury needed someone to write lyrics for his music. *Is this my answer?* she wondered.

She went home to ponder the possibility. For so long she had felt no real hope for her future. But now as she thought about Bradbury's hymns, a miraculous vision came.

Her senses more fully alive than ever before, Fanny was spiritually transported to a large observatory. A friend instructed her to look through a giant telescope in a certain direction. There she focused on a brilliant, captivating star. As she looked, she moved toward it—past other stars and celestial scenery too wonderful to describe.

Then she came to a river and paused there. "May I not go on?" she asked her guide.

"Not now, Fanny. You must return to the earth and do your work there before you enter those sacred bounds; but ere you go, I will have the gates opened a little way, so you can hear one burst of the celestial music."

Soon the air was filled with music more beautiful than any Fanny had ever heard. Then the music ended, the vision ended, and Fanny abruptly returned to the shabby apartment. But the thrill of the heavenly music continued to course through her. With it came certainty that at last she knew what to do with her life.

Her anticipation mounted as the date of her meeting with Bradbury neared. At last, February 2, 1864, arrived and she went to his office at the Ponton Hotel. Though she couldn't see his face, she immediately felt his goodness. He greeted her warmly.

"Fanny, I thank God that we have at last met, for I think you can write hymns; and I have wished for a long time to have a talk with you."

The time passed quickly as they discussed collaborating. Bradbury asked Fanny to return in a week with a sample hymn.

Back in her apartment the music seemed to flow through her, bringing the perfect words with it. In three days she was ready to show her poem to Bradbury. The delighted musician wasted no time promising Fanny a lifetime partnership.

Fanny wanted to dance for joy. At last she had found her life's work.

For the next fifty-one years, Fanny Crosby knew beyond a doubt what she was living for. During that time she wrote thousands of songs. Though she was never paid more than one or two dollars for her lyrics and never made more than four hundred dollars per year, Fanny felt rich. She was doing what she loved—listening for heaven's music and putting it into everyday words that common people could sing.

She cared little for anything material. Out of her modest income she found ample to share with the poor. She considered them her foremost ministry and refused to alter her life-style in any way that would distance her from them. At the same time, she felt comfortable with the most affluent, gifted, and famous people of her day.

So popular and beloved did she become that on her eighty-fifth birthday a "Fanny Crosby Day" was instituted in churches around the world. Her best loved songs were translated into many languages and still grace the pages of most church hymnals. For the past one hundred years people have been won to Christ, strengthened, and comforted by singing such favorites as: "God Will Take Care of You," "Blessed Assurance," "I Am Thine, O Lord," "Jesus, Keep Me Near the Cross," "Pass Me Not, O Gentle Savior," "Draw Me Nearer," and "Rescue the Perishing."

Rather than destroying her life, Fanny's blindness shut out enough of the world so she could hear the music of heaven. She said, "Sightless, I see, and, seeing, find soul-vision, though my eyes are blind." That vision strengthened her to work until the age of ninety-one. She worked tirelessly, writing, speaking, ministering in the slums and missions of New York City, and praying for those spiritually blinded by sin.

When she died at age ninety-five, the simple tombstone erected on her grave captured the essence of her life: "Aunt Fanny. She hath done what she could."

What We Can Learn from the Life of Fanny Crosby

When someone wins the affection and acclaim awarded Fanny Crosby, the word *handicap* loses much of its meaning. Not only did she enjoy popularity, she cultivated a deep spirituality and left a body of work that has continued to minister for generations. We are so awed by the achievement that it's easy to forget the cost in terms of pain, frustration, and disappointment.

Human nature likes the hosannas and hoopla of welcoming a winner, especially one that surmounted incredible odds. But with the waving palms of triumphal entries, there are desert experiences and Gethsemanes of relinquishment. Rather than becoming part of the fickle cheering throng, we profit more from searching the lives of overcomers for keys to handling our own handicapping circumstances. Particularly in the area of physical limitation, Fanny Crosby's life serves as a model for healthy, productive living. Let's take a look at the weights she had to throw off in order to run her race.

◆ *Physical handicaps put painful limits on life.* In terms of education and employment, the prospects for the blind in Fanny's day were extremely grim. Our society has come a long way, but it still struggles with bringing equal opportunity to the handicapped. Those with physical limitations must have strong determination to enter and stay in the mainstream of life.

Fanny had a brilliant mind, but, without eyes to study, she had limited means of increasing her knowledge. She partially satisfied her desire to learn by listening to others read and by memorizing as much as she could.

One of Fanny's most remarkable childhood achievements became central in her personal and artistic development. She committed to memory the first four books of the Old Testament, the four Gospels, many Psalms, the book of Proverbs, the Song of Solomon, and Ruth. For the rest of her life, she could reach into this sacred treasure chest for resources to help overcome her limitations.

No handicapped person can afford to overlook the wealth available to him or her in the Bible. Its truth has power to enlarge our horizons, strengthen our wills, and fuel our creativity. It will also drive us to dare amazing things because it reveals that our sufficiency is in God rather than ourselves.

In addition to spiritual aid, Fanny had a brave and loving mother who encouraged her efforts. While a young girl, Fanny learned to ride horseback, climb trees, and play outdoor games with sighted children. She also began composing poetry and playing the guitar.

As Fanny entered her teens, she grew more frustrated by her lack of educational opportunity. God answered her heart cry by opening the door for her to enroll in New York's pioneer Institution for the Blind. She quickly distinguished herself as a gifted student and then as a teacher. Still, she remained dependent on readers and scribes throughout her life. Her courageous independence had to be balanced with a healthy willingness to accept help.

Achieving that delicate balance between dependence and autonomy is no easy matter. Not only must the handicapped struggle to achieve it, but also those involved in their lives must learn when to lift and when to let go. Three qualities are essential to the process: dignity, diplomacy, and determination.

◆ *Physical handicaps raise questions about God's love.* Not every person who struggles with a less-than-whole body draws closer to God as Fanny Crosby did. Some handicapped people and their families actually lose faith as they question how a just God can allow the innocent to suffer.

Jesus' disciples looked at a man born blind and asked Jesus about the cause of his malady. "Is it because he or his parents sinned?" they asked. They made a false assumption that many still make; they assumed that physical impairment had a burden of guilt attached to it. Although sin can produce sickness and disease in the lives of those who harbor it, many of the afflicted are free of such guilt. The Lord responded by saying that neither the man nor his parents had sinned and that his condition would be a means of demonstrating God's glory and power.

There aren't any easy or complete answers to the whys of broken and impaired bodies. Fanny never pretended there were. She knew the sting of life's unfairness. Her blindness was the result of an incompetent doctor's prescription of hot poultices for an eye infection she contracted at six weeks of age.

In one of her best poems, "Samson and the Philistines," Fanny captured the agony of blindness:

O to be left at midday in the dark!
To wander on and on in moonless night!
To know the windows of the soul are closed,
And closed till opened in eternity!
They who have felt can tell how deep the gloom,
And only they who in their souls have learned
To walk by faith and lean on God for help,
To such a lot can e'er be reconciled.

Fanny's family dealt with any uncertainties they had about the justice of God by relying on their stoical Presbyterian faith. When eye specialists told Fanny and her mother that there was no hope of restoring her vision, Grandmother Crosby reasoned, "If the Lord does not want you to have what you have prayed for, then it is best for you not to have it." Rugged Puritan determination was the hallmark of their lives.

Of a gentler, more sensitive disposition, Fanny came to terms with God's will in a somewhat different way. "The idea is repulsive to me that the Lord looked down on baby Fanny Crosby and ordained that she should be blind for life," she said. She saw her infirmity as a direct consequence of the doctor's blunder but believed God had helped her turn the blindness into a blessing.

Whatever the theological means of coming to terms with suffering, a firm conviction of the Lord's love and participating presence in pain is essential to health. Faith reaches for a complete cure. Patience perseveres in the dark. Hope looks through the prison windows into paradise.

◆ *Physical handicaps often elicit negative responses from others.* Fanny experienced the full range of unpleasant reactions to her blindness. She encountered people who pitied her and tried to shield her from life, offering unnecessary help. Fanny ignored or, if necessary, actively resisted those who deterred her pursuit of rigorous service to God.

"A great many people sympathize with me," Fanny said, "but although I am grateful to them, I really don't need their sympathy. What would I do with it?" She had no memory of being sighted and had spent her life surmounting whatever difficulties blindness presented with fortitude and a large supply of humor.

Those who treated her as a curiosity and put her talents on display were harder to deal with. Only by God's grace and her mother's watchful care did she escape life as one of P. T. Barnum's circus attractions. At the Institution her poetic talents were often merchandised and dwarfed. While many extolled her gifts as "the blind poetess," few understood her needs and feelings. In a moment of deep frustration Fanny said, "Some people seem to forget that blind girls have just as great a faculty for loving and *do* love just as much and just as truly as those who have their sight."

In spite of these misunderstandings, Fanny forgave people. She never tired of reaching out to anyone who would let her. Some of her closest friends were wealthy New York Christians. Her deepest affection, though, went to poor and downcast people of her city. After the age of sixty, she considered her ministry in the Bowery District, New York's worst slum area, her primary calling.

Wherever Fanny went, she purposed to show kindness, believing it to be the greatest tool for leading people to Christ. Having felt the sting of unkindness, she knew how great the gift of thoughtfulness could be.

◆ *Physical handicaps compound life's sorrows.* For those who must tackle each day with battlefield heroism, little energy remains for dealing with added crises. There isn't room for one more problem or grief or disappointment. But, no matter how loudly we cry, "Foul!" the poison darts keep flying.

Fanny certainly understood about having sorrow on top of sorrow. In addition to her blindness, she grew up fatherless and in poverty. Her heart nearly broke when she had to say good-bye to her mother at fourteen in order to get an education. As a young woman she was grieved as her mother's second marriage was torn apart by a cult. The stress on Fanny became so great at one point that she became ill and had to leave her teaching position at the Institution. Many of her friends there expected her to die rather than return, but God had other plans.

She also suffered in her marriage to a man she rapidly grew away from in interests and friendships. Her marriage eventually ended in permanent separation. This sorrow, as well as the death of her only child, hurt too much for Fanny to share with anyone but God. Rather than talking about her grief, she cheerfully busied herself with the needs of others.

Blessed with good health, Fanny outlived most of her closest friends and family. She mourned deeply the difficult passing of cherished giants like D. L. Moody and Ira Sankey. Eventually, she had to resign herself to leaving her beloved New York City to live with relatives. The opportunities for bitterness were plentiful.

But Fanny was not bitter. What was the secret of her remarkable endurance? "One of my earliest resolves . . . was to leave all care to yesterday, and to believe that the morning would bring forth . . . joy," Fanny explained. Her life echoed the determination of the apostle Paul, who said, "One thing I do: Forgetting what is behind and straining toward what is ahead, I press on toward the goal" (Phil. 3:13-14).

The lines of her songs were her lifelines in this pursuit. Out of her broken heart came the words:

Perfect submission, all is at rest,
I in my Savior am happy and blest;
Watching and waiting, looking above,
Filled with His goodness, lost in His love.

She was not repressing memories and emotions; she was burying them in the ocean of God's love. "The Lord planted a star in my life," she said, "and no cloud has ever obscured its light." He had answered her prayers in a way that exceeded her highest aspirations. No wonder her motto was Trust God and Take Heart.

We can expect God to plant a guiding star in our lives as well. He may not do it through a vision or other dramatic means, but his light will shine in such a way that we are beckoned to follow. Our creative outlet may not be songwriting, but we can have a song in our heart as we do whatever the Lord calls us to.

In *Notable American Women, 1607-1950: A Biographical Dictionary* (Harvard U. Press, 1971), Fanny Crosby is written off as a prolific poet who "was unable to rise above the conventional; her claim to distinction must rest not upon the quality but the quantity of her achievement and upon her attractiveness as a curiosity."

Countering that low estimate of Fanny's worth, Christian historian Ruth A. Tucker writes, "Preachers, theologians, and Bible scholars, who would not permit a woman to speak or teach in a worship service, week after week sang her hymns and profited by her ministry."

During her lifetime, critics labeled her poems and hymns as sentimental and clichéd. Fanny sloughed off the criticism and kept going. Never mind that they said she couldn't do better; she knew she could. Her intelligence and musical ability were unquestionable. In the spirit of Christ, she deliberately chose simple words that the sick and distressed could sing with ease. What a shining example of living for the purpose of God rather than the praises of people.

Like another songwriter, the Psalmist David, Fanny could say, "Lord, you have assigned me my portion and my cup. . . . The boundary lines have fallen for me in pleasant places" (Ps. 16:5-6). Handicapped? Hardly!

Steps to Spiritual Greatness
- Discover your destiny through prayer and the Bible.
- Discipline yourself to make the most of what you have been given.
- Devote yourself wholeheartedly to God and others.
- Determine to make your life count for the kingdom.
- Defy the devil and all his discouraging helpers.

I pray that the eyes of your heart may be enlightened in order that you may know the hope to which he has called you, the riches of his glorious inheritance in the saints, and his incomparably great power for us who believe. (Eph. 1:18-19)

CHAPTER 9
Streams in the Desert

Lettie Cowman sighed. *Rest. I must rest in God and trust him to provide the money,* she thought. *And rest, Lord, send rest to my beloved Charles.* The demands of the Japanese gospel literature campaign seemed insurmountable. *But with God nothing shall be impossible,* she reminded herself. The reports coming to their temporary headquarters in Kuamoto were encouraging. Still she struggled against worry.

She looked down at her open diary. There were no words for the concern she felt. Tears slid down her cheeks and spattered the page. Hearing Charles enter the room, she quickly brushed them away.

"Sweetheart, keep tonight for me," he said. "I want to walk up the hill with you this evening. I have a secret to tell you."

The rest of the day Lettie puzzled over his mysterious words. Had an offering come in the mail in answer to their prayers? Did he have some wonderful news?

The hours seemed to drag on as she worked. But then as the sun set, she and Charles trudged up the nearby hill. Lettie looked up expectantly at her husband. "Well, what is this surprise?"

Charles answered in a solemn voice. "I have been having such heart pain at night. If I go on with this crusade, I fear I will die.

If I do not go on, there are millions that will die without hearing of Christ."

The words broke her heart. She knew there could be only one decision for a servant of God like her Charles: *Onward!* She could do nothing but cry out to the Lord for help and healing.

In the following weeks, Lettie learned to dread the nights. Each brought another vigil with Charles through hours of sleepless agony. The pain in his chest kept worsening.

Then at last the campaign was completed. Looking back over their seventeen years in Japan, Lettie realized that much of the foundation for the Oriental Missionary Society had been laid: establishing the Bible institute, training national workers, and placing Scripture in more than 10 million homes. No wonder Charles's heart was worn out.

Sadly, they packed to return to the States, leaving their work in stronger hands. As they sailed away, their prayers for healing and a speedy return flew up to God.

Charles groaned as pain ripped through his chest. The train sped down the track toward their speaking appointment in Owosso, Michigan. Lettie prayed Charles would make it to the next stop and a doctor. He had been so much better the past few months, so eager to be back about his Master's business. She hadn't dreamed he was near collapse. But all the speaking and preaching and praying, the traveling cross country . . .

As soon as the train stopped, Lettie slipped her arm around Charles and helped him detrain. She sent for a doctor immediately, all the while calling on the Great Physician.

The doctor arrived and examined Charles. Finally, he looked up. "Sir, I'm sorry, but your work is finished. Go home."

Six years. Six long years of living hell. Watching Charles burn up what little strength he had in trying to carry on the work of OMS through article writing, interviews, financial oversight, and letters. Each night wondering if he would have another attack. Sleeplessness. Tears. Searching the Scripture. Trusting God more each day for complete healing. Watching for some sign of his answer. All the powers of darkness seemed determined to destroy their faith in God's love.

How much more can Charles bear? Lettie wondered. One attack last night, three attacks tonight. No longer able to lie in bed, Charles rested what little he could in a large chair in their living room.

Night after night he sat in his chair and looked at the maps of the world hanging on their walls. All his desire reached out to the harvest fields where souls waited to hear of Jesus' love. He could not go now. But he could pray. Lettie watched through the night hours with him, listening as he poured out his requests to God. "Lord, awaken a sleeping church. Help us to do what we could if we only cared. Help us, in this generation, to obey thy command to preach the gospel to every creature."

When Charles wasn't praying or dozing, Lettie read to him. Endlessly collecting books and magazines, she searched for words of encouragement. Out of the dark mine of her sorrow she dug golden nuggets of hope to share with Charles. And together they searched the Bible to find God's will for their lives.

Increasingly certain that the Lord desired Charles's total healing, they stopped asking and started praising. Still the symptoms continued. *Why does God delay in answering?* Lettie and Charles wondered. *Are we being disobedient in some area?* They humbled themselves in deeper consecration than ever before. Friends visited to pray with them, and, as they talked about the Lord's provision for healing, Charles cried. They couldn't want it more, but they didn't know what else to do to receive.

In an effort to act on his faith, Charles tried to walk in the neighborhood each day. Often, after only a block, weakness and pain forced him to sit on the curb an hour or more before he could return home. Still, his faith in God's love and healing power endured. Refusing to complain, he filled the hours with song and Scripture. During those dark days, a question began pricking Lettie's mind. *Am I more concerned about healing than about God's working out his purpose through the illness and testing?* She determined to trust that God would eventually reveal the reason for the fiery furnace.

A period of improvement came only to be followed by worse attacks than ever. A stroke paralyzed Charles' right side. Lettie grew more and more exhausted. Then peace came flooding over her, refreshing her weary spirit and body. "Lord, I have no request; I have no desire. My will is lost in Thine," she prayed.

Later, standing beside Charles's bed, she quoted Psalm 23 to him.

"Am I a lamb?" he asked.

"Yes, you are, Charlie. You are God's lamb."

"I am a sick lamb," he said in a whisper. "I don't want to go and leave you alone in this cruel world, Lettie." She leaned down to accept his kiss and then retreated to pray.

The Lord's word came to her: "Thy Maker is thy husband." So Charles was going to his reward, healed in the arms of the Great Shepherd, but not in Lettie's arms. He had been her sweetheart for forty-one years, her husband for thirty-five. Only God could take his place.

Soon Charles slipped away into the presence of Jesus, leaving behind his body—an empty, shattered husk. Lettie found his last words to her on a slip of paper in his Bible: "Go on with my unfinished task."

Lettie Cowman didn't see how she could carry out Charles's request. She was a fifty-four-year-old widow, more poet than organizer, and devastated by grief. In her weariness, she longed for the Lord to take her home too. But through God's grace she rose to the challenge Charles had given her.

From 1925, when Charles died, until 1949, she stood faithfully at the helm of the Oriental Missionary Society (OMS), first as its vice-president and later as president. When she retired from that post, she launched a new ministry, World Gospel Crusades, based on the single objective of mass literature distribution.

In addition to her missionary work, Lettie Cowman wrote several devotional books that have comforted and sustained believers around the world. *Streams in the Desert* has been translated into more than a dozen languages. In its 100 English printings, it has sold more than 3 million copies.

Lettie Cowman's lifelong commitment to prayer anchored OMS through World War II, the Japanese occupation of China, the Great Depression, the Chinese Communist revolution, and many other crises. Her commitment to personal sacrifice provided constant inspiration, and her captivating speaking ministry rallied workers for many major evangelistic thrusts.

Today hundreds of missionaries carry on the work of OMS, which has planted churches and schools in over a dozen countries. Still a nondenominational faith mission as envisioned by the Cowmans, OMS is engaged in radio and TV broadcasting, theological education, evangelism, medical assistance, training of national workers, and church support.

It's doubtful if "Charlie" Cowman ever dreamed just how far his precious Lettie would run with the torch he handed her. She went out weeping, but the precious seed she carried was watered by her tears and produced an abundant harvest.

What We Can Learn from
the Lives of Lettie and Charles Cowman
Throughout their ministry the Cowmans had believed in, experienced, and taught divine healing. Charles liked to use

Jesus' definition of healing, calling it "the children's bread." During the early part of his illness, he wrote a manuscript entitled "The Bible Readings on Divine Healing or Studies from the Scriptures."

In this study, Cowman set out to show "six principal causes of sickness; six specific reasons why we may be healed; and six divinely authorized methods we may employ to obtain the benefit." The central verse in his discourse was 3 John 2: "Beloved, I wish above all things that thou mayest prosper and be in health, even as thy soul prospereth" (KJV). He directed his and his readers attention to Scripture's promises that state Jesus' wounds have healed ours (Isa. 53:4-5; 1 Pet. 2:24).

Neither Lettie nor Charles could understand what prevented healing from flowing into Charles's broken body. One day as he hovered at the point of death, Lettie read the story of the apostle Paul's experience of storm and shipwreck on the way to Rome (Acts 27). Her attention was captured by the words "no stars in many days." Of course, the stars still shone, fixed in their heavenly courses, but Paul couldn't see them.

"Just think," she said, "Paul was called to the mission field! And yet, here he was 'many days' doing nothing, just floating about in an old boat." In this precarious situation, Paul was able to say with calm faith, "Be of good cheer, the Lord is at hand." Charles was so inspired by the passage that he wrote an article based on it entitled "Sail On! Sail On!"

Chronic illness and disease truly are like a night without stars. The twinkling lights we've depended on to navigate by are veiled in darkness. In these times the fundamentals of our faith in God are tested to the limits.

◆ *Pain attacks our spiritual confidence.* In an effort to account for the illness, we ask endless questions: Did I miss God's will at some crucial point? Is it my lack of faith? Am I harboring sin? How long will this last? What should I be doing that I'm not?

Self-examination easily deteriorates into self-accusation.

Even when we experience grace to rest and wait for God to make his will clear, well-meaning family and friends may not. They encircle us with cure-alls, advice, interrogation, and reproof until the free air of the Spirit is stifled. We may come to feel increasing guilt and responsibility for our sickness in such an atmosphere. Fuller Seminary President David Allen Hubbard warns such unwelcome sickroom visitors that "blame bordering on rejection is no comfort to those whose sense of worth is already worn paper thin by the chafing cords of pain and inadequacy."

Whether the attacks come from outside or inside ourselves, the Lord of Life would have us resist them. Even when he needs to use his rod of correction on us, he will never do it without simultaneously rescuing us with his staff. His Spirit is rightly called the Comforter.

♦ *Pain blocks us from constructive activity.* The work that we've delighted in doing for God often becomes impossible. Frustration compounds our physical distress as we watch others burdened or see needs go unmet. For those of us who base our sense of worth largely on visible accomplishments, lowered self-esteem adds to the burden.

Charles Cowman recognized that his affliction was due in part to overwork aggravated by lack of workers and funds. But he saw as well that the Lord healed ailing workers in order to prevent their partners in ministry from also becoming overburdened and sick (Phil. 2:27). Watching Lettie grow more exhausted each day and seeing the needs of the mission, he must have been painfully aware of the stress his illness was creating. What he didn't immediately comprehend was that, seated in his chair in a little brown bungalow in Los Angeles, he would do his greatest work for world missions. God sustained him through those six agonizing years that he might pray. After Charles died, Lettie left his large maps on the walls of the living room. She delighted in telling visiting missionaries, "You will never go to any land, any country, any island of the sea, but that I have seen the map of it upon these walls, and Charles would be here before it pleading for someone to evangelize those people, to give them the Word."

Satan thinks he is destroying our usefulness by destroying our bodies; he thought that about Jesus too. In actuality, he puts us in situations where God uses us more. No circumstance that our enemy engineers can separate us from the Lord and his loving purpose for us.

◆ *The quest for healing dims the joys of heaven.* It's not too hard to be happy when we're comfortable. It's not even too difficult when we feel that our temporary discomfort is accomplishing something worthwhile for the kingdom of God. But when we lie sick, our spiritual vision projects about as far as ceiling level. How can we talk about victory and triumph and glory when we can't conquer our own bodies?

It isn't easy to imagine yourself seated in heavenly places in Christ when you're flat on your back in bed! But it isn't impossible either. Jesus makes it clear that situations of need and distress are doorways into spiritual joy (Matt. 5). He says, "Rejoice and be glad, because great is your reward in heaven" (v. 12). Then he went before us, willingly enduring the cross for the joy set before him (Heb. 12:2). Children of the heavenly King need not fear thorny crowns. Willingness to suffer with him is, in fact, the prerequisite to reigning with him.

◆ *Death is often equated with failure and defeat.* We talk about how we anticipate our arrival in heaven, but we're apprehensive regarding the means of transportation. We would much rather reach paradise via a luxury cruise than to feel like damaged freight on a dilapidated tugboat.

Most of us will go to almost any expense to regain our health and stay earthbound a little longer. There's nothing wrong with that; God designed us with a fierce survival instinct. As Bruce Barron states in his penetrating analysis *The Health and Wealth Gospel*, "God seems to prefer a faith that seeks to change things rather than a resignation sanctified as submission to God's will."

In an effort to neutralize the healing issue, some Christians actually praise pain and death. They may go so far as to call them gifts of God or blessings in disguise. Anyone who has endured day after day of illness or mourned the loss of a loved one knows better. "Doctors and research scientists dedicate their lives to the eradication of disease as a dread enemy," writes Robert H. Culpepper. "The church must not glorify it as a benign friend!"

In the Old Testament there is a stinging indictment of those who shun divine healing. King Asa of Judah became afflicted with a serious foot disease. He had already been reprimanded by God for depending on political and military alliance rather than asking for divine assistance. But somehow the message didn't get through to him. Scripture tells us that "though his disease was severe, even in his illness he did not seek help from the Lord, but only from the physicians" (2 Chron. 16:12).

We're correct in perceiving death as an enemy. Our mistake is failure to recognize that death is a vanquished enemy. The horror of the tomb is swallowed up in the glory of the Resurrection. We aren't mouthing cemetery platitudes when we say, "To die is gain." Physical healing is a marvelous gift of God, but it pales in comparison to eternal life.

After several years of encouraging a greater openness to miraculous signs and wonders (including physical healing) through a laboratory class, the faculty of Fuller Seminary stepped back to evaluate the program. They found that, while many sought healing as a means of experiencing more fully the life of Christ, frequently a demand for "pain-

free, disappointment-free, and frustration-free life" domi-
nated. In their report, *Ministry and the Miraculous*, they offered
the following insight:

> When miraculous healing becomes the cutting edge of
> faith, people ask: "Why should we suffer?" When disci-
> pleship becomes the cutting edge of faith, we ask: "How
> can we turn our suffering to the service of our neighbor,
> to our growth, and to the glory of God?"

One of the Cowmans' greatest gifts to the church was their
relentless honesty. They admitted their doubts and fears, their
hopes and their disappointments. They let others see that the
way of faith is not easy. When criticized for sharing with the
public how bleak some situations were, Lettie Cowman simply
strode to the podium and said, "Brethren, we have made a
colossal blunder in not letting you share with us some of the
hardness."

We don't have to fear the darkness or whistle false tunes to
keep our courage. We don't have to sugarcoat our Christian
experience. No matter what hurricane hits our lives or our
theology, the same hand that firmly holds the stars in place
holds us safe. Sailing in a seemingly starless night, Charles
Cowman wrote:

> We have never undertaken a work for the Lord under
> His direct guidance for the liberation of precious souls
> that Satan has not fought us inch by inch, but in the
> midst of the battle, as we have gone along with God, our
> spirits have been hushed and a sweet still voice has whis-
> pered to our inmost hearts, "I am on board, there is no
> wind wild enough, no wind high enough, no storm fierce
> enough to wreck the vessel which carries the Lord of the
> earth and sky. Sail on, sail on."

Steps to Spiritual Greatness

- Seek his unique will for your situation.
- Search out every means of health.
- Speak his promises as an antidote to despair.
- Submit to his loving, though sometimes mysterious, purpose for your life.
- Sing praises to the Author and Finisher of your faith.

Though outwardly we are wasting away, yet inwardly we are being renewed day by day. For our light and momentary troubles are achieving for us an eternal glory that far outweighs them all. So we fix our eyes not on what is seen, but on what is unseen. For what is seen is temporary, but what is unseen is eternal. (2 Cor. 4:16-18)

Section Four

◆◆◆◆◆◆◆◆◆◆◆◆◆◆◆

SHATTERED DREAMS

CHAPTER 10
Bound in Chains

"Good morning! Welcome to the house of God." The young black preacher beamed at his African brothers and sisters as they flocked into St. George's Methodist Episcopal Church of Philadelphia. How their numbers had grown in the months he had been there! And the church had profited too. Thanks to its new black supporters, the building had a new gallery, new floors, and other improvements.

He thanked God for bringing him from his former slave master's farm in Delaware. And, thank God, the elders had been kind in letting him preach each Sunday morning at five o'clock to his people before the regular morning worship service. He knew the white folks were becoming uncomfortable with the growing numbers of blacks, but God could take care of that. For with the Lord, who had brought him out of slavery and made him a gospel preacher, nothing was impossible.

He only wished the elders would give their blessing for an independent black church where the people could feel truly free to worship God as they chose. But they refused, so he had to do his best here—at least until God showed him another way. Maybe his good friend Bishop Asbury would help somehow.

Allen filled his lungs like the bellows in the blacksmith's shop. His listeners warmed to the Word of God as it hammered off their chains. The knowledge that Christ died for them made them sit up tall in the pews, their faces shining with joy. They were children of the King of heaven, no matter what others might say.

Then the early service concluded and time came for the main worship service. The black believers took their usual seats around the wall, behind the pews of the whites. The church sexton walked toward them. "You must take your seats in the gallery," he said. "Go and you will see where to sit."

They made their way to the gallery and sat down. The service began. People's voices blended as one in songs of praise to God. After the singing, the presiding elder said, "Let us pray." The people knelt quietly to seek the Lord, but their prayers were disturbed by scuffling and loud voices.

Richard Allen raised his head and looked to see who was disturbing the peace of God's house. To his horror, one of the church trustees was trying to pull Absalom Jones, a respected black leader, from his knees.

"You must get up. You must not kneel here!" the trustee commanded. Jones resisted. "Wait until prayer is over. Then I will get up and trouble you no more."

The frustrated trustee motioned for assistance. Another trustee came and began pulling on William White, who knelt near Absalom Jones.

By that time, the prayer was over. Richard Allen, William White, and Absalom Jones stood to their feet and led the black worshipers out of St. George's. They wouldn't stay any longer in a place where they could not worship in dignity.

From the day Allen and his followers walked out of St. George's Church, they experienced terrible opposition to forming an independent church. Richard Allen was welcome to use his gifts in preaching to whites and blacks and in filling the seats and coffers of the church. Leadership was another matter. Determined to minister to the needs of Philadelphia's blacks, he rented a store-room where they could meet for worship and preaching. Several Methodist leaders threatened to excommunicate those involved if they did not return to the discipline of St. George's Church.

Allen firmly refused, pointing out that they had been treated worse than heathen at St. George's. As to the threat of excommunication from the Methodist denomination that he so dearly loved, Allen replied, "If you deny us your name, you cannot seal up the Scriptures from us and deny us a name in heaven. We believe heaven is free for all who worship in spirit and truth."

Along with Absalom Jones, Allen helped establish the Free African Society. Its members made a regular financial commitment to care for the needy among them. They also served the community at large, black and white. The African Free Society held the uncompromising belief that "every pious man is a good citizen of the whole world."

During a yellow fever epidemic in 1793, Philadelphia appealed to its black residents to aid the sick and bury the dead since it appeared their race was highly resistant to the illness. Richard Allen and Absalom Jones led their people in a ready response. While large numbers of whites fled Philadelphia or hid in their homes in terror of the plague, the courageous black Christians labored for seventy days. Their only earthly rewards were criticism in the city newspaper for alleged profiteering, a financial loss of more than 170 pounds, and untold hardships to themselves and their families. In 1794 Philadelphia's mayor gave them a tardy commendation.

After over six years of such discrimination, Allen managed to buy an old frame building with contributions from blacks and whites. At last he could welcome the people of God to worship in full liberty. Bishop Francis Asbury dedicated the new church, named Bethel, in July 1794 and later ordained Allen. Still the persecution continued. After failing to convince Allen and his followers to sign their property over to the Methodist Conference, a Methodist official offered to help the group incorporate. They accepted his assistance but discovered ten years later that the incorporation papers placed the property completely under the control of the Methodist Conference. Only a ruling by the State Supreme Court prevented a white takeover.

Word spread of the independent black church in Philadelphia. Soon similar groups formed in Baltimore, Salem, Wilmington, and other major cities. By 1816 the churches united under the name of the African Methodist Episcopal Church. This black organization differed little from its white counterpart in doctrine and practice. It was simply a visible expression of the unwillingness of whites to accept their black brothers and sisters as equals. The group elected Richard Allen as bishop, an office he held until his death in 1831. By the 1880s, the church he began in Philadelphia seated over three thousand.

The African Free Society and the African Methodist Episcopal Church played an important role in firmly anchoring the black community in evangelical Christianity and in ending American slavery. Richard Allen, once a slave without education or hope, became the leader in the first and strongest independent black Christian organization. The only chains that bound him were the chains of love.

What We Can Learn from the Life of Richard Allen

Only the most calloused heart could go unmoved by the suffering of Richard Allen and the millions of blacks he represents. Born into slavery, Allen experienced enough oppression in his early years to drive him to despair or angry retaliation. Instead, his heart opened to the love of God. In that unconditional love he found fresh hope and confidence that his situation would change.

Torn between patient waiting for deliverance and impatient doubt and confusion, Allen learned to lean on God as his sole support and helper. He resisted the victim mentality and stretched himself to become a victor. During his enslavement, strength of character formed in Richard Allen that later would be essential to his leadership of the black church.

In every generation and place, individuals and groups have felt the sting of similar prejudice. The issue is not always race or skin color; sometimes it is religious affiliation, political alliance, or economic status. Almost any aspect of human identity can be used by corrupt individuals as an excuse to walk over others. Unfortunately, the church is not free of such attitudes. But God is. As Richard Allen testified, God is the defender of the downtrodden. More than just a page from history, Allen's story offers hope to all who suffer from prejudice and abuse today.

Victimization forges chains around lives. Some of those chains are visible. Most of them aren't. The world is full of people chained by sin and oppression. For this reason Christ suffered and reclaimed the keys of death, hell, and the grave. He helps us see our chains and then hands us the keys to unlock them.

◆ *Christ releases us from the chains of oppression with the key of forgiveness.* Unlike indentured servants, slaves had no legal right to purchase their freedom. They were bound for life unless a kind master set them free. Every member of the human race is born into similar bondage under sin. The wonder of Christ's suffering for us is that the wealth and power of heaven became available to us. The full pardon of God's forgiveness gives us liberty. In light of this, our physical situation diminishes in importance because we know it is only temporary.

Richard Allen pointed out to slaves that, no matter how their masters and mistresses treated them, they could experience "the favor and love of God . . . which will be a consolation in the worst condition . . . and no master can deprive you of it." Jesus

Christ's triumph guarantees us a place in heaven, where, as Allen said, "the power of the most cruel master ends, and all sorrow and tears are wiped away."

God's forgiveness in our lives gives us the strength to forgive the wrongs done to us. It's difficult to say thank you to God as he wipes your record clean and then refuse to clear off the list of offenses you hold against others. While we can't absolve sin, we can make sure that we aren't holding anyone in bondage through our unforgiveness.

◆ *Christ releases us from the chains of revenge with the key of loving service.* When Richard Allen became a child of God through faith in Jesus, he received a new heart of love. He could look at his master and see a man who needed Christ, a man who had terrible financial problems, a man who struggled to do what was right. He didn't see an enemy any more.

Allen worked harder after his conversion because he wanted his master and any other observers to see that knowing Christ made a difference. This attitude won him favor and resulted in the master's conversion and the slave's release. If Allen had slacked off in his work or used his new Christian freedom as a weapon against his master, the results probably would have been much different.

People who experience the love of God should become eager servants. We should obey, the apostle Paul wrote, "like slaves of Christ, doing the will of God from your heart" (Eph. 6:6). Rather than looking for ways to get even with those who have wronged us, we should look for opportunities to express God's love for them. Out of this attitude came the willingness of Richard Allen and his fellow believers to spend themselves caring for white Philadelphians suffering from yellow fever.

As long we keep rehearsing the wrongs we have suffered and fill our minds with plans for evening the score, creative ideas can't come. But when we shift our confidence to God's eternal and perfect justice in our behalf, we begin to see fresh possibilities for today. Only God can ever settle all the wrongs in life. It is more than enough for us to discover ways we can overcome evil with good in our daily situation (Rom. 12:9-21).

◆ *Christ releases us from the chains of inferiority with the key of renewed esteem.* Some people resist the idea of being slaves of Christ. "Christians aren't called to be doormats," they protest. And they are right about that. The Lord doesn't want us to see how low we can go in self-abasement. He wants to make us more than conquerors. By breaking our chains, he sets us free to serve.

Jesus is King of the universe, yet he washed dirty feet. True servanthood flows from the inner strength of knowing that the One living inside us is greater than all that is in the world. We are released from the struggle for preeminence or power. We owe no man anything but love—and that is everything!

The opposite attitude appears all too frequently in today's church, as it did in Richard Allen's time. Sometimes, in a quest for seats of honor, Christians forget their call to serve. They look for ways to gain advantage over one another. Allen called this approach "spiritual despotism" and renounced its hold. Scripture confirms that God's people should not lord their position over others (1 Pet. 5:2-3), nor should they allow themselves to be victimized by those who struggle for power to achieve their own ends.

◆ *Christ releases us from the chains of false accusations with the key of truth.* In our world, the reward for doing right is often slander. Allen and his helpers discovered this after their heroic effort during the yellow fever epidemic. Critics seized on the greed of less than a half-dozen Philadelphia blacks and used it as a reason to condemn the whole group. In the same spirit of righteous indignation that motivated the apostle Paul to defend his ministry, Allen refuted the lies circulated in the press.

As Christians, we are to avoid self-commendation. We should long to be like Christ who "was oppressed and afflicted, yet he did not open his mouth; he was led like a lamb to the slaughter, and as a sheep before her shearers is silent, so he did not open his mouth" (Isa. 53:7). Often this is the correct response, particularly when our personal reputation or status is the only thing at stake. But this isn't how Jesus handled all criticism. Frequently he responded in order to bring sharp confrontation between truth and error (Matt. 12:1-13).

When false charges defraud an entire group of the respect they deserve, an answer is especially in order. Paul countered the criticism aimed at his ministry because of the threat it represented to the church's well-being. He knew that unscrupulous people sought to discredit him so they could usurp his leadership and thus take advantage of the people of God. He wrote to the Corinthian church, "We are not trying to commend ourselves to you again, but are giving you an opportunity to take pride in us, so that you can answer those who take pride in what is seen rather than in what is in the heart" (2 Cor. 5:12).

Richard Allen followed Paul's example of confirming the character of black ministry in Philadelphia by listing the risks and hardships endured for others. "We wish not to offend," Allen said, "but when an unprovoked attempt is made to make us blacker than we are, it becomes less necessary to be overcautious on that account. . . ." Faced with constant interference in the affairs of Bethel Church by white Methodist leaders, he appealed his case to the Pennsylvania Supreme Court.

While we must leave our vindication to God, we must also raise the shield of faith and the testimony of a clear conscience against the fiery darts of satanic accusation. Through knowledge of truth, freedom comes. Our job is to boldly declare the truth.

◆ *Christ releases us from the chains of prejudice with the key of affirmation.* In the body of Christ, two life principles merge:

unity and diversity. We are made one through the blood of Christ that was shed to purchase our freedom. At the same time, we are released to express our unique gifts and abilities. This is the church as God intended it. Too often we ignore his pattern. Our narrow range of experience and understanding tempts us to make unfair judgments about others. Somehow we equate "different" with "bad." Instead of dazzling the watching world with God's matchless variety of grace and gifts in our lives, too many Christians turn into stunted church clones. We measure ourselves against ourselves and then wonder why we grow inward instead of outward and upward. The more threatened we feel, the thicker our walls of bias and criticism become.

This appears to be what happened at St. George's Methodist Episcopal Church. Initially, the congregation welcomed black worshipers, but as their numbers grew so did white members' discomfort. Whites drew dividing lines and removed freedoms in an effort to maintain absolute control. Their actions created hostility where none had existed and raised walls of division and misunderstanding.

A similar crisis developed among the black believers who left St. George's. Not long after their exodus, they became divided over whether to follow Methodist doctrine and practice or to align themselves with the Episcopal church. Richard Allen and his followers went one way; Absalom Jones and his followers went the other. Wall building never stops.

Christ died to tear down these walls. All that separated us from God and one another was destroyed by his suffering on the cross (Eph. 2:14). The good news is that, when we were nobodies, Christ chose us to be somebodies. And whatever he has cleansed, we dare not call common or unclean, including ourselves (Acts 10:15; 11:9).

Richard Allen modeled Christian maturity in his responses to persecution and oppression. He forgave those who caused his pain. He worked for reconciliation and unity. He affirmed and expressed gratitude for all the good that had come to his life, particularly through those who brought him pain. He persevered in fulfilling his God-given destiny without regard for opposition.

Nehemiah, the city builder, and Richard Allen, the church builder, have a lot to compare notes on in heaven. They share similar experiences and responses. If they could send us a guide for dealing with critics and oppressors, it would probably offer the following advice: Don't be afraid; remember the Lord (Neh. 4:14). Exhibit your faith in God by confident action (Neh. 4:20). Don't be distracted from God's work (Neh. 6:2-4). Don't run, and don't sin; renew your strength in God (Neh. 6:8-11). Give God time to put your enemies to shame (Neh. 6:16).

With the keys of forgiveness, loving service, esteem, and affirmation grasped firmly in our hands, we can face any kind of opposition and win. When Christ is our confidence, we don't have to fear anyone's opinion or oppression. We can speak the truth of God's freedom, both spiritually and physically, knowing that he has committed himself fully to our deliverance.

Steps to Spiritual Greatness
- ◆ Release your debtors from any unsettled obligations.
- ◆ Redeem the situation by returning good for evil.
- ◆ Redefine your worth in the light of God's love.
- ◆ Remove the walls of prejudice from your life.

It is for freedom that Christ has set us free. Stand firm, then, and do not let yourselves be burdened again by a yoke of slavery. (Gal. 5:1)

CHAPTER 11
Missionary Shipwreck

Norman Grubb struggled to make his wife, Pauline, understand his weariness and frustration. He admired C. T. Studd as a great man of God and valiant missionary. He also respected him as Pauline's father. But he didn't think he could stand being caught between Studd and the wrath of World Evangelization Crusade's (WEC) home committee much longer. All he wanted was to be an effective missionary to Africa. Instead he spent his time shuttling back and forth between opposing forces on impossible diplomatic missions. He was miserable here in London and equally miserable in the Congo.

Why should he go on like this, especially now that he had an opportunity to become partner in a new work in West Africa? C. T. was the warrior; let him fight it out with the committee over policy and doctrine. When the time came to leave London, he and Pauline could say good-bye to the WEC problem and start fresh in West Africa with her sister and brother-in-law.

While he still struggled with words to explain his feelings, Pauline seized the conversation. She might be the youngest and most timid of the Studd girls, but she unleashed her fury at the idea of betraying her father's trust.

"Norman, you came home as Father's ambassador. An ambassador is honor-bound to report back to the authority who sent him. You cannot in honor run away like this. You must go back, tell him how you feel, and then do as you like."

As much as he hated to admit it, Pauline was right. C. T. was too great a man to treat with anything but complete respect. Besides, Norman didn't agree with the committee. It wasn't right to criticize C. T. for his all-out commitment to the Congo work. Nothing short of his consuming zeal could get the job done. And the high demands he made on workers and converts for lives of holiness and sacrifice helped ensure the work would endure. It made no sense for the stay-at-homers to dictate to the ones on the front line.

Still, he wished C. T. would write the committee with a pen instead of a sword. How could a man make peace with those flaming letters of C. T.'s in his hand? Letters that offered not an inch of room for compromise or negotiation. Letters that incited the committee to ever greater disdain for C. T.'s position. He must try to convince C. T. of the wisdom of toning down his responses. It might cost him any advancement in the Congo work; it might pitch him out on his ear with the other malcontents. But for honor's sake he would try.

On returning to the Congo mission base, Norman encountered the sword he had dreaded. Rather than agreeing to temper his correspondence, C. T. rebuked him and withdrew the promised field leadership position. For days no one spoke to Norman. Only a deep assurance that Christ was going through this with him held him there.

Gradually the white-hot conflict passed as Norman's devotion won out over the disagreement. With the passing of time, though, it became clear that C. T. had shifted his nurturing of a successor to another young missionary, Jack Harrison.

Jealousy ate at Norman. Jack was from a poor family; he had no education, no background for such responsibility. *So much for trying to do the honorable thing!* he thought. *I might just as well have gone to West Africa.*

Then one day C. T. called him into his little hut for a conference. The haggard, disease-ridden old man looked across his makeshift table at Norman. "Jack is doing very well here, but we still need to decide what you're to do."

A strange mixture of exhilaration, suspense, and anxiety swept through Norman. He had little trouble telling that his father-in-law had called him to announce a decision. The only "we" in such matters was C. T. and God.

"I want you to go home and be ready to take over the office there when I die. You and Pauline will make a good team at that end."

So he was being sent away, trusted as a diplomat but not as a battlefront soldier. Norman shook his head. "You know I can never go back on my call to the Congo. I came here to stay."

"You also agreed to obey your leader," Studd reminded him. "You will either keep that commitment and go back to represent me with the committee at the home office, or you will be dismissed. Make your decision."

Later that day Norman returned with his answer. "After much prayer I am ready to do as you wish. The Lord has made it clear to me that I must be ready to take any part in this worldwide work that he chooses."

Years earlier he and Pauline had buried their first-born son in a tiny grave there in the heart of Africa. Now Norman Grubb dug a different kind of grave and buried his expectations. The tombstone read: 1928. No turning back.

Norman and Pauline Grubb walked toward C. T.'s little hovel. Missionaries around the Ibambi station called joyful greetings to the couple who had supervised the WEC office in England for the past two years and had now come to visit.

Studd answered the door. "What are you two doing here?" he exploded.

"You asked us to come," they answered with one voice.

"No, I didn't!"

Norman reached into his pocket and handed his father-in-law a letter. "See it there in your own handwriting. Besides, it was God's time for us to come. We have a lot to talk about."

For the next few hours the three discussed the mission committee's intention to bring about drastic moderation and reform as soon as Studd died. "They don't understand why you preach such a hard gospel, why you demand so much. And they're especially offended by your booklet D.C.D.* Then there's the matter of your morphia tablets."

"You know what I think of all that," Studd retorted. "Thank God for the morphine. I'm a dying man, but with those tablets I can still work a twenty-hour day. And I meant what I said about being one of those who doesn't care a damn except to give my life for Jesus and souls. D.C.D. to the end!"

"We understand, Father, but the committee thinks you are becoming profane and a dishonor to the mission," Pauline said.

"And they intend to remove you and us from all leadership," Norman added.

"We will see about that." Then Studd called the other missionaries together.

By unanimous decision they confirmed Jack Harrison as God's man to continue the Congo work. The Grubbs were ordered back to the home office to fight for WEC's original vision.

Norman and Pauline Grubb might as well have been told to walk into a fiery furnace. They were virtual outcasts in British evangelical circles because of Studd's extreme behavior and their loyalty to him. But they held their ground. Finally the WEC committee conceded that it had no power to oust Studd or the Grubbs from leadership since Studd held veto power.

*D.C.D.: Don't Care a Damn. Studd chose this title to reflect the all-out commitment necessary of a soldier in wartime. "I want to be one of those who doesn't care a damn except to give my life for Jesus and souls," he had said.

The majority of the committee members broke off to form a new mission and left the Grubbs to pick up the broken pieces of WEC.

One day as Pauline and Norman prayed about how to proceed, Pauline received a clear impression that her father had died. It was confirmed two days later by a telegram from Jack Harrison which read, "Bwana glorified July 16. Hallelujah."

With those words, Norman and Pauline were free to find a new beginning for WEC. Counting themselves, there were four workers in the home office. Funds were nonexistent, and the world was suffering from depression. The picture could not have been more grim. But Norman Grubb challenged the little band to trust God and go forward boldly as Joshua had after Moses' death.

Today the combined legacy of the Studds and the Grubbs is a missionary organization that reaches around the globe. There are more than one thousand missionaries in its ranks, all living on faith and sacrifice as Studd taught. The Worldwide Evangelistic Crusade marches on, while the old warrior bends over heaven's balcony to shout, "Hallelujah!"

What We Can Learn from the Lives of
C. T. Studd and Norman and Pauline Grubb

Whether C. T. Studd was right or wrong in the administration of his God-given commission is something only God can truly judge. One thing is clear from this side of eternity: Studd had tremendous compassion for souls and wanted to see Jesus honored in all he did. But the intense way he pursued his heavenly vision didn't take into consideration the personalities and maturity levels of his co-workers.

Studd's demand for holiness and total sacrifice failed to recognize that we all are people in process. If his spiritual vision and energy hadn't been so compelling and attractive, his harshness would have driven everyone from him. Those hurt worst by him were among his most ardent supporters. They point out that it takes someone with Studd's kind of consuming zeal to birth a cutting-edge ministry. In relating the pain of working with C. T. Studd, Norman Grubb frequently seemed apologetic for himself rather than his father-in-law.

Most readers of Grubb's moving biographies of Studd and other missionary leaders never guess the price team members pay for such a ministry. The excitement of working in a frontline ministry, shoulder to shoulder with a spiritual giant, has great appeal. But there are few men and women who can endure the rigors of such a life. A week of the kind of stress Norman Grubb regularly experienced would send most of us packing.

When the disciples asked to share Jesus' heavenly glory, he asked if they were also willing to share his cup of suffering. Let's look at some of the bitter dregs in the cup of ministry.

◆ *Pain may result from differences in ministry.* Ministry is best defined as loving service. But what we mean by *love* is as varied as our fingerprints. Is love an action, an emotion, or both? Some measure their love by the amount of industry directed toward others, some by the amount of feeling they have.

C. T. Studd leaned so far toward the action end of the spectrum that more expressive and tender people like Norman Grubb found dealing with him difficult. This doesn't mean that either had the wrong concept or approach. The African people understood that Studd loved them. His self-sacrifice proved it. Their culture didn't demand words or a show of emotion. On the other hand, Grubb's did. A stress point developed where these two approaches to ministry collided.

◆ *Authoritarianism produces pain for both leaders and followers.* Obviously, someone has to chart a clear course for a ministry amid the crosscurrents of conflicting views and personalities.

Submission to divinely instituted authority is a wonderful biblical principal that can diminish stress. It can also increase tension if the call for submission becomes a dictatorial decree.

Those who worked for C. T. Studd did it his way or didn't do it. He was the consummate admiral, able to translate his convictions into decisive commands. He interpreted criticism as mutiny and accommodation as weakness. He was perfectly willing to go down with his ship rather than alter his course. Even when the WEC "ship" started sinking, no one could convince him there were more positive alternatives.

This position caused Studd more grief than any other sacrifice he made for missions. He watched, heartbroken, as beloved mission coworkers—some of them close family members--abandoned ship. But rather than recognizing his flawed leadership, he saw himself as the injured party. Those who deserted him were, to his mind, refusing to submit to God-given authority.

This type of Christian leadership is common. It's often justified by pointing to the apostle Paul's forceful command of church affairs. However, we must remember that, while Paul could be a stern disciplinarian, he was also able to say, "We were gentle among you, like a mother caring for her little children," and "we dealt with each of you as a father deals with his own children, encouraging, comforting and urging" (1 Thess. 2:7, 11).

♦ *Lack of communication brings pain.* Studd issued ultimatums that made two-way communication virtually impossible. Those who tried to express their thoughts or feelings to him often encountered silent rebuff or stinging rebuke. He believed he had heard from God and that those under his leadership should trust his divine guidance.

This leadership model is more characteristic of the Old Testament order than that of the New Testament church. When the people of God (Israel) refused to communicate with God directly, he gave them prophets, judges, and kings to receive and dispense his word. With the restoration to God's fellowship brought about by Christ's death and resurrection, the lines of divine communication were restored. So, in the New Testament church we see a more corporate structure built on cooperation, spiritual gifts, and consensus (Acts 6:1-6; Eph. 4:1-13).

When leaders reject the participation of even their most trusted helpers in forming policy or making critical decisions, unity is destroyed. Workers' motivation and esteem is undercut and hostility frequently results. This was the condition in WEC under Studd's rule.

◆ *Pain results from unfulfilled expectations.* Finding a place of ministry should be every Christian's ambition. Whether in a local church or on a mission field, it's exciting and rewarding to do something for God. What isn't so exciting is finding out how far short of our ideals our fellow ministers fall.

During difficult times, we may feel that, instead of having the proverbial "feet of clay," our leaders are made of mud—hard as rock when dry but apt to crumble. The one who once seemed tender and gracious now seems harsh and demanding. The door that always stood open to us is now always closed. Performance and priorities eclipse understanding and compassion.

Added to this is the painful realization that all ministry is nine-tenths hard work and one-tenth pleasure. Tempers flare with fatigue. Days become filled with routine and responsibility rather than inspiration and fellowship. Failure seems to be the most frequent teacher. Doubt, fear, resentment, and loneliness tempt us to resign. "It's not supposed to be like this if you're in God's will," we may reason.

There is a strong tug to be angry with God as well as people. *Why did he allow me to come here? Why doesn't he do something to change things?* we wonder.

If we give in to the enemy's persistent knock on the door of our emotions, we may react in ways that will sever relationships and damage the work of God. On the other hand, if we deny our feelings without resolving them, we may become sick or ineffective in ministry. Crushing the will, the mind, or the emotions doesn't result in Christ-likeness or creativity. We must confront our disappointments honestly and prayerfully.

Perhaps we will find our expectations were unrealistic. Maybe we will become an instrument for needed change in the situation. Or, God may release us to work in a ministry where we experience less conflict. But no matter where he leads us, we must come to a place where we aren't easily discouraged by people or circumstances. It is there we find Jesus as our true source of encouragement. Norman Grubb testifies to the essential nature of this process: "We have to go through our 'wilderness' experience . . . with constant failures, self-disgust, strains and stresses we cannot handle. . . . After the . . . collapse, we are conditioned to see and affirm Himself replacing ourselves."

◆ *Balancing personal, family, and ministry demands can be painful.* C. T. Studd had a simple approach to dealing with conflicting responsibilities: He turned his back on everything except fulfilling his call to evangelize Africa. That meant years of separation from his wife, refusal to return home for proper medical treatment, and living in extreme physical deprivation. His wife and other family members supported him in these decisions.

The crisis within WEC occurred when Studd tried to force that same life-style on all workers. Not everyone, even in the same ministry, is called to the same sacrifice. God knows our temperament and needs well enough to custom-make the commitment he requires of us. Our job is personal obedience. Whether others understand, agree with, or follow our example should be left with God.

There is no standard operating procedure for disciples. Jesus made this clear in a conversation with Peter. After giving Peter some insights regarding his future, Jesus had to deal with Peter's curiosity about how his life would compare with that of John. Jesus answered, "What is that to you? You must follow me" (John 21:20-23).

While the Lord does ask for total, unquestioning surrender to his will, no one should feel guilty about fulfilling legitimate personal and family obligations. Jesus left us a healthy model for spiritual living. He spent time with God the Father, renewing his inner being and receiving direction. He cared for his body by sleeping and eating and enjoying some leisure. He cultivated close relationships and never let his eternal mission dim his love for the individual.

On the other hand, Jesus did many things that were misunderstood and misinterpreted. Those about him sometimes experienced confusion and hurt as their desires crossed purpose with God's will. He made demands on himself and on his followers that involved considerable cost. His obedience to the cross would never have earned the endorsement of a success-oriented management committee. No matter what personal life-style or leadership style we follow, conflict will still arise at times. The key to mastering the storm is not throwing some people out of the boat, but rather sitting down together as servants of the Most High and receiving his direction for blending our gifts, abilities, and efforts. God won't remove our personalities, but he does want to free them from the domination of selfishness.

In evaluating his and Studd's lives and their relationship, Norman Grubb offers the following penetrating observation:

> There is no doubt that when all the cards are on the table, there are sides of all our lives which others find difficult to take and wish were different. But the great necessity is to keep the true perspective. We are each as God has created us, and He lives in us as He pleases. . . .

years have passed since [Studd] went to be with the Lord, and still that life cuts deep furrows for God, where most of his contemporaries are forgotten.

The same could be said of Norman Grubb, a brokenhearted man who was brave enough to hold on when hope seemed gone. His affirming attitude made him a minister of reconciliation rather than an instrument of destruction. May the same be true of us in the place God assigns us.

Steps to Spiritual Greatness
- Humble yourself before God and accept correction.
- Honor the diversity of others and God's work in and through them.
- Hear the pain in others' lives.
- Help repair damaged relationships and ministries. Do not rejoice in anyone's decline.
- Hope in God rather than in human ability.

The Lord will continually guide you, and satisfy your desire in scorched places, and give strength to your bones. . . . And you will be called the repairer of the breach. (Isa. 58:11-12, NASB)

CHAPTER 12
Sentenced to Scrub

Gladys walked down the hall of the China Inland Mission Training School. After three months as a student, she felt at home in the London school. But as she entered the Candidates' Committee office, anxiety filled her. *Will they let me stay on in spite of my bad grades?* she wondered.

The committee chairman greeted her warmly, but he did not smile. The concern in his eyes told Gladys the verdict even before he spoke the words.

So little time here and already a failure. How will I ever get to China now? she wondered. She had tried hard, but the lessons made no sense. No tutoring, explaining, or reading helped. It just wouldn't go into her brain.

Gladys tried to listen as the chairman talked about the problems that loomed between her and China. Her age—already twenty-eight and just beginning three years of training. Her lack of academic ability—how would she ever learn a complex language such as Chinese? Her simple background in domestic service . . .

Why didn't he mention the fire that burned inside her, that relentlessly commanded her to go to China? What about the way she got along with everyone? And what about her willingness to work hard at any job that needed doing? Didn't these things count?

"Miss Aylward, I'm sorry, but it seems best that you look for some other way to serve God, something more suited to your abilities," the chairman said. "Do you have any plans?"

Plans? Yes, she thought, *to go to China!* But she said, "No, not now."

He suggested she consider domestic work for an elderly missionary couple recently returned to England. Gladys cringed at the thought of being a parlormaid again. But she took the job because she didn't know what else to do.

To her surprise, the dear old couple became a gift from God. Every day they talked about how God had taken care of their needs and helped them work for him. It soothed Gladys's aching heart. They gave her a little card that said, "Be not afraid, remember the Lord." Armed with it and her Bible, Gladys set out determined to find what a not-too-bright, poor, British spinster could do for God.

For a short time she helped in a hostel for working women. From there she went to serve the down-and-out in Swansea, Wales. Then she took a job as assistant matron for the Sunshine Hostel, a ministry to rescue women from prostitution.

She walked the docks of Swansea, looking for girls in trouble. Her heart bled over the poverty and suffering of the city's unemployed. Here was a work to do, yet she was not content. *It has to be China. Somehow I've got to get to China.*

But how? No mission board would send her. The words from the little gift card came back to her: "Be not afraid, remember the Lord." She didn't have to depend on others; God and her own hard work would send her to China!

Gladys applied for domestic work in London. The agency placed her in the home of a famous author and explorer.

In spite of this new situation, she felt crushed by discouragement. The butler showed her to the plain, tiny bedroom with a bed and washstand and little else.

She sat on the edge of the bed. *A parlormaid again. And China still so very far away.* Gladys reached for her suitcase and pulled out her Bible, her devotional book, and the bit of money she had. She opened the Bible and put the few coppers on top of it.

"Oh, God! Here's me. Here's my Bible. Here's my money. Use us, God! Use us!" Gladys prayed.

A knock came at the door, and then in popped another maid to say that the lady of the house wanted to see her downstairs. Gladys wiped away her tears, straightened her cap, and went down.

The mistress welcomed Gladys and then said, "It is my practice to pay the fares of my maids when I engage them. How much was your fare from home?"

"Two and ninepence," Gladys said with surprise.

"Here are three shillings, then," said the mistress and handed her the money.

Gladys flew up the stairs to put the coins with the pennies she had tucked away. In those few minutes she had gained ten times what she had prayed over. Maybe China wasn't so far away after all!

For several months Gladys took extra jobs in addition to her regular employment. Every penny she could save from her wages went to the ticket master, who held her dreams of China in his hand. By October 1932 she had enough money to finish paying for a one-way, third-class ticket on the Trans-Siberian Express.

The railroad trip across Europe, war-torn Russia, and Siberia qualified as a first-class nightmare. On reaching Vladivostok, Gladys learned she could go no farther by train. So she took a steamer to Japan, another boat to China, and a bus from the harbor city, deep into central China. Then she joined a mule caravan for the final leg of her journey to Yangcheng. The trip took more than a month.

The rest of Gladys's life was filled with daring journeys. She trekked to villages throughout the area, sharing the gospel by means of her captivating and highly dramatic Bible stories. The language posed no barrier to her; she quickly learned it by mimicking the Chinese, something she never could have accomplished with a book.

The local mandarin gave Gladys another reason to travel in Shansi Province by making her the official foot inspector. To her was entrusted the duty of making sure Chinese mothers stopped the terrible practice of binding baby girls' feet to keep them from growing. The mandarin also talked often with Gladys about the Christian faith. He eventually became a convert.

During the Chinese-Japanese War, Gladys added spying to her evangelistic work. A naturalized Chinese citizen, she was fully committed to the Nationalist Chinese cause. She related all she learned of Japanese troop strength and movement to Nationalist intelligence officer Colonel Lin. Linnan, as Gladys called him, soon claimed her heart, but the war made any future together an impossible dream.

The atrocities of war left many homeless children. Gladys soon had over two hundred in her care. In addition to caring for the children, she also provided crude hospital care for soldiers in the war-ravaged compound. Just before the compound had to be evacuated, God sent a tremendous revival to the people of the province, who had gathered there for a Bible conference. When the Japanese discovered her activities, they offered a reward of $1,000 for her capture. Gladys had already sent one hundred of the children with a Chinese evangelist to one of Madame Chiang Kai-shek's orphanages over the mountains in Free China. Upon learning of the bounty on her head, Gladys asked God's direction and received instructions to flee to the mountains.

With almost no provisions, on foot, and with more than a hundred children ranging in age from three to sixteen and only one adult assistant, Gladys made her longest and most difficult journey of all. The story of how she brought the group to safety in Free China parallels her favorite Bible story of the Israelites' deliverance from Egypt.

The trip took a month and almost cost her life. For the next several years her physical and mental health suffered greatly from the effects of typhus, which she contracted on the trek.

In spite of her broken health, Gladys remained in China and continued her missionary work until 1947. Upon returning to England, she found herself a stranger, far more Chinese than British. She began ministering to the Chinese refugees, reaching out to Chinese students and Liverpool's Chinese seamen. During this time, Alan Burgess, a BBC reporter, discovered her story and told it in the book *The Small Woman.*

Gladys returned to the Orient in 1957, this time to Taipei, Formosa (Taiwan). She founded an orphanage there and in Hong Kong. The rest of her life was spent working in the Taipei orphanage or traveling in America, Canada, England, or Australia, where she told the amazing miracles God had worked in the life of one simple young woman who dared to take him at his word.

Gladys Aylward's life prompted several biographies, a major motion picture (*Inn of the Sixth Happiness*), and a *This Is Your Life* production. She commanded the respect of all who knew her. She died in Taipei on January 1, 1970.

What We Can Learn from the Life of Gladys Aylward

Most of us want to be used by God. His call to service comes in many ways—as a gentle drawing, a tender nudging, a burning desire, or a firm tug. However we experience it, we know it's there. What we don't always know is *what* to do or *how* to do it. Most of us don't have a problem identifying with Gladys's cry, "Here's me! Use me!" But we have the struggle of a lifetime with getting beyond that point.

Though Gladys was blessed with unusually clear direction regarding her place of ministry, she didn't find the road to realization smooth or straight. Her experiences point out some pitfalls, roadblocks, and detours we can avoid on our journeys.

♦ *We must watch out for potholes of negative expectation.* While some people seem to have mountains of confidence, others feel too weak and insignificant to be used by the Lord. And, besides our attitude toward our capabilities, there are the limiting concepts others may have of us. Between the two, many people trip at the starting block.

Looking at the call of various Bible giants can give a boost to our confidence in God and ourselves. Moses said, "Not me, Lord. I don't speak well." Solomon said, "I'm just a little child. I don't know even know how to go in and out when I should." Isaiah said, "I am a man of unclean lips." Paul said, "I am the chief of sinners, the least of the least." Each felt inadequate and unprepared, yet God used them to change the world.

That same Paul reminded the church of the source of genuine confidence. He wrote:

> Think of what you were when you were called. Not many of you were wise by human standards; not many were influential; not many were of noble birth. But God chose the foolish things of the world to shame the wise; God chose the weak things of the world to shame the strong. He chose the lowly things of this world and the despised things—and the things that are not—to nullify the things that are, so that no one may boast before him. It is because of him that you are in Christ Jesus, who has become for us wisdom from God—that is, our righteousness, holiness and redemption. (1 Cor. 1:26-30)

In other words, we have no grounds for confidence except in the Lord. Eventually God shines his spotlight on all our weaknesses and deficiencies, not to hurt us but to show us that whatever we accomplish of eternal good comes from his power in us. Servants like Gladys, whom the system stamps "reject," just get the message a little quicker.

It's important to remember that the Lord's spotlight also illuminates our gifts and abilities. He delights in affirming and nurturing the unique talents he has given us. Gladys couldn't learn from a book or behave like a refined lady of society, but she could "spin a yarn" that became a net to catch people for Christ. Her simplicity, dramatic flair, and imagination made her an effective missionary as no classroom could.

♦ *We must not mistake mirages for true spiritual visions.* Gladys's dream of working in China could have been nothing more than a fantasy. It had to be proved and tested before it could be fulfilled. Considerable tension exists between dealing responsibly with reality and obeying our heavenly calling. Those without spiritual vision look at the life of faith as a great delusion. They warn us to look at the facts and be reasonable. Yet we know that the ways of God often defy human logic.

At the same time, we must recognize the potential for being led astray by delusions of grandeur. If our notions of ministry are inflated with ego or desire for self-promotion, we may wander a long time on the desert before the Lord humbles us to the point of obedience. We must line up our divine "call" with godly advice, circumstances, and general scriptural principles.

The following questions provide a basic checklist for separating visions from mirages:

1. Is this feeling born out of a deepening fellowship with God and a sensitivity to his voice?
2. Is my desire based on a genuine love for people? Or do I simply want to display my knowledge or ability?

3. Would I be willing to fulfill my call if I never received any recognition for my labor?
4. Am I willing to be trained and disciplined by the Lord in order to increase my effectiveness, even if I look like a failure in the process?
5. Is the pull to this ministry so strong that no other Christian service fulfills me?
6. Am I attracted to this work because God has planted it in my heart or because I feel others expect me to do it? Am I driven to it by God's grace or by my guilt?
7. Do I think of ministry as a means of gaining power over others or as a method of serving others?

It pays to search out the answers to these issues in the company of a loving and honest spiritual mentor.

◆ *We must not despair from delays.* God's timing and ours may be years apart. His destination and ours may be miles apart. The Lord doesn't wait until we get our timetable and road map in perfect alignment with his before he starts us on the journey.

In the flush of our early zeal and commitment, he lets us step out in faith, and then he restrains us through some circumstance or misgiving. "Be still before the Lord and wait patiently before him" is often the only direction we receive.

While we wait, three essential things happen. First, our desire to discover what God wants us to do drives us to his Word. As we search, the Word cleanses and refines us, preparing us for what lies ahead. Second, we recognize that he is placing before us immediate opportunities for ministry. Though they may not be our specific life's work, they are given to us to do with all our might for the moment. Third, we gradually develop the gifts and abilities that will carry us on to our destination.

Before God allowed Gladys to go to China, some critical

signposts were passed. She deepened her faith in God's promises through fellowship with other believers. She worked with rescue missions in Wales. She humbled herself and returned to domestic service. Repeatedly she obeyed the following biblical command: "Whatever your hand finds to do, do it with all your might" (Eccles. 9:10). Each "delay" made her more effective when she reached the land of her vision.

♦ *We must beware of the detour of doubt and despondency.* Sometimes our pathway seems to be through a rolling sea instead of on solid ground. At such times our emotions churn like white-water rapids. These feelings of anxiety, frustration, or disappointment are a normal part of being human. What we must beware is the deadly undertow of despair that rips the oars of faith out of our hands and peels the life jacket of trust off our backs.

Sometimes God commands the winds and waves to be still and they obey. At other times he allows them to drive us along. Occasionally, in our desperate search for a safe harbor, he comes to us walking on the same water we thought would bury us. Hymn writer William Cowper expressed it well:

> *God moves in a mysterious way,*
> *His wonders to perform;*
> *He plants his footsteps in the sea*
> *And rides upon the storm.*

During Gladys's harrowing journey out of war-torn Yangcheng with more than one hundred orphan children, she grappled with despair as never before. After passing a sleepless night, she faced the morning with no hope of reaching safety. A thirteen-year-old girl in the group reminded her of their much loved story of Moses and the Israelites crossing the Red Sea.

"But I am not Moses," Gladys cried in desperation.

"Of course you are not," the girl said, "but Jehovah is still God!"

This same God is Lord of our rocking boats and bids us walk with him, as Peter did, on the shifting waves of emotion and circumstance. If we allow our attention to slip back to the path beneath our feet, we will fail. But if we keep our eyes fixed in trust on our Guide, he will bring us safely to shore. We don't have to be equal to the situation; we only have to know that Jesus is.

In order to be used by God, we need our hearts and minds united in a single focus. Otherwise, our cries for direction and deliverance become little more than superstitious grasping of a good-luck charm. Scripture warns double-minded people not to expect anything from the Lord and to recognize that they will be continually unstable in their Christian walk (James 1:6-8).

◆ *We must scale the mountains of hardship and cross the valleys of loneliness and misunderstanding.* To assume that because God calls us to his service he will not allow things to go wrong is a dangerous error. Regardless of how much faith we have, trials will come.

These painful obstacles come for three main reasons: (1) God wants to teach us something; (2) Satan wants to block us from any godly activity; and (3) we sometimes get in our own way. Not only must we confront the mountains, we must also determine their source. Is this a mountain to camp by until the Lord gives us clearer direction? Is this a mountain we should order to be cast into the sea by faith? Is this a mountain that grew from some molehill we stubbed our toe on yesterday?

Gladys not only faced these mountains, she also walked the gorges between them. There were hidden valleys of loneliness and relinquishment that only God shared. She never experienced the fellowship and belonging that those who are part of a mission organization enjoy. The war tore her from the man she planned to marry. Her daring rescue of the orphans broke her health, leaving her deathly ill for months and impaired for life.

Writing to a close friend during a particularly difficult experience, Gladys revealed the depths of her pain:

> This has been my most terrific year, and I do not believe I could stand another one like it. It seems as though everything I do is wrong, and only my faith in a Loving and Living God keeps me going. . . .
>
> I believe God has called you and me, and it is not to walk as other people have walked in a nice, rosy way, but just along the way He walked to Calvary; and one day we will be able to look back and understand why all these things have had to be.

Near the end of her life, Gladys reflected on the day she boarded the train to begin her long trek to China. She thought of the little cluster of family and friends who had come to see her off and the sorrow she felt at parting. Rather than crying, she had silently told the Lord, "I'm giving up my mother and my father—I want mothers and fathers wherever I go! There's my sister and my brother—Lord, I want sisters and brothers wherever I go! I'm giving you my friends, Lord—Lord, I want friends wherever I go. . . ."

That quaint little parlormaid marched over the mountains of impossibility, down the road of self-denial, and through the valley of death. And as she walked, a multitude followed her into the kingdom of God. Those are footsteps worth following.

Steps to Spiritual Greatness

- ◆ Validation. Make sure your chart and compass have the heavenly seal of approval.
- ◆ Vigilance. Hold fast to your vision and move toward it

as steadily as allowed.

- ◆ Valiance. Fight the good fight of faith.
- ◆ Victory. Claim the prize reserved for those who finish the course.

The Lord be with you, and may you have success and build the house of the Lord your God, as he said you would. May the Lord give you discretion and understanding. . . . Be strong and courageous. Do not be afraid or discouraged. . . . Is not the Lord your God with you? (1 Chron. 22:11-13, 18)

Section Five

◆◆◆◆◆◆◆◆◆◆◆◆◆◆

DIVINE
SILENCE

CHAPTER 13
Running Ahead of the Spirit

"You are going to be a father soon, George," Elizabeth said in her dear, straightforward way.

Whitefield thought his heart would burst with joy. Thanks to God's blessing on his ministry, he had thousands of spiritual children throughout England, Wales, Scotland, and America. But now he was to hold a wee babe of his own. His hearty laughter told Elizabeth the depth of his pleasure at the news.

It will be a boy. He was sure of it. *And he will be a great evangelist someday.* The knowledge settled into his heart like a word from Scripture.

Still, he couldn't help worrying about Elizabeth's well-being during the long months of her pregnancy. Every illness seemed to threaten the vision Whitefield cherished of his son's future. Added to that was Elizabeth's age—ten more than his twenty-seven years. So many women past thirty died in childbirth. Surely God would not allow . . .

It was September 1743. Only one more month until the baby's arrival. The doctor said Elizabeth was fine. "Just see to it she gets plenty of fresh air," he told Whitefield. So the happy young father-to-be borrowed a one-horse chaise and took Elizabeth for a drive.

As they rode down the London streets, Whitefield's thoughts drifted. He was startled by Elizabeth's cry and felt her arm go across the chaise in front of him. To his horror, the horse began slipping down into a wide drainage ditch. The ditch dropped fourteen feet. *Too late!* He tugged on the reins, knowing he was helpless to stop their terrifying descent.

The chaise crashed to the bottom of the ditch, knocking the Whitefields about violently. Only Elizabeth's grip on the side of the chaise kept them from being thrown out.

"They're killed!" he heard a passerby shouting. Then a man scrambled into the drain to hold the horse. Whitefield struggled to climb up on the horse's back so he could reach the long whip someone was holding down to him.

He pulled himself up on the bank and looked down to see what could be done for Elizabeth. She was already standing on the overturned chaise, and men were lifting her slowly out of the ditch.

In a daze the two walked to a house nearby where kind folks washed their cuts. Meanwhile, the battered chaise and horse were rescued from the ditch and righted for the Whitefields to return home.

As they drove back to the house, they rejoiced in their miraculous deliverance from death. Elizabeth assured him that the baby seemed fine, still kicking and thumping inside her. Whitefield was more certain than ever that this child would grow to be a great world evangelist.

"We will call him John," he announced to the people of his church, "after John the Baptist who prepared the way of the Lord." Newspaper critics mocked his prophecy, but he was not shaken in his confidence. He felt sure God had a special purpose for this child.

Since Elizabeth showed no ill effects from the accident, Whitefield decided to spend the weeks remaining until the child's birth on a short preaching tour. Word came to him that his son had been born, and he rushed back to London.

The baby John's baptism was a great event at Whitefield's church. He felt a mighty anointing as he proclaimed the works God would do through the child. He made the sign of the cross over John "in token that he shall not be ashamed to confess the faith of Christ crucified, and manfully to fight under his banner against sin, the world, and the devil: and to continue Christ's faithful soldier and servant unto his life's end."

Of course, it would be years before the child could preach the gospel, so his father had to carry on. He bade Elizabeth and the baby good-bye, and resumed his work as an itinerant evangelist.

After a lengthy preaching tour, Whitefield returned to his family. He was delighted that John was growing and appeared quite healthy. Unfortunately, Whitefield's purse was anything but healthy. He could not afford to continue renting the room they had been occupying, so he made plans for Elizabeth and baby John to meet him at the Bell Inn, his boyhood home in Gloucester, now managed by his brother. From there they would continue together to Abergavenny, where Elizabeth still owned a cottage.

Whitefield went on ahead of them, preaching throughout the countryside until the time set for their reunion.

With eager and happy heart, he dismounted at the Bell Inn in Gloucester on the eighth of February. He could hardly wait to hold his son in his arms again. *But what was this?* There stood his brother in the doorway, his face white as death, his eyes brimming with tears.

"I have bad news for you, George," his brother said in a husky voice. Whitefield saw his mother sobbing just inside the door. "The child has just died. There was nothing we could do. A seizure came upon him suddenly and he was gone."

Pain ripped through Whitefield's heart. *Scarcely four months old. What of God's promise?* He stumbled into the room and gathered his family about him for prayer. He tried to comfort Elizabeth, but his own heart was breaking.

The next day he had commitments in nearby village churches. *How can I preach with such sorrow welling up inside me?* he wondered. *But preach I must.* "As Matthew Henry says, 'Weeping must not hinder sowing,'" he told the family as he left Bell Inn.

He preached twice that day and twice the next. As he preached from the text "All things work together for good to them that love God," his words were interrupted by the tolling of the bell for baby John's funeral service. Sorrow swept over him beyond enduring.

"God, help me," he prayed and then concluded his message. "These blessed words, 'All things work together for good,' make me as willing to go to my son's funeral as to hear of his birth." They were hard words to speak, but by faith he willed them to be true.

The Whitefields committed tiny John's body to the earth and his spirit to God. They knelt weeping a long time by the little grave. But at last, tears were dried and duties resumed.

Whitefield's thoughts turned often to his glowing prophecies concerning his son's future ministry. *Where did I go wrong?* He did not know.

All he could do was pray that the lesson would leave him more sober-minded, more experienced in Satan's devices, and, somehow, more useful in his future labors to the church of God.

George Whitefield was the first Christian evangelist to span the Atlantic, the leader of the evangelical revival in England, and the central figure in America's Great Awakening. Most of his sermons were delivered outdoors due to church censorship of his revolutionary revival message on the new birth. Wherever Whitefield preached, thousands gathered to listen. He is remembered as one of the greatest orators of the eighteenth century.

A focal point of Whitefield's ministry was the flourishing Bethesda Orphan House in Savannah, Georgia, which he built from money raised in his meetings. In addition to his extensive evangelistic ministry and charitable work, Whitefield also established two large churches in London. Although he died at the age of fifty-six, it is estimated he preached more than thirty thousand sermons in his lifetime.

George and Elizabeth Whitefield lived another twenty-five years after their son died. Their lives were filled with the work of God; their arms were never again filled with a baby of their own.

What We Can Learn from the Life of George Whitefield

Medieval theologians debated about the number of angels who could dance on the head of a pin. We probably could debate just as long and as futilely about Whitefield's mistaken prediction. In such a situation, the possibilities are staggering: Did Satan destroy Whitefield's son to thwart God's plan? Was the child's death the result of Whitefield's neglect? Was the impression of his son's future greatness merely Whitefield's desire to prolong the acclaim of his own name?

And all the time we're asking those questions, we're dodging the issues that really matter: (1) Does God speak to us personally? (2) Can we trust our ability to hear his voice? (3) If we are deceived, will God abandon us for our presumption?

We don't enjoy admitting our capacity for garbling God's messages to us. It's more comfortable to judge the blunders of George Whitefield and other misguided prophets than to deal with the pain of our own failures in hearing the voice of God. Some people find their own fallibility so painful that they quit listening for God's voice, preferring silence to risk.

Whatever Whitefield did wrong, his desire to hear his Master's voice was perfectly right. It takes courage to speak the truth we believe God shows us. When God sent the angel Gabriel to tell Zechariah that he would become a father in his old age, the priest didn't have the faith to share the good news (Luke 1:5-25; 2:57-80). Gabriel told him, "You will be silent and not able to speak until the day this happens, because you did not believe my words, which will come true at their proper time." Whitefield was not bothered by such timidity.

Unfortunately, his brave forecast, unlike Zechariah's vision, didn't come to pass. Was Whitefield a false prophet who deserved God's wrath? Hardly! His life evidenced a sincere love for Christ and an intense desire to obey him in everything. Early in his ministry, he prayed, "Lord, show that Thou dost love me, by humbling and keeping me humble as long as I live. The means I leave to Thee."

This painful event was just such a discipline as Whitefield had requested. It revealed an area of spiritual immaturity, a point where Whitefield could be tempted to presumption. He longed so deeply for intimacy with God, desired so ardently to change his world for the Savior, that he mistook emotional impressions for divine inspiration.

We can be certain that the error cost him dearly. He compromised his credibility with his wife, his congregation, and the public. He compounded his grief because of the tremendous fall from the pinnacle of his expectations to the valley of death. In short, he failed. And sometimes so do we. Such defeats leave us crushed and broken.

Depending on our individual personalities and situations, we may struggle with emotions ranging from doubt to total cynicism. Embarrassment prompts many of us to wonder, *What will people think of me?* Confusion swirls around us, blurring our view of what to do next and leaving us helpless. Disillusionment whispers, *You can't hear God's voice,* and discouragement joins in with, *You'll never be the kind of person God can trust.* We may counter such attacks with defensive responses, trying to justify or explain away our failure. The ultimate temptation is to decide that there is no God or that he has no desire to talk with any of us.

Whitefield's reaction to his failed prediction offers us a lift out of this emotional quicksand. He didn't give up on God or himself. He didn't wallow in despair. He simply prayed that his crushing experience would make him a wiser, more effective Christian. He kept moving forward with his trusted Guide—more determined to watch the path for potholes, less confident in his own perceptions, fully convinced God would keep on picking him up.

We can learn several important lessons from Whitefield about the challenges of hearing and responding to the voice of God. Let's examine a few of them:

◆ *God wants to speak to us from the Scriptures and deep in our hearts.* Jesus described himself as the Good Shepherd whose sheep recognize and respond to his voice. When he talks about our relationship with him, communication is central. Scripture promises that we can expect to be led by God: "Whether you turn to the right or to the left, your ears will hear a voice behind you, saying, 'This is the way; walk in it'" (Isa. 30:21).

If we rule out everything other than the Bible as a means of hearing from God, we create a long-distance relationship. That's not what God has in mind. He put his promises in writing to anchor our lives. They keep us from sailing off on false courses under the wind of our own thoughts and feelings. But he also longs to talk with us, to surround us with his presence and power. We are sternly warned not to put out the Spirit's fire or treat prophecies with contempt. Instead, we must test them carefully and hold on to what is good (1 Thess. 5:19-21).

◆ *Much of what God speaks to us as we draw closer to him will consist of fresh inspiration and insight from his written Word.* Just as God breathed into the dust and brought man to life, his Spirit breathes into the Scripture and brings truth to life in us (2 Cor. 3:6). The Holy Spirit guides us into truth and protects us from error (John 16:13). He enables us to progress in our knowledge and application of God's written Word in our lives.

We don't need special insight into the future or revelations of new truths nearly as much as we need the Spirit's simple words of encouragement and correction. There are few places in the New Testament where the future of individual believers' was foretold. Instead, there are repeated assurances that wherever the future leads and whatever it brings, the Lord will be there to guide and uphold.

If we focus too much on receiving personal information, it's possible our motives need examination. Proverbs 27:1 cautions, "Do not boast about tomorrow, for you do not know what a day may bring forth." Do we want to hear God's voice so we can prove our spiritual superiority? This is pride. Are we so uncertain of God's direction and blessing that we need a sign of some sort to reassure us? This is unbelief. Do we want God to guarantee us everything is going to work out great without action on our part? This is laziness.

♦ *We must beware of deception.* George Whitefield was warned early in his ministry by the famous American preacher Jonathan Edwards that he was trusting his impressions too much. His emotions carried him along. He became intoxicated with his perception of God's will. No wonder he prayed to be more sober-minded!

John Wesley cautioned, "Do not hastily ascribe things to God. Do not easily suppose dreams, voices, impressions, visions or revelations to be from God. They may be from him, they may be from nature, they may be from the devil. Therefore, believe not every spirit, but try the spirits, whether they be from God."

In a letter to a friend several years before his own major blunder, Whitefield said, "Follow after, but do not run before the blessed Spirit; if you do, although you may benefit others, and God may overrule everything for your good, yet you will certainly destroy the peace of your own soul." He proved the truth of those words.

Often silence is the best way to respond to what we believe is a special message from God. Like Mary, the mother of Jesus, we can treasure up God's promises in our hearts and wait to see how he will fulfill them (Luke 2:19). When we feel the Lord wants us to share what he has spoken to us with others, we should do so in a way that encourages the listener to seek God personally rather than accepting us as an ultimate authority. If George Whitefield had exercised similar caution in predicting his son's future, much unnecessary heartache could have been avoided.

♦ *Our humanity affects our ability to receive God's direction.* In his excellent book *Voice of God,* Herman H. Riffel discusses how the various dimensions of our personalities make us able to hear God and, at the same time, capable of fabricating or distorting spiritual insight. God speaks to us through our spirit, but the message filters through our thoughts, emotions, senses, and will.

For instance, emotion-centered people believe they have heard God because it feels right. Logic-oriented individuals accept the message because it makes sense. The highly intuitive depend on a mystical inner knowing. Those with a strong will and ambition are apt to accept messages that line up with their plans. Sense-dominated people test everything against circumstance. In addition, there are the voices of authority, upbringing, and past experience. And joining in with every misleading inner voice is the voice of Satan, the father of lies.

No wonder Paul wrote, "For we know in part and we prophesy in part. . . . Now we see but a poor reflection as in a mirror; then we shall see face to face" (1 Cor. 13:9, 12). God is infinitely patient with our human limitations. When we are sensitive to him, he can speak softly and still get an obedient response. But when we get off track, he must sometimes shout to us through our pain, as C. S. Lewis so aptly put it.

George Whitefield wrote in his journal, "Suffering times are a Christian's best improving times; for they break the will, wean us from the creature, prove the heart."

◆ *In spite of our capacity for deception, we must not give way to fear.* This is summed up well by John White in his book *The Fight:*

> At the back of your mind you may feel that following Christ is like walking a tightrope. One false move and you're done for. Yet if the sheep strays a little, the Eastern shepherd, who knows his sheep by name, will not abandon him to his false course. He will call him, and if the sheep fails to respond to the call, he will go and fetch him. Guidance is not walking a tightrope.

That doesn't mean we should be casual or careless about hearing from and speaking for God. Whitefield's experience underscores the costliness of error. But we can be confident that the safety net of God's grace holds firm to keep us from destruction. Through trial and error we grow in strength and skill. "If the Lord delights in a man's way, he makes his steps firm; though he stumble, he will not fall, for the Lord upholds him with his hand" (Ps. 37: 23-24).

The secret of discerning God's voice is not being perfect; it is keeping our hearts pure and responding to his loving discipline. God promises that as we return to him for cleansing and correction, he will teach us to separate the precious from the worthless (Jer. 15:19). Through Bible training and practice in right living, we acquire a spiritual sense of good and evil (Heb. 5:13-14). This exercise best prepares us to speak for God.

Steps to Spiritual Greatness

- ◆ Confirmation. Submit the messages you receive from God to the testing of trusted spiritual counselors.
- ◆ Caution. Refrain from sharing the secrets God whispers to your heart. Wait for further insight and guidance.
- ◆ Confession. When you mistake your own thoughts or desires for God's voice, humble yourself and accept a course correction.
- ◆ Courage. Regardless of how many times you misunderstand, doubt, or disobey, keep listening!

I am still confident of this: I will see the goodness of the Lord in the land of the living. Wait for the Lord; be strong and take heart and wait for the Lord. (Ps. 27:13-14)

CHAPTER 14
Out of the Ashes

D. L. Moody closed his Sunday evening sermon. He gave the invitation for sinners to come to Christ. Ten hands went up immediately. Ira Sankey began singing, "Today the Savior calls: For refuge fly . . ."

Moody could sense the Spirit of God drawing people to the Lord Jesus across the vast congregation of more than three thousand that filled Farwell Hall. Then the clang of a city fire alarm drowned out Sankey's voice. Soon bells tolled throughout Chicago, including the great city bell at the courthouse. Noisy fire engines rushed past outside the meeting. Moody recognized the general alarm's severity and quickly dismissed the crowd to seek safety without finishing his altar call.

The two evangelists went out on a back stairway of the building and spotted the fire's ominous glow on the southwest edge of the city. Sankey decided to go see what help he could give at the scene of the fire. Moody hurried away to his home on the North Side, where Emma and the children waited for him. As he walked, a strong southwest wind blew and the sky glowed with flying embers and bursts of flame. The fire was headed for the heart of Chicago. When Emma welcomed him into their home, Moody could offer her no hope. "The city is doomed," he said.

He grieved for his beloved city, but took comfort that the fire lay across the river from his family. The children slept in their beds, safe from the inferno. He and Emma went to bed after midnight when word came that the fire was under control.

In the wee hours of morning a loud knock came at the front door. Moody opened the door to a policeman.

"The fire's crossed the river. You'd better get out of your house right away," the weary officer said. "It's moving this way fast."

Moody told Emma to wake the children and get them ready to leave. She dressed them in two of every garment and then stood with them at the French windows in the drawing room, watching the fire. Meanwhile, Moody located a neighbor who was taking his family to safety in a horse and buggy. "Is there room for my family?" he asked. The neighbor shook his head. "What about just our little son and daughter?" As soon as he had a yes, he hurried back for the children.

He and Emma put a few valuables and their Bibles into the baby carriage. Then they hurried off on foot to Emma's sister's home in a westside suburb.

The fire raged all day Monday and into Tuesday. The Moodys rejoiced when, after twenty-four hours of anxious waiting, they learned that their children were safe in the home of friends in a northern suburb.

By Wednesday the fire had burned itself out. Moody walked city streets of hot, cracked, and blackened brick, strewn with coils of burned telegraph wire. Whichever way he looked, the city lay in ashes. Gone were his elegant new home, his church and mission Sunday school, handsome Farwell Hall, less than a year old and built at great personal cost to him. Thousands wandered about homeless and disoriented.

News reports gradually revealed the dimensions of the disaster: 250 dead; 150,000 homeless; 2,100 acres burned; 17,450 buildings destroyed, including 50 churches; $192 million in property damage. October 8, 1871, would surely be remembered forever as the darkest day in Chicago's history.

Moody gazed at the desolation, his mind overwhelmed at the thought of what it would take to rebuild. He felt like an old man at thirty-four, exhausted and empty.

With a heavy heart Moody sat down in November to write to prominent men in the East. He was desperate for financial aid and eager to get away from Chicago's bottomless pit of need for a little while. Perhaps a fund-raising tour would help him overcome the discouragement he felt.

"One thousand children and their parents are looking to me for another building," he wrote. For years now Chicago had been looking to D. L. Moody. His life was an endless string of committee meetings, fund-raisers, conventions, and pastoral duties.

It wasn't just the fire that had him down. He had been at low ebb for months. Maybe those two women who had told him he needed the Holy Ghost were right. Something had to account for his lack of fruitfulness, his complete sense of helplessness.

He wept alone in prayer, asking God to fill him with his Spirit. No relief came.

By sheer force of will Moody traveled east. Large donations from businessmen in Philadelphia should have lifted his spirit. Instead he became increasingly miserable. He arrived in New York City and sought out opportunities to preach in addition to his fund-raising work. After a dry sermon or two, his audience dwindled to less than twenty.

He cried out as never before for God to fill him with the Holy Spirit. Pacing the streets of New York City one miserable night, Moody suddenly felt an overpowering awareness of God's presence. It was as if he had come to the burning bush and stood on holy ground.

He had to find a place to be alone. He hurried to the closest home of a friend. "I want to be alone," he told the bewildered man. "Let me have a room where I can lock myself in." His host quickly complied.

Alone with God, Moody felt his self-will, his ambition, his pride in achievement swept away by holy fire. He knew at last that it was not what he could do for God but what God could do for him that mattered most.

When he left that room, he knew that he wouldn't have to spend the rest of his life trying to pump water out of a dry well. He wouldn't be tugging and carrying buckets to quench the thirst of others. At last he had the water of life springing up inside him!

"God revealed Himself to me, and I had such an experience of His love that I had to ask Him to stay His hand," D. L. Moody said when questioned about his transformation. "I went to preaching again. The sermons were not different; I did not present any new truths, and yet hundreds were converted. I would not now be placed back where I was before that blessed experience if you should give me all the world—it would be as the small dust of the balance."

Moody's heartstrings had been torn from Chicago. He was set free to go wherever God led. He soon sailed for England as a traveling evangelist, leaving the fund-raising and rebuilding to others. He lost interest in everything except preaching the Word and working for souls. As never before, Moody knew who Christ was, who he was, and what his purpose in life must be. His rebirth of confidence made him equal to the demands of international evangelism.

The next twenty-eight years of ministry made the name of Dwight L. Moody legendary. He remained active until his death at age sixty-two.

In addition to his remarkable Sunday school and YMCA work, he traveled an estimated one million miles and preached to more than 100 million people. He also started several schools, including Moody Bible Institute, which has prepared thousands of men and women to continue his evangelistic ministry around the world.

What We Can Learn from the Life of D. L. Moody

Americans are famous for frenetic activity. Consider the following description of our national life-style:

> In the United States a man builds a house to spend his latter years in it and he sells it before the roof is on: he plants a garden and [rents] it just as the trees are coming into bearing. If his private affairs leave him any leisure, he instantly plunges into the vortex of politics; if at the end of a year of unremitting labor he finds he has a few days' vacation, his eager curiosity whirls him over the vast extent of the United States and he will travel fifteen hundred miles in a few days. . . . He who has set his heart exclusively upon the pursuit of worldly welfare is always in a hurry for he has but a limited time at his disposal to reach it, to grasp it, and to enjoy it.

Those words were penned in 1835 by Alexis de Tocqueville, a visiting French statesman. Their ring of truth is clearer than ever. Whether our ambitions are worldly or heavenly, they relentlessly drive us.

America didn't invent this state of mind, however. While the term *burnout* is relatively new, the condition dates back at least as far as Moses. In his effort to lead the Israelites, he became overwhelmed with daily responsibility. His visiting father-in-law watched the spectacle and then responded with a stern correction: "What you are doing is not good. You and these

163

people who come to you will only wear yourselves out. The work is too heavy for you; you cannot handle it alone" (Exod. 18:17-18).

Moody learned this principle the hard way. A careful look at his life reveals how he burned out and how God relit his fire.

◆ *Mistaking outward success for inner fulfillment produces painful burnout.* D. L. Moody was a remarkably gifted leader. Throughout the 1860s, his ambition for increasing the kingdom of God on earth knew no bounds.

Moody's mission Sunday school gained such fame for transforming the lives of Chicago's street children that President Abraham Lincoln paid it a visit. During the Civil War Moody also ministered to troops at forts, front lines, and hospitals. He became head of Chicago's YMCA and launched an ambitious fundraising campaign to erect the country's first YMCA hall (Farwell Hall). His tract campaign aimed at distributing a million pages of Christian literature each week, and he was the guiding light of the American Sunday School movement. He pastored a large church and prided himself on his physical and emotional endurance, demonstrated by such feats as once making 200 pastoral house calls in a day. He served on a dozen important religious and governmental committees. Influential men began pressing him to consider the good he could do in the political arena.

By 1871 Moody could accurately say, "The zeal of the Lord's house has consumed me." His perpetual motion continued, but the gears were grinding. In a letter to his brother he complained, "It is eleven to twelve every night when I retire and am up in the morning at light. Wish you could come in sometime about one to three o'clock my office hours & see the people waiting. I do not get five minutes a day to study so I have to talk just as it happens." On another occasion he said, "If a man came to talk about his soul, I would say: 'I haven't time: got a committee to attend.'"

That same year two humble Christian women approached Moody with a message similar to the one Moses' concerned father-in-law gave him. They said, "Mr. Moody, you need the power of the Spirit." He huffed at the suggestion that he needed anything. But the women persisted in prayer and in confrontation.

Gradually Moody became aware how right they were. He was physically exhausted, mentally confused, emotionally undone, and spiritually dry. He repeatedly cried out to God for a fresh infilling of the Holy Spirit. Nothing happened. He soon felt that he didn't want to live without supernatural empowerment for service.

But he also didn't want to let go of his own agenda. "God was calling me to higher service," Moody said later, "to go out and preach the gospel all over the land instead of staying in Chicago. I fought against it." He had yet to realize that "God sends no one away empty except those who are full of themselves."

Then the fire came. Not the fire of the Holy Spirit but a consuming fire that reduced Moody's achievements to an ash heap. God didn't send fire to Chicago, but neither did he shield Moody's monuments of ambition from its flames. Sometimes our outward success must be stripped away before we clearly discern our inner poverty.

◆ *Commitment to conflicting causes and kingdoms destroys inner harmony.* The apostle Paul warned that good soldiers don't entangle themselves in distracting duties, and prize-winning athletes don't break the rules (2 Tim. 2:4-5). Many Spirit-filled Christians find themselves with serious "leaks" through directing their talents and affections in too many directions.

Moody faced just such a dilemma. His success in Chicago had made him a popular candidate for every righteous cause the city needed championed. He wholeheartedly desired to serve Christ, but he became confused about how many ways he could effectively do that. Would he be only an evangelist or could he also work as a social reformer? Should he concentrate on Chicago, where his efforts seemed destined to prosper, or should he venture into new areas that tested his faith? Would he be a man of wit or a man of the Word?

Such turmoil is compounded by overcommitment that keeps one too busy to wait for God's direction. A large portion of today's church leads this fragmented life instead of the fragrant life that attracts others to Jesus. It's hard for anyone to believe his yoke is easy and his burden is light when they see us crushed by the load.

We can resolve the conflict and throw off the unnecessary burdens by obeying one essential command: "Since we live by the Spirit, let us keep in step with the Spirit" (Gal. 5:25). He knows the right path and the right pace.

♦ *Substituting human energy for divine anointing leads to exhaustion and fruitless living.* It's possible to know how to do the work of God too well. Moody brought his effective business skills into the kingdom and assumed they would do just as good a job there as they had in the world. Meanwhile, he became like a mainspring that's been wound too tight. Tension and restlessness filled him. Each day became more miserable.

"Why should God have to lead us thus, and allow the pressure to be so hard and constant?" asks another remarkable servant of God, A. B. Simpson. Because "he wants us to stand, not with a self-constituted strength, but with a hand ever leaning upon his, and a trust that dare not take one step alone."

God puts us in the school of trial to teach us this trust. Simpson continues, "The lesson of faith, once learned, is an everlasting acquisition and an eternal fortune made; and without trust even riches will leave us poor."

When the Holy Spirit filled Moody, replacing his ambition and drive with inspiration and peace, the yoke of weariness was broken. He received strength to obey his Master's command to go into the world with the gospel message, to minister to those who found him crude and uncouth, to resist the pull of conflicting priorities.

If we suffer from chronic weariness in well-doing, it's a fairly good clue that the oil of God's Spirit has burned low in our lamps. Instead of offering light to those around us, we may be stifling them with the smoky fumes of our frustration.

A Spirit-transformed Moody was able to say, "When God wants to move a mountain, he does not take a bar of iron, but he takes a little worm. The fact is, we have too much strength. We are not weak enough. It is not our strength that we want. One drop of God's strength is worth more than all the world."

◆ *High performance does not equal spiritual perfection.* In fact, it can actually diminish it. God doesn't want us to learn how to *do* good as much as he wants us to *become* good. As one minister put it, "Before God calls us to destiny, he calls us to delight."

When King David decided to build a permanent home for the ark of God's presence, the Lord let him know who was the real builder (2 Sam. 7). "Are you the one to build me a house to dwell in?" God asked. Then he reminded David of his humble beginnings as a shepherd boy and how divine providence had lifted him to the throne. God's word to David was, "You aren't building my house; I'm building yours."

We have difficulty admitting that the Lord can achieve his purposes without us. Certainly he wants us to give our best, but he also wants us to recognize that we have nothing to offer him that didn't come from his infinite riches. When we are gone from the scene, his work will still proceed as divinely planned.

Like many Christians today, Moody became caught up in spiritual empire building. He felt a constant need to do more and to do it faster and better than others. He bragged about the size of his audiences and drooped when the numbers went down.

Looking back on his early ministry, Moody said, "The Chicago

Fire was the turning point of my life. . . . In my ambition to make my enterprises succeed because they were mine, I had taken my eyes off from the Lord and had been burdened in soul and unfruitful in my work. When the Fire came, as a revelation, I took my hat and walked out!"

Many of us would do ourselves and God a favor by walking out of the performance trap and back into his presence. Instead of an endless quest to prove our worth and a constant fear of failure or criticism, we need to cultivate the ability to sit quietly at Jesus' feet. There we will discover that it's "not by might nor by power" but by the Spirit of God that anything of eternal good is accomplished (Zech. 4:6).

Those afire with the Holy Spirit need not fear burnout. His flames consume sin and self-will, leaving behind cleansed vessels fit for the Master's service. "I do not know of anything that America needs more today than men and women on fire with the fire of Heaven," Moody said, "and I have yet to find a man or woman on fire with the Spirit of God that is a failure."

Steps to Spiritual Greatness
- Recognize that you are running on empty.
- Resist the temptation to fill your life with something besides God's Spirit.
- Renew yourself through spiritual, mental, and physical rest.
- Receive the Holy Spirit's indwelling enablement.
- Rejoice in his power as an antidote to your problems.

Even youths grow tired and weary, and young men stumble and fall; but those who hope in the Lord will renew their strength. They will soar on wings like eagles; they will run and not grow weary, they will walk and not be faint. (Isa. 40:30-31)

CHAPTER 15
Night without Morning

Catherine Marshall LeSourd kept vigil beside the heat table where her six-week-old granddaughter lay. A network of tubes attached to Amy Catherine's tiny body substituted for the work her damaged organs could not do. Meanwhile, a network of unbroken prayer went up for her healing. The nurse carefully lifted the infant up from the table and indicated that Catherine could hold her.

The baby's color is worse today, Catherine noted, as she took her from the nurse. How she and her daughter-in-law, Edith, and son, Peter, had come to treasure these holding sessions. Catherine snuggled the infant as close to her as the tubes would allow. Sometimes Amy Catherine snuggled back, but today there was no response.

The heart monitor is back on too, Catherine observed. She glanced back down at the baby. "You'll make it, little one. I'll fight with you. Two Catherines slugging it out together." While she willed the baby's fighting spirit to respond, Amy Catherine began crying as loudly as she could.

"Please, stop!" Catherine begged the nurse who was pumping bile from Amy Catherine's stomach. The nurse kept pumping. The baby became increasingly distressed. The nurse took a quick look at the heart monitor and then insisted on placing

Amy Catherine back in the heated crib. That done, she raced out in search of the doctor.

Moments later the doctor bent over Amy Catherine, examined her, and then said, "The baby has expired. I'm sorry."

Edith began crying. Catherine could not.

Expired. Expired. The word was so final. So empty. Why, God? Why? Catherine had given all she had to the battle. She had stretched her faith to the limit, never doubting God's power or willingness to heal. And now, total defeat. The darkness closed around her.

Week followed weary week with no change. Catherine's closest companions were depression, grief, sleeplessness, anger, and humiliation. Whenever she tried to write, the image of Amy Catherine crying out for help overwhelmed her.

Even after the initial grief and anger began to subside, Catherine experienced a total absence of the sense of God's presence in her life. Her granddaughter's death had uncorked a stream of questions: *Have I ever really known God deeply? How many other times have I mistaken what I wanted for divine direction? Is God's judgment against me for marrying a divorced man?*

Her husband, Len, tried to comfort, to confront, to reason. Nothing worked. Added to Catherine's inner turmoil were a host of disappointments and frustrations. MGM decided not to make her novel *Christy* into a movie. The new novel she had been struggling to write for three years, against her editors' advice, had to be abandoned. The dishwasher wouldn't work; the plumbing leaked; the car broke down.

After six months of misery, Catherine was reduced to a shell of her former self. Then Len and two of her closest friends confronted her. As they talked, she felt withdrawn and hollow.

They pointed out her self-pity and rebellion against God. She admitted they were right. They encouraged her to repent of the sins so God could restore her. She assured them she had done this repeatedly, and he had not answered.

"I've never, ever lived in this kind of vacuum before. I talk, I pray. Nothing." The tears flowed as she poured out her agony over losing the battle for Amy Catherine. "I didn't ask for anything for myself, only that a tiny baby be healed, and God not only refused that request, but turned his back on me. I don't understand."

"Maybe it's that insistence on understanding that's the problem, Catherine," one friend said.

With those words a shaft of light broke through the darkness. Her depression didn't leave, but the next morning she felt an inner prompting—the first since her granddaughter's death—to read Isaiah 53.

As she read, Catherine understood in a brand new way that Christ's suffering was the heart of God's perfect plan. Yet Jesus had felt completely forsaken in his time of greatest pain. The disciples had responded much like she had to Amy Catherine's death. They couldn't understand what was happening, couldn't see any way it could be good or bring glory to God.

Finally Catherine saw what had walled her off from God. She had insisted on understanding what he did and why. She had demanded, presuming she knew his will. Maybe she had even tried to *be* God for Amy Catherine, to make her live. No wonder God had been silent.

On her knees with tears streaming down her face, she prayed, "I need you and your presence in my life more than I need understanding. I choose you, Lord. I trust you to give me understanding and an answer to all my whys—only *if* and *when* you choose."

Then she heard the inner Voice. "I, your God, am in everything. The baby died, but Amy Catherine is with me. And while she lived, she ministered to everyone who prayed for her. You, alone, Catherine, were too stubborn to see it."

Out of that long dark night, Catherine Marshall LeSourd emerged stronger, wiser, more tender, more creative than ever.

For many weeks she continued to struggle with insomnia and spiritual emptiness. The journey back into the light was not easy, but it was filled with new insights and hope.

After reordering her personal life and renewing her fellowship with God, Catherine experienced healing in her marriage and other relationships. She received clear direction for writing that would minister to others at levels of deep pain and questioning. She experienced relief from her unyielding perfectionism and need for control.

Between 1974 and early 1983 Catherine wrote eight books. She and her husband, Len, worked closely on all of them. She enjoyed her family; Peter and Edith Marshall were blessed with two healthy children, who helped to fill the void felt after the loss of Amy Catherine. She and Len started a book publishing company and founded a nationwide intercessory prayer ministry. Grief had cut her deeply, but the pruned tree bore much fruit.

What We Can Learn from
the Life of Catherine Marshall

"No discipline seems pleasant at the time, but painful. Later on, however, it produces a harvest of righteousness and peace for those who have been trained by it" (Heb. 12:11). To say that the Lord's chastening isn't pleasant must qualify as one of the Bible's greatest understatements. Most of us dread it worse than we did the spankings, lectures, and long silences of our childhood.

People like Catherine Marshall who have enjoyed deep fellowship with God and a flow of his power in their lives feel the pain of his discipline in a profound way. It's like being evicted from the Garden of Eden. The Bible assures us that God's correction comes in love so that we may reap the maximum in life. But our emotions tell us something far different. We're apt to feel humiliated, abandoned, and disoriented. We usually cry out for the pain to cease, but God loves us too much to listen.

Our heavenly Father knows what's best. He knows that we'll be able to echo the Psalmist David's words some day: "It was good for me to be afflicted so that I might learn your decrees" (Ps. 119:71). In the meantime, he puts up with our screams and whimpers and patiently waits for us to learn our lessons.

We can take courage in realizing that Jesus also suffered in order to come to the place the Father designed for him. "Although he was a son, he learned obedience from what he suffered and, once made perfect, he became the source of eternal salvation" (Heb. 5:8-9).

God's discipline in our lives comes in many forms. Most of the time it's a gentle prodding through the commands of Scripture and the conviction of the Holy Spirit. Sometimes it's like sandpaper as the circumstances of life wear down our rough edges. But at some point most of us experience the searing pain of plunging into a crucible of trial beyond our worst nightmares. Catherine Marshall's experience gives us a penetrating look at how God cleanses and refines his chosen vessels.

♦ *He allows us to experience the crucible of unanswered prayer.* We have a hard enough time with situations where God seems to be saying, "Wait," "Not now," or "We'll see." Then we can prayerfully persist in a kind of spiritual arm wrestling. But when an avalanche of tragedy buries our prayers, we're caught between the dilemma of thinking we've failed God or he's failed us.

At such times we dredge through the lives of everyone involved looking for the sin and unbelief that would account for God's silence. Sometimes we find it, and sometimes we don't. Either way we eventually have to deal with our attitude about God and our degree of confidence in his love. This process purges away careless living and spiritual pride, bringing us back to the fundamentals of Christianity. It reduces us to the diaper stage where we become once again totally dependent on God's grace and ability rather than our own.

We like power. Learning spiritual principles and becoming proficient in Christian living gives us a sense of power. When we forget where that power comes from and try to work independent of God, he lets us fall on our face. His central desire is not our quality of service or our accomplishments but our intimate knowledge of him.

In her book *The Freedom of Obedience*, Martha Thatcher identifies one of the most common causes of God's silence:

> Herein lies the root of our discouragement: We are listening for *something*, not *someone*. We are, as it were, trying to hear the *voice* of God, not the voice of *God*. This difference is subtle but pivotal.

To ask why our prayers were not answered is legitimate. But if this further asking is also not answered, we have no choice but to continue until God's reason becomes clear. "For the revelation awaits an appointed time; it speaks of the end and will not prove false. Though it linger, wait for it; it will certainly come and will not delay" (Hab. 2:3).

◆ *God leaves us in the crucible of trial to purify our theology.* We practice theology in everything we do. Our knowledge of God and his ways affects our thoughts, speech, and actions. What we learned from the Lord yesterday is what we can live out today. There is tremendous excitement in seeing Scripture come alive in our daily walk.

Catherine Marshall practiced a lively theology. She expected to see God at work in every area of life. She had learned to expect miracles. But, like most of us, she became absorbed in certain aspects of God's working to the exclusion of others. Her theology of healing and prayer impaired her ability to accept the diversity of divine purpose and action.

God will not allow us to manipulate him with our understanding of Scripture, past spiritual triumphs, or daring faith. He refuses to be put in the box of our limited expectations. He is forever the God of surprises. Just when we think we have him figured out, he says, "You do not realize now what I am doing, but later you will understand" (John 13:7).

In the crucible we rediscover who is master and who is student.

♦ *God permits us to sink to the depths of our crucible.* Realizing that our trials come to teach us, we quickly respond, "OK, Lord, explain this to me and I'll learn it right away." After all, how can we understand him better if he doesn't explain himself? When he leaves us with no answers or insights, the night closes in around us.

Not only are we devoid of answers, we lack even the comforting awareness of God's presence. After the death of his wife, C. S. Lewis experienced this terrifying spiritual void: "A door slammed in your face, and a sound of bolting and double-bolting on the inside. After that, silence. . . . Why is He so present a commander in our time of prosperity and so very absent a help in time of trouble?" We must remember this is the voice of emotion, not faith. Lewis did, in fact, find the Lord to be helper and healer in his grief, as did Catherine Marshall. But they and many others have had to endure a total absence of emotional reassurance of God's presence.

One of the hardest spiritual battles we ever fight is the battle to lay down our right to know what God is doing. William Gurnall addresses this special test:

> It takes a submissive faith for a soul to march steadily forward while God seems to fire upon that soul and shoots His frowns like poisoned arrows into it. This is hard

work, and will test the Christian's mettle. Yet such a spirit we find in the poor woman of Canaan, who caught the bullets Christ shot at her, and with a humble boldness sent them back again in her prayer (Matt. 15:22-28).

Two anchors hold our faith secure at such times: (1) God's vow that he will never forsake us or leave us orphaned, and (2) the testimony of our experience and history.

♦ *God lets the crucible get hotter.* As long as he sends one problem at a time, we handle it fairly well. We pray, seek counsel, work through the difficulty, and move on. What we may not realize is how large a collection of little disappointments we're accumulating—things we don't want to deal with, attitudes we think we shouldn't have, doubts about the goodness of God.

The Lord doesn't want us weighed down with all that, so he allows the heat to be turned up in life's pressure cooker. He carefully watches the gauge, knowing exactly how much we can bear. As the pot boils, some poisonous gases start to bubble up. Reeling from the foul odor that permeates our lives, we cry, "Where did all this come from?" Sometimes we discover we've been building a temple to God on a toxic waste dump of unresolved hurt.

Then the Holy Spirit makes himself known to us as the refining fire rather than the gentle dove. He burns away the stench of rebellion, unforgiveness, pride—whatever is polluting our lives. He cauterizes the wound amid our screams. Finally, he pours in the oil of healing and restores our joy.

♦ *God allows Satan to fuel the fire.* During these times of painful discipline, Satan tempts us to believe several lies. He tells us our past experiences with God were only fantasies. He tries to convince us that we have permanently cut ourselves off from the Lord. He reminds us of sins that God has forgotten. He points to the doors of addiction and self-destruction as ways of escape. In God's silence, the devil's voice sounds louder than ever.

Does this mean Satan is stronger than God? Can evil ultimately win in the lives of those who belong to the Lord? If it were not for the death and resurrection of Jesus Christ, the answer would be yes. But he won the supreme victory over all the power of hell. His nail-scarred hands are in control of every circumstance we encounter.

Our loving heavenly Father would never allow such testing in our lives if it were not essential to our spiritual development. He isn't tempting us to forsake him. He simply wants us to trust him for no other reason than who he is. No conditions. No options. No arguments.

This Divine Alchemist knows just the right moment to turn down the heat. He won't leave us on his back burner. He's standing near, whether we feel his presence or not, watching for just the right moment to lift us out of trial into triumph.

Steps to Spiritual Greatness
- Let go of your demands on God, others, and yourself.
- Listen until you're able to hear the still, small voice of direction and comfort.
- Learn to see God at work in tragedy and failure.
- Laugh at the idea of giving up on God.
- Look forward to the time when your song returns.

Let him who walks in the dark, who has no light, trust in the name of the Lord and rely on his God. (Isa. 50:10)

Section Six

••••••••••••••

DEATH, THE FINAL ENEMY

CHAPTER 16
A Grain of Wheat

Another fit of coughing racked David Brainerd's frail body with pain. He covered his mouth with his handkerchief. Lowering it, he saw the now familiar spattering of blood. The smell of meat roasting on the fire turned his stomach.

He and his little band of Indian converts had been gone from home almost a month. They had traveled the easy route from Cranbury, New Jersey, to the Susquehanna River. But even without the rigors of the mountains, the trip had been too much for him.

Upon reaching the river, they had traveled upstream into the wilderness. Night after night Brainerd camped on the damp ground. Day after weary day, he hung in the saddle, traveling to remote Indian settlements with the gospel. He could feel his life ebbing away with each difficult mile.

He struggled to record a few lines in his diary. His only achievement for the day was to talk of spiritual things with his Indian companions and a few camp visitors. His heart was heavy. Grief poured from his pen.

"6 Sept. 1746. Had, by this time, very little life or heart to speak for God, through feebleness of body. Was scarcely ever more ashamed and confounded in myself than now," he wrote. If the people who supported him through the missionary society

181

could see him lying here, helpless and undone in body and spirit, they would regret ever having sponsored him, he thought. Returning to the day's entry, he added, "If God's people knew me as God knows, they would not think so highly of my zeal and resolution for God as perhaps they now do! . . . If they saw the smallness of my courage and resolution for God, they would be ready to shut me out of their doors, as unworthy of the company or friendship of Christians."

He had intended to linger much longer in the area before returning home. Time was so short, and so many had never heard of the Savior. But he couldn't hold up much longer, and some of his companions were ill too. They would have to return soon—if he could.

Two weeks later Brainerd arrived back in Cranbury. He found the faithful Indian converts there praying when he arrived. After giving them a brief report on his journey, he retreated to his hut and collapsed. He lay there thinking of the many hardships and distresses he had endured. He struggled to thank God for his mercy in it all.

Tomorrow is the Lord's day, he thought. Would he be able to preach? He cried out to God for strength. His prayer echoed the words of the apostle Paul, "O that whether I live, I might live to the Lord; or whether I die, I might die unto the Lord; that, whether living or dying, I might be the Lord's!"

A year had passed since that final missionary journey along the Susquehanna River. Brainerd no longer lay beside campfires. He no longer preached. He couldn't even climb the stairs to his room in Jonathan and Sarah Edwards's home. He felt useless.

He lay in bed praying for the Indian believers in Cranbury. His brother John had replaced him as their pastor in April, but he still felt the weight of their well-being. Sorrow filled him as he thought of the long winter months when they had been left alone while he struggled to regain his health in the home of a dear friend. He had returned to them briefly in the early spring but found he was still too weak to minister. In a last desperate attempt to overcome the illness that had him in a death grip, he had set out for New England on horseback in March.

He had been here in Northampton, Massachusetts, in Jonathan Edwards's home since May. He had been near death most of that time. His worst suspicions had been confirmed by Dr. Mather's able diagnosis: he had advanced tuberculosis. The Edwardses had graciously made their home his, and their seventeen-year-old daughter, Jerusha, nursed him daily.

As he thought of his weakness and the end of his mission work, strong encouragement began flowing into his heart. Something he had realized several months earlier and recorded in his diary came alive inside him: "The Redeemer's kingdom is all that is valuable in the earth, and I could not but long for the promotion of it in the world. I saw also, that this cause is God's; that he has an infinitely greater regard and concern for it than I could possibly have." Yes, God would finish what he had begun.

In confirmation of it, his brother John arrived from Cranbury with an encouraging report and David's private papers and diaries. He drew strength from John's presence at his bedside and from the good news of his beloved Indian friends. He also took courage from reading in his diaries of God's mercy in his life in times past.

John could only stay a week, but soon their brother Israel arrived from Yale to spend whatever time remained to David on earth. Israel—soldier of God—the name fit the capable young ministerial student. What a comfort to have him near to talk and pray with, to write in the diary when David was too weak to try.

The glory of heaven seemed to fill the sickroom. The guilt, doubt, and discouragement that had plagued him so much of his life gave way to peace. Though he could no longer minister in preaching or missionary service, he could pray—for his congregation, for the outpouring of God's Spirit on the earth, for the building of the kingdom. How he longed for death, but he determined to persevere in prayer.

In late September he revived enough to correct a small volume of his writings for publication. With that accomplished and all his personal affairs set in order, Brainerd felt his work was done. "O, why is his chariot so long in coming? I long to be in heaven, praising and glorifying God with the holy angels," he cried out again and again.

By early October the pain became so unbearable he feared he might fail God by his inability to endure it patiently. He said his final farewells to his brothers Israel and John, who had returned from Cranbury, and to Jerusha Edwards, who had become so dear to him over the past nineteen weeks. Looking at her devout and lovely face, he said, "If I thought I should not see you, and be happy with you in another world, I could not bear to part with you. But we shall spend an happy eternity together!"

On October 9, 1747, David Brainerd's deepest longing was granted. He entered God's eternal glory. Though only twenty-nine years old, his race was finished. The outcome was up to God.

David Brainerd was a most unlikely candidate for wilderness missions. He suffered poor health, unstable emotions, and spiritual uncertainties. He had no facility for learning the Indian languages and no experience in primitive living, and he was too independent to serve under a veteran missionary who could train him and protect him from his ignorance. Yet his intense determination to evangelize the American Indians kept him from accepting calls to pastor white congregations for which he seemed ideally fitted by his background and education.

After he had worked four years among the Indians, his health was wrecked and his missionary career ended. But David Brainerd's life became the grain of wheat that fell into the ground and produced an amazing harvest of missionaries around the world. In the capable hands of Jonathan Edwards, the Brainerd diaries and papers became the first full-length missionary biography. It quickly gained international recognition. Readers were moved to prayer and service of a caliber that changed the world for God.

The Life of David Brainerd found its way into the hands of William Carey of England, who served forty years in India and is called the father of modern missions. Henry Martyn read it and responded as a missionary and Bible translator to India in 1805. Samuel Mills and other American students read it, committed their lives to missions, and helped birth the first foreign missions boards in America. Adoniram Judson Gordon, whose place of service was sophisticated and predominantly Unitarian Boston, kept *The Life of Brainerd* on his desk for ready reference. Gordon's comment on the book reveals why it has impacted so many so deeply. "When we shut the book we are not praising Brainerd, but condemning ourselves, and resolving that, by the grace of God, we will follow Christ more closely in the future." That is the legacy of David Brainerd.

What We Can Learn from the Life of David Brainerd

The majestic creativity of God finds its greatest demonstration in human personality. In spite of all we have in common, no two people who have ever lived are exactly alike. Some personalities are bold and abrasive like C. T. Studd. Some are moderate and controlled like Susanna Wesley. Others are tender and easily grieved like David Brainerd.

Each personality could be thought of as a unique stroke of the Master on the canvas of life. The richness of life results from the careful blending of a myriad of colors. In thinking of David Brainerd's place in God's painting, the color blue immediately comes to mind. The shadings of his life ranged from the blue-black of night's deep depression to the true-blue of devotion to the unclouded blue of heaven's canopy.

God's sensitive servants like Brainerd have great capacity for compassion and self-sacrifice. They also have unique temptations, hurts, and difficulties. David Brainerd's life illuminates the struggle many tenderhearted Christians experience. For the sober, introspective melancholic, it's never easy to enjoy meaningful service, emotional stability, and God's peace. But this personality type belongs to some of the Lord's choicest servants.

Turning the pages of David Brainerd's life story takes the reader on a journey through several kinds of pain. Rather than feeling depressed by that, however, we rejoice as we see the gold edges of God's grace on each of those pages. But we cannot fully appreciate that grace without seeing the tear stains from Brainerd's trials.

♦ *Childhood suffering sets the stage for a life of struggle.* Brainerd's father died when he was only eight years old. His mother died when he was fourteen. Though he inherited a sizable estate, he lost the parental love and affection that is so essential to a child's happiness and security.

In his book *Creative Suffering*, noted Christian physician and counselor Paul Tournier makes some interesting observations on deprivation. He relates the startling fact that a large portion of the greatest world leaders share the experience of having been orphans. This is confirmed in numerous studies of high performers. As many as three-fourths of those who become celebrated achievers are estimated to have suffered serious emotional deprivation or hardship in childhood.

Commenting on this phenomenon, Tournier says, "The person matures, develops, becomes more creative, not because of the deprivation in itself, but through his own active response to misfortune, through the struggle to come to terms with it and morally to overcome it."

Scripture seems to confirm this. Consider the life of Moses. Deprived of his parents and ethnic identity, he became a young man consumed with the desire to exercise power on behalf of his downtrodden people. Only a very sensitive, compassionate young man could grow up as an Egyptian prince, yet choose to suffer with the enslaved Jews as Moses did (Heb. 11:24-25). His desire for justice had a strong element of anger in it, as we see in his murder of an Egyptian oppressor. His actions resulted in exile to a lonely desert where he at last clearly heard the voice of God.

David Brainerd's youth closely parallels that of Moses. The loss of both parents plunged him into a period of deep grief and introspection. He searched for meaning in Christianity but often felt abandoned. Like Moses, he was easily moved by others' needs, responded passionately to life, and despaired of his own ability.

Thanks to improved medical technology and health care, fewer children today experience the grief of becoming orphans. But many are "orphaned" by divorce, their parents' addictions, and workaholism. The current phenomenon of latch-key kids is producing an appalling number of lonely, emotionally deprived children. The pathways of overperformance ("Maybe I can win their affection.") and rebellion ("I'll get even with them for abandoning me.") are particularly enticing to them.

◆ *Rejection produces anger and estrangement.* Like many orphaned and neglected children, Brainerd felt an unusual burden of guilt, almost as if he had been responsible for his parents' deaths. After years of spiritual struggle, at age twenty-one Brainerd was able to believe himself forgiven and accepted by God. His immediate response was full commitment to Christian service and enrollment at Yale University (then a leading school for ministerial preparation). While a student there, he became increasingly angry at the gap between his perfectionistic expectations and daily realities. Disappointment with God, with people, and with himself filled his being.

Highly critical of the apathy of professing Christians, Brainerd became attracted to the Whitefield revival. While his experience in this move of God increased his spiritual passion, it also encouraged his verbal violence against those he saw as spiritually dead. He soon found himself following Moses' footprints into exile. The brilliant young man who should have graduated at the head of his class was permanently expelled from the university.

In the physical realm, pain results when food and water are denied. In the spiritual and mental realm, rejection produces a similar pain. Everyone needs acceptance and approval. For people with a temperament like Brainerd's, the absence of affirmation is particularly damaging. Rejection creates uncertainties about ability and worth. Festering wounds of inferiority can easily cut off fellowship and creative abilities.

In this pain we can learn to look to Christ for the approval we need. Rather than being people pleasers or revolutionaries, we learn to focus on pleasing the Master. We may *feel* unworthy, but we *know* that God fully accepts us on the merits of Jesus. Our Lord understands our feelings of rejection. He came to his own chosen people and they refused to receive him. He "suffered outside the city gate to make the people holy," and those who identify with him often will be outcasts too (Heb. 13:12-14).

◆ *Focusing on failure burdens us with guilt and self-doubt.* Realizing the magnitude of his error in judgment at Yale, Brainerd turned his frustration and anger completely inward. Still earnestly desiring to be used by God, he applied for the most sacrificial form of ministry he could find—wilderness living as missionary to the American Indians. He felt himself unworthy for ministry and accepted the mission board's appointment with serious misgivings.

By the end of his second year of missionary work, the depressed young man was ready to resign his position. Brainerd's failure to convert the Indians convinced him that his small stipend from the mission board amounted to theft. Only his devotion to Christ and his strong drive to make his life count for the kingdom of God kept him from quitting. His despair, mingled with unwillingness to accept defeat, filled the pages of his journal. "My soul longed for more spirituality; and it was my burden that I could do no more for God," he wrote. "Oh, my barrenness in my daily affliction and heavy load! Oh, how precious is time, and how it pains me to see it slide away, while I do so little to any good purpose."

Many Christians experience these same painful uncertainties about their usefulness to Christ. Failure produces guilt and self-doubt, which in turn lead to more failure. We can break that negative cycle by recognizing our true source of competence. In defending his ministry, the apostle Paul confidently wrote, "Not that we are competent in ourselves to claim anything for ourselves, but our competence comes from God. He has made us competent as ministers of a new covenant—not of the letter but of the Spirit; for the letter kills, but the Spirit gives life" (2 Cor. 3:5-6).

The letter of guilt that grinds us to powder was nailed to Jesus' cross. He doesn't want us to rip it down and try to use it as a guide for Christian service. We have been called to love and to obey, not to constantly evaluate our worth to the kingdom of God. If Paul, an apostle and central figure in New Testament church building, could say that he was inadequate to accurately judge himself, how much more should we resist that temptation? "Therefore, judge nothing before the appointed time; wait till the Lord comes. He will bring to light what is hidden in darkness and will expose the motives of men's hearts. At that time each will receive his praise from God" (1 Cor. 4:5).

◆ *Perfectionism robs us of God's rest.* Throughout his twenties, Brainerd subjected himself to such harsh demands that his inner peace and physical health suffered immeasurably. The Holy Spirit repeatedly made real to him Christ's sufficiency, but Brainerd's personality pulled him back to self-effort. By late 1746 his greatest fear had come upon him; he had become an invalid—too ill to preach, teach, or pray.

The young man who had exhausted himself trying to serve God perfectly then had to learn his hardest lesson. He had to learn to lie down and receive the loving service of others. He had to let go of his need for performance. Day by day, his desire moved from *serving* God through action to *glorifying* God through attitude.

As he became weaker physically, Brainerd's confidence in the Lord's faithfulness to accomplish his will in human affairs increased. During the last two weeks of his life, Brainerd repeatedly voiced his confidence that his work was finished. "I am almost in eternity; I long to be there," he said to those by his bedside. "I long to be in heaven, praising and glorifying God with the holy angels. *All my desire is to glorify God.*"

Consumed with pleasing his heavenly Father, David Brainerd had spent most of his twenty-nine years focused on the need to suffer in the flesh that he might cease from sin (1 Pet. 4:1). God honored his zeal and commitment by making his presence known to Brainerd in many moments of majestic fellowship. But only as death drew near did he learn the reality of God's rest. All deficits and disappointments fell away, leaving only the sweet song of loving adoration.

The impact of Brainerd's life story on generations of readers reveals the universal need to be accepted by God. It was not his missionary toil that made the greatest impact. The intimate revelation of his daily walk with the Lord communicates and convicts as his labors never could. As P. T. Forsyth said, "Christ can do without your works; what he wants is you." If we learn to live in and for the glory of God, even in death our life will speak for him.

Steps to Spiritual Greatness
- Accept your strengths and weaknesses, life's hardships, and God's encouragement.
- Adapt your expectations to fit life's realities.
- Advance, even in the face of discouragement. Keep moving.
- Affirm the goodness of God, your daily blessings, and each victory over despair.
- Adore Christ, in whom you enjoy full acceptance. Center your life in his worthiness.

There remains, then, a Sabbath-rest for the people of God; for anyone who enters God's rest also rests from his own work, just as God did from his. Let us, therefore, make every effort to enter that rest, so that no one will fall. (Heb. 4:9-11)

CHAPTER 17
The Fellowship of Suffering

Lydia and Peter Vins carefully snipped pages of the New Testament into small pieces. Lydia glanced up from her work at their nine-year-old son, Georgi. He must surely know what it meant, this cutting up of the Bible late at night. Police coming, coming to take away Christians, to take away his preacher father again.

When they had the precious bits of God's Word ready, Lydia began stuffing them here and there inside Peter's clothes. With needle and thread she bound them into his coat collar, inside his heavy quilted pants, anywhere they could be hidden. With more arrests in Omsk every day, they knew it would not be long until Peter's turn came. So they would be ready. If he must go, he would go with the bread of life to feed his soul.

"Come, Georgi, sit here on my lap," Peter said. His arms snug about his son, he said, "Remember, Georgi, it is better to suffer with God's people than to enjoy earthly treasure." Then he began to hum his favorite hymn, "I Love Thy House, O Lord." Soon the three were singing the words together, smiling through their tears.

While they waited for the inevitable, there was so much work to do that there was little time for family activities. Peter labored long hours at his job and then spent evenings visiting the believers in Omsk. It was no small job to be their shepherd since their numbers had swelled to a thousand in the year since the Vinses had arrived. With no church services allowed, the Vinses had to teach and encourage them house by house. There could be no resting. The night was coming. . . .

And then one evening, with the unrelenting severity they had learned to expect, police arrived at the Vinses' home to take Peter away. No time for anything but a hug and a quick prayer.

It has been true what Peter promised when he proposed, Lydia thought. The words echoed in her memory: "If you are willing to die in the mud, the swamps, and the forests of Siberia, then marry me." Ten years of marriage stood as witness to his words.

Already Peter had served almost four years in prison and labor camps. But there had been much joy in their home too, joy she would not exchange for any comfort.

Lydia began the familiar task of packing parcels to take to the jail. "Come, Georgi, your father will need these things," she called. Georgi hurried to help.

Each carrying a small package, mother and son walked to the Omsk prison. At the prison gate they were stopped by a guard who questioned them and took the parcels.

"No visitors allowed," he said when Lydia asked to see her husband. She knew better than to argue. Leading Georgi away from the gate, she walked on down the street beside the prison. As they walked they noticed a prisoner on the fourth floor waving his arms. They struggled to see his face.

"Perhaps it is your father, Georgi," Lydia said. They both waved back at the man in the tall prison. He waved again in response.

"It must be Father," Georgi said, scanning the prison. "No one else waves to us from the other windows."

Lydia pointed to a bench at the gate of a nearby house. "Let's sit here with your father. It will give him courage." Several hours passed. Then Lydia said, "Georgi, we must go home now."

"We will come tomorrow, won't we, Mother?" Georgi asked, his eyes bright with tears.

"Of course, we will."

Every free day they walked down the street beside the prison, waving and watching for Peter's face. Then one day they noticed workmen building covers for the windows on the first floor. Soon the men finished and went on to the second and then the third floor. In a few days they were on the fourth floor, at the window next to Peter's cell.

Lydia and Georgi looked up at Peter, their hearts aching with love and sorrow. Tomorrow they wouldn't be able to see him. No more walks down the street to assure him of their love and prayers with their eager waves. Lydia traced the dim outline of his face with her eyes, burning it into her memory, wondering how long.

After that day in 1937, Lydia and Georgi never saw Peter's face again. She made endless attempts to learn what had happened to him. Finally she was told that he had been transferred to a Siberian camp for the socially dangerous to serve his ten-year sentence. Letters and visits were forbidden, so she filled her days with prayer and worked hard to care for Georgi and minister to other believers. Just surviving was difficult, since anyone aiding a Christian was considered an enemy of the government.

In 1941, the same year Germany attacked the Soviet Union, Georgi Vins dedicated his life to Christ. World War II and reconstruction brought a softening in the government's treatment of Christians. Georgi grew up and followed in his father's footsteps as a Baptist minister. The time for Peter Vins's release came, but he didn't return to his family. They were given no explanation. Then in 1959 the government launched a new program for the removal of all religion from the Soviet Union. They expected to achieve their goal by 1980.

Along with all other full-time Christian workers, Georgi Vins was labeled a "parasite" by the communist government. The All-Union Council of Churches became a puppet of the government, and the past decade's gains in religious freedom were swept away. Older Christians who had served prison sentences and young people like Georgi whose parents had suffered for the gospel found it hard to accept the government's new restrictions. They began to unite and take action against the antireligious government policy.

Georgi Vins helped establish the All-Union Council of Evangelical Christians and Baptists. Hundreds of churches across the Soviet Union joined, withdrawing from the old union. Their actions set off a frenzy of arrests, tortures, and executions.

Seeing the enormous suffering of their fellow believers, in 1964 Georgi Vins and other Christian leaders organized an All-Union Conference of Baptist Prisoners' Relatives. The group crusaded for human rights, networked with local churches to provide information on arrests and imprisonments, and gave aid to families of those arrested. Lydia Vins became the group's leader at the age of fifty-seven. Having only recently learned of her husband Peter's death in a Siberian camp in 1943, her heart blazed with compassion and holy anger.

For the next fifteen years Lydia, Georgi, Georgi's wife, and their four children repeatedly faced prison, financial hardship, and death. Georgi served three prison sentences, totaling eight years. Separated from him as she had been from her husband, Lydia poured out her love to her daughter-in-law and grandchildren. She also wrote words of comfort to her son:

> The day after tomorrow is the anniversary of your imprisonment, both sad and happy. Be strong, my child, for on that day you acted nobly as the son of your father. . . . Your father and I used to sing this song:

"He knows how we tire along the way,
How rarely we rested,
Carrying the cross.
He will take our burden when he comes,
The time of bliss is near,
The Lord is coming!"

Now I sing it with you. In heaven, we three will sing it together.

In 1970, at age sixty-three, Lydia was arrested and sentenced to three years in a labor camp for her ministry to prisoners and their families.

The commitment to suffer for the gospel was passed on to a third generation of Vinses. Georgi's son Peter, named for his martyred grandfather, followed the familiar path to prison. He was beaten so badly that he was declared unfit for labor and released, only to be arrested and imprisoned again in a short time.

Then in 1979, U.S. President Jimmy Carter's administration, working with the Soviet Union, obtained Georgi's release. The Vins family was then exiled to America. Transplanted to a free country, they began using their new freedom to work for the suffering church.

Until her death at age seventy-eight, Lydia Vins devoted herself to traveling and speaking in the United States and Europe. She urged Christians to wake up to the agony of persecuted believers around the world. Georgi Vins and his family continue the work for aid to the suffering church through Russian Gospel Ministries International in Elkhart, Indiana.

What We Can Learn from
the Lives of the Vins Family

In the late 1920s the persecution of the Russian Church became intense. Peter Vins was one of an estimated twenty-two thousand Christians who gave their lives for the gospel.

Peter and Lydia Vins could have escaped the persecution by going to the United States, but they chose to stay in Russia. They felt it would be hypocritical to challenge Soviet believers to stand for the faith and then run themselves. Their courageous sacrifice strengthened thousands for the purge that followed.

Today Christians in the Soviet Union enjoy increased liberty to practice their faith. They welcome it joyfully but with a certain cautious reserve. Who knows when the pendulum will swing back toward repression? they reason. It would be dangerous and foolish to grow soft now.

Believers in other parts of the world have experienced similar suffering for their Christian convictions. They have done nothing to provoke persecution other than worshiping, studying Scripture, and spreading the message of salvation—freedoms we take for granted. When will it be our turn? What can we learn from our persecuted brothers and sisters?

◆ *Christ's cross and crown cannot be separated.* As Christians we wholeheartedly embrace the truth that Jesus came to conquer sin and Satan. Since suffering and sorrow are the fruit of sin and Satan, many further reason that Christians have been set free from pain. Doesn't God want us to be victorious, to overcome all evil?

The answer that reverberates from the open tomb is *yes!* We are more than conquerors over all the works of the devil through the power that raised Jesus from the dead. But we only experience that power as we are willing to also experience the journey to Gethsemane and Calvary. In the midst of the present warfare between the kingdoms of darkness and light, we cannot expect to be soldiers without taking the risks of combat.

If this doesn't sound too glorious, remember the apostle Paul's words to persecuted Christians in Rome: "We also rejoice in our sufferings, because we know that suffering produces perseverance; perseverance, character; and character, hope" (Rom. 5:3-4). He went on to say that he considered "that our present sufferings are not worth comparing with the glory that will be revealed in us" (Rom. 8:18).

Jesus left his disciples with the warning, "In this world you will have trouble" (John 16:33). Later the apostle Peter wrote to the church, "Dear friends, do not be surprised at the painful trial you are suffering, as though something strange were happening to you" (1 Pet. 4:12). The surprising thing is how little some of us have ever suffered for our faith in Christ!

Make no mistake, our suffering is not a condition of our salvation. The Scripture makes it clear that our pain as Christians is not a means of atonement or a necessary proof of love for God. We are never to self-inflict it or invite it through reckless behavior. But we can't consistently retreat from the cross and expect to wear the crown.

◆ *God cautions us to count the cost of our commitment.* Some of us have prayed, "Lord, I'll go where you want me to go and I'll do what you want me to do," in a burst of emotion. Then the feelings subside, and we start hoping that God wants us to go to Hawaii and meditate on the beach. Commitment must be more than emotion or it is meaningless.

Peter Vins's dedication to the Lord didn't dodge the prospect of suffering and death. He carefully chose a godly wife with the same level of commitment. Both ministry and family would have suffered immensely without this mutual consecration. The marriage of Lydia and Peter was a threefold cord, a union with God strong enough to withstand the tug of doubt and fear.

Serving the Lord is serious business, and only serious commitments will withstand the ravages of life in a spiritual combat zone. We need a firm resolve that, though we may stagger under the weight of the cross, we will not throw it down and run.

♦ *Bearing up under persecution provides others with Christlike role models.* This is particularly evident in the tremendous influence godly parents have on their children. Peter Vins was the eighth generation of preachers in the Vins family. Peter and Lydia Vins's consistent devotion to Jesus inspired their son, Georgi, to serve the Lord in a similar way. Georgi and Nadia Vins's children followed in the same footsteps, partners in suffering and ministry.

While it is certainly true that God has no grandchildren, it is also true that we can leave a legacy of Christian faith, hope, and love for others. The apostle Paul commanded believers to follow him as he followed Christ (1 Cor. 4:15-16). His most faithful pastoral assistant was Timothy, a young man who had developed a genuine experience with God through his mother and grandmother. Young people respect and respond to those who pay the price of their commitments.

Lydia's granddaughter Natasha, now a vital part of Russian Ministries International, says of her grandmother, "She always had time for us. She taught us with her life. Her highest priority was the Lord. And she always cared for people; she put their needs much above her own." Now Natasha follows that example as she works with her father in Christian ministry.

♦ *Persecution sifts and strengthens the church.* One of the most commonly used excuses for rejecting Christianity is the large number of "phonies" or hypocrites in its ranks. Tough times have a way of reducing that number dramatically.

When persecution strikes the church, the lukewarm and halfhearted find the nearest exit. Those who remain grow deeper day by day in their love for God and one another; they must to survive. In the early days of the Christian church, oppressed believers opened their hearts, their homes, and their bank accounts to one another. One of the mysteries of Christian suffering is its ability to produce an active compassion that seeks out and strengthens other sufferers.

In Lydia Vins's bereavement and hardship, she found courage and purpose through her work to aid prisoners and their families. She became "Babushka" (grandmother) to countless hurting Christians. When Lydia was sentenced to prison, rather than stopping her work, the government found they had only multiplied her ministry. Ten women immediately dedicated themselves to take her place.

No government will ever legislate love for God out of the human heart. "Before him all the nations are as nothing" (Isa. 40:17). The Soviet Union's twenty-year program to eradicate religion failed to take into account the work of the Holy Spirit in sustaining and empowering believers. China and other lands have experienced the same purging and strengthening. These Christians know what it is to have hell come against them and lose. No wonder they are bold for Christ.

Perhaps it is the freedom and ease of our materialistic Western society that provides the greater threat to church purity and power. Mikhail Khorev, a blind Soviet minister who has endured tremendous suffering at the hands of the government, spoke this stern warning to believers: "Our enemy is at work today, trying to lead the church into a quiet rut, a life with no struggles and no victories. Beware of this."

♦ *The body of Christ must share the mark of his wounds.* Jesus suffered once and for all in his earthly body on the cross. But in his spiritual body, the church, his suffering continues.

If we ignore the wounded body of Christ in our world, we are really ignoring him. When Jesus confronted Saul on the Damascus Road, he said, "Saul, why do you persecute me?" Since Jesus had already ascended to heaven in his resurrected body, what did he mean? He was clearly linking himself to the Christians Saul sought to imprison and kill.

One of Lydia Vins's favorite parables was that of the Good

Samaritan who rescued the wounded traveler. She liked to compare the man left beside the road for dead to persecuted Christians. She said, "God's Word teaches that all believers in Jesus Christ are members of one body. In the Soviet Union many of God's children are suffering. Beatings, arrests, prison, concentration camp, confiscation of Bibles, psychiatric hospitals, and orphanages are familiar to active believers in my homeland. . . . Do you see the need? Don't walk on by."

Someday each of us will stand in Jesus' presence and hear him ask us how much we cared for the prisoners, the orphans, the sick, the needy. We have a command to "remember those in prison as if you were their fellow prisoners, and those who are mistreated as if you yourselves were suffering" (Heb. 13:3).

In his letter to the Christians at Colosse, Paul said, "Now I rejoice in what was suffered for you, and I fill up in my flesh what is still lacking in regard to Christ's afflictions, for the sake of his body, which is the church" (Col. 1:24). This kind of suffering has one specific goal—upbuilding the church.

No church ever becomes mature and healthy without leaders who are willing to suffer for its sake. As Lydia Vins observed in a letter to Georgi, "The way of honesty is difficult. I am not speaking of honesty with money, but of spiritual honesty, looking straight ahead, not warping the soul, not doing things for personal gain. Many have walked such a path, but compared to the masses, they are few."

◆ *The same persecution that strengthens may also embitter.* The Vinses experienced conditions that brought out the best and worst in people. While they held onto their faith, many around them despaired. Anger, bitterness, and hatred for their persecutors corroded the hearts of some prisoners and their families until the presence of Christ could no longer penetrate.

Lydia Vins wrote to Georgi in prison:

Your path is hard; I know you have times of bitter loneliness when it seems you will fall beneath the weight of the cross. Don't be depressed; be assured that the sun is shining behind the clouds! You are young, and if God so wills, you will survive and even forget this time of suffering. You will remember only the lessons learned. . . .

Among all the adversity, may God preserve your soul from evil and hardness and protect your life in perfect well-being.

After his exile to the United States, Georgi Vins said, "Soviet prisons are full of people who have lost everything, including any faith they may have had."

Why does one man stand up under adversity and another become an embittered atheist? The answer is not simple. Remaining tender to God and others in spite of persecution seems to revolve around the ability to look beyond the circumstances with hope. Persecuted Christians cherish thoughts of heaven and take great comfort in knowing that even if they are killed their persecutors do not win.

Like the New Testament church's fearless servant Stephen, these suffering Christians look through their pain to the face of Christ. As the stones fell on him, Stephen's words declared an enduring message for oppressed believers. First, he proclaimed Jesus as the King, Lord of all creation. Next, he affirmed his own eternal being and committed his safety to God. Then, he prayed for mercy for those who were taking his life. Scripture tells us that, having done this, Stephen "fell asleep." Not just a euphemism for death, that expression refers to the perfect peace with which he could release his mortal life.

God's suffering church around the world reminds us that our true citizenship is in heaven. We are strangers in a world that is passing away. Knowing that, let us do all we can to cultivate a faith that cannot be shaken. As Paul wrote to the Corinthian church, "The time is short. From now on those who have wives should live as if they had none; those who mourn, as if they did not; those who are happy, as if they were not; those who buy something, as if it were not theirs to keep; those who use the things of the world, as if not engrossed in them" (1 Cor. 7:29-31).

Rather than spending ourselves in trying to create a paradise on earth, let us arm ourselves for the struggle. Let us pour out our lives for the glory of Jesus Christ and the good of one another. Let us seek to follow the large footprints left before us by our brothers and sisters on the Calvary road.

Steps to Spiritual Greatness
- Anticipate deliverance and future blessings.
- Assist others in need.
- Appreciate the small daily tokens of God's love.
- Aspire, dream, dare to soar in your spirit, which knows no prison.

Let us hold unswervingly to the hope we profess, for he who promised is faithful. And let us consider how we may spur one another on toward love and good deeds. Let us not give up. . . . (Heb. 10:23-25)

CHAPTER 18
To Die Is Gain

The people of peaceful Tsingteh in China's southern Anhwei Province trembled with fear as the invading communist army overran it. The streets jammed with people fleeing to safety. The district magistrate was one of the first to run. Crumbled down, comfort-loving Tsingteh was no match for two thousand soldiers enraged by their expulsion from the neighboring province.

Betty Stam had been bathing baby Helen when the messenger arrived at the mission house with the grim news. Now she hurriedly packed diapers and a clean nightie for the baby in case they could get away. Certain the soldiers would take any money they found, she pinned two five-dollar bills inside the diapers. Her husband, John, had ordered transportation for their escape. Until it, or the army, arrived, there was nothing more to do but wait and pray.

John and Betty Stam called the terrified house servants together for prayer. "For this cause came I unto this hour. Father, glorify thy name." Long dear to them, Jesus' words as he faced death now pulsated with meaning. Had they come to Tsingteh as missionaries and young parents only to die less than a month after arriving?

Loud banging at the door told them the communist soldiers had arrived. John walked calmly to the door and invited them to be seated in the simple living room. Betty quickly brought the customary tea and cakes. The soldiers demanded money and valuables. John responded politely. It did no good.

Soon the soldiers tied John's hands behind his back and took him away to the communist headquarters. Betty prayed and waited. Before long they returned for her and the baby.

"Please take us too," the cook and maid cried, beside themselves with concern for their beloved Betty and baby Helen. The soldiers pushed them away and raised their guns to settle the matter.

Betty and the baby were taken to communist headquarters, where John was being held. After several hours of questioning and imprisonment, the commander let John go to their house for the baby's formula and some clothes. On his return, he told Betty how the house had been ransacked and everything of any value taken. He'd had his hands full in the brief minutes there trying to comfort the weeping cook and maid.

"I told them, 'God is still on the throne. These little things do not matter: our heavenly Father knows.' Then I sent them to stay with old Mrs. Li." *Our Heavenly Father knows.* Betty and John comforted themselves with the thought as they waited.

Their captors made their demands clear—$20,000 dollars ransom for their release. John sat at a small table and wrote to the brothers at the China Inland Mission (CIM) headquarters in Shanghai:

> All our possessions . . . are in their hands, but we praise
> God for peace in our hearts and a meal tonight. God
> grant you wisdom in what you do, and us fortitude, cour-
> age, and peace of heart. . . . As for us, may God be glori-
> fied whether by life or by death.

By the next day, the communist army in the district had risen to six thousand. Having plundered Tsingteh, they prepared to march on to Miaosheo, twelve miles across the mountains.

Soon the order came to leave the makeshift headquarters. Tsingteh had become the graveyard of many, and many more were now captives like the Stams. They would have plenty of company on the trek. As they waited to depart, the soldiers began discussing what to do with baby Helen.

"Let's kill her now. She'll be nothing but trouble on the road," one said.

"Yes, better we shoot her than listen to crying all day." While the soldiers laughed and taunted John and Betty, a Chinese man stepped forward to plead for the baby's life.

"She's done nothing worthy of death," he said.

"Then it's your life for hers!" the soldiers shouted.

The old farmer stood his ground. "I am willing," he said. His words earned him almost instant death.

John held the baby tightly to him as they started the trip to Miaosheo. Betty was given a horse to ride part of the way. The small act of kindness didn't reassure the couple regarding their captors' intentions. As they traveled, they silently prayed for their coworker, Evangelist Lo, and his family, who lived in Miaosheo. *God give them time to escape!*

On arriving in nearly deserted Miaosheo, soldiers took Betty and John to the postmaster's shop. The postmaster knew them from their mission work in Miaosheo. As they passed he asked, "Where are you going?"

"We do not know where they are going," John answered, and gestured toward the soldiers, "but we are going to heaven."

In the postmaster's office, John wrote another note to the CIM office in Shanghai while Betty nursed the baby. More waiting. More prayer. "Glorify thy name, Father."

When the troops finished looting Miaosheo, attention shifted back to the Stams. Orders came to move John, Betty, and baby Helen to a small room in an abandoned mansion. A soldier bound John's wrists tightly, but Betty was left free to care for the baby. Several guards stood just outside the room.

Through the long, cold winter night they waited to learn what would be done with them. Then the beauty of dawn broke over the mountains. With it came soldiers who stripped them down to their underwear. Betty's hands were tied. Baby Helen lay on the bed in her cozy bunting. Betty took a final loving look at her precious child.

The soldiers marched John and Betty out of the house and down the street of the city. There was no sign of Evangelist Lo. The communists shouted insults at them and called the residents to come and see how these stupid white people with the strange God would die. Many of the people still in Miaosheo knew and liked them. Too terrified to make a sound, they watched as the couple was led out of the town to Eagle Hill.

Then a Christian doctor rushed forward and fell on his knees before the soldiers. "Please, spare their lives," he begged. The soldiers pushed him away, but he kept crying out. Angered at his boldness, the soldiers arrested and removed him.

John turned to the commanding officer to plead for the doctor's life. Before he could speak, the commander ordered him to kneel. With a quick flash of the executioner's sword, John Stam entered paradise.

Betty quivered and fell on her knees beside him. The sword flashed again, severing her head from her body and uniting her spirit with John in the presence of Christ.

John and Betty Stam had one consuming desire—to give their lives to God for his glory. They believed his plan for them was mission work in China. They spent years preparing to answer that call, checking and rechecking their guidance over and over. They willingly relinquished their desire to marry until they were positive it would not hinder their work for God. They submitted to the wisdom and direction of more experienced missionaries. They consulted with Chinese government officials before moving to Tsingteh. And then they died before their thirtieth birthdays, leaving behind a three-month-old daughter.

The Christian community in China and the United States reverberated with the shock waves at the senseless crime. The Stams' deaths prompted a sharp increase in student prayer meetings at Moody Bible Institute and Wilson College. Many offered themselves to take the Stams' place in mission service. The China Inland Mission received more donations in 1935 than it had since the stock market crash of 1929. The first biography of the Stams quickly went through nine printings, igniting thousands of readers' hearts with a fresh vision of Calvary love and missionary zeal.

After the Stams' beloved Chinese associate Evangelist Lo found the couple's bodies and buried them, he preached a short message to the crowd that had gathered to watch. He said:

> You have seen these wounded bodies, and you pity our friends for their suffering and death. But you should know that they are children of God. Their spirits are unharmed and at this moment in the presence of their Heavenly Father. They came to China . . . not for themselves but for you, to tell you about the great love of God, that you might believe in the Lord Jesus and be eternally saved. You have heard their message. Remember, it is true. Their death proves it so. Do not forget what they told you—repent and believe the gospel.

Many of his listeners cried as he spoke, a response rarely if ever seen by Christian missionaries. Through vivid examples of Christian commitment like those of the Stams and others, many Chinese were converted, and believers were steeled to endure as an underground church.

One missionary to China commented, "A life which had the

longest span of years might not have been able to do one-hundredth of the work for Christ which they have done in a day."

What We Can Learn from the Lives of the Stams

The Bible relates dozens of stories that leave us asking, "Why did you do it that way, Lord?" Why should God choose Abraham and Sarah to parent a holy nation after they were withered with age? Why did he appoint Moses, a stuttering fugitive, as leader of a bold slave uprising? Why would he send the Messiah to the cross rather than to the throne of Israel?

God doesn't respond with apology or extended explanation. He simply says, "As the heavens are higher than the earth, so are my ways higher than your ways and my thoughts than your thoughts" (Isa. 55:9). He also leaves us with his promise to bring beauty out of ashes and joy out of mourning (Isa. 61:3). The Lord guarantees that his plan for us is good and that nothing will ultimately thwart it.

Still, only the heart convinced of his love and committed to his will endures in spite of unanswered questions. John and Betty Stam had such hearts. Something deep in their spirits called them to love people they did not know, to love even in death. Out of their complete devotion and sacrifice come profound lessons about trusting the plan of God in pain.

◆ *God treasures our tears.* He knows their cost. The Psalmist David was so confident of this that he asked the Lord to catch his tears in a bottle (Ps. 56:8, KJV). Only a Father God who watched his Son die on the cross could feel what John and Betty Stam felt when they left their baby alone in a hostile environment. Because they knew him as a kind and faithful father, they could trust baby Helen to his care.

This God of ours is the one who numbers the hairs on our

heads, who has carved us into the palm of his hand, who keeps our faces ever before him. He walked with Betty and John to their execution. He cradled their baby in his love during her thirty-hour abandonment. He guided Evangelist Lo to rescue her and bury her parents. He protected Lo, his wife, and his young son as they made a dangerous 100-mile journey on foot to deliver the Stam baby to missionary authorities.

Betty's sorrowing parents received the best comfort imaginable when baby Helen came to live with them. They wrote, "Everything about her deliverance tells of God's love and power. And we know that if He could bring a tiny, helpless infant, not three months old, through such dangers in perfect safety, He could no less surely have saved the lives of her precious parents, had that been in His divine plan for them."

◆ *God never wastes our sorrows.* The Stams were young, vibrant, full of potential. Their martyrdom could be seen as a total waste of talent and ability, especially in our culture where the twin goals of personal success and pleasure reign.

Did the Stams suffer for nothing? Their families didn't think so. Betty's father, Dr. Charles Scott, said, "They have not died in vain. The blood of the martyrs is still the seed of the church. If we could hear our beloved children speak, we know from their convictions that they would praise God because he counted them worthy to suffer for the sake of Christ."

John's father, Peter Stam, wrote, "The sacrifice may seem great now, but no sacrifice is too great to make for Him who gave Himself for us. We are earnestly praying that it will all be for God's glory and the salvation of souls."

During college years, Betty's writing often revealed the values system that later enabled her to face death bravely. "When we consecrate ourselves to God," she wrote, "we think we are making a great sacrifice, and doing lots for Him, when really we are only letting go some little, bitsie trinkets we have been grabbing, and when our hands are empty, He fills them full of His treasures."

John shared her convictions. In a letter to his parents, he commented on the growing tensions in China: "One never knows what one may run into. But we do know that the Lord Jehovah reigns. . . . If we should go on before, it is only the quicker to enjoy the bliss of the Savior's presence, the sooner to be released from the fight against sin and Satan."

For them, as for the apostle Paul, to die was gain. They knew the One in whom they had believed, and were convinced that he would guard all they had entrusted to him (2 Tim. 1:12).

◆ *The kingdom of God grows through Christians' dying.* It seems a paradox that the death of Christians could be the key to church growth. Yet as surely as the cross of Christ was essential to our salvation, the sacrifice of believers is crucial to world evangelism. That is as true today as ever.

In fact, the rate of Christian martyrdom has risen dramatically in recent years. The World Evangelization Research Center estimates that there were approximately 35,600 Christian martyrs in 1900 compared to an estimated 325,000 in 1989. Martyrdom is a fact of life in at least fifty countries. The Center concludes from its research that out of the two thousand or so plans for global evangelization by A.D. 2000, "martyrdom is probably the most potent and significant factor of all."

Our response should not be to seek martyrdom, but we should not avoid it either. The display of love at great cost so completely shown on Calvary's cross must also be displayed in the lives of Christians. We love *because* Christ first loved us; we love *as* he loved by laying down our lives.

In his speech to the Moody Bible Institute graduates of 1932, John Stam said:

Let us remind ourselves that the Great Commission was never qualified by clauses calling for advance only if funds were plentiful and no hardship or self-denial involved. On the contrary, we are told to expect tribulation and even persecution, but with it victory in Christ. . . . It is ours to show, in the salvation of our Lord Jesus Christ, and in personal communion with Him, a joy unspeakable and full of glory that cannot be affected by outside circumstances. . . .

Sometimes we draw back from this level of commitment because of its impact on others. The pebble tossed into the waters of sacrifice by John and Betty Stam made far-reaching ripples of grief and pain. For their daughter, parents, brothers, and sisters, the cost was great. But rather than feeling betrayed or deserted by these two who left all to follow their Master, the family responded with tearful rejoicing and renewed personal commitment. John's father said, "We were honored by having sons and daughters minister for our Lord among the heathen, but we are more signally honored that two of them have received the martyr's crown."

That special crown of martyrdom doesn't belong to every Christian. Many of us are called to work for God in places where our lives aren't threatened. But no matter where he plants us, we must die many little "deaths" to be fully available to him.

◆ *God prepares us to endure pain.* Facing the executioner's sword isn't exactly Discipleship 101; there are many lessons on the way to that point. John and Betty Stam practiced obedience to the Lord's will in various aspects of their lives, taking ever larger steps of faith. The Lord promises never to allow more to come our way than we can bear. That means he's committed to developing our stamina before testing it.

In an Easter meditation on John 12:24-28, John Stam wrote about God's loving supervision of our lives:

Whatever we face we may say, "For this cause came I unto this hour." All our social, church and family background, all of our training, conscious and unconscious, has been to prepare us to meet the present circumstances, and to meet them to the glory of His Name.

Lesson by lesson, the Lord leads us to deeper trust and obedience. We can also rejoice in the process as evidence of God's faith in us. "What a blessed thing it is that God thinks it worth while to test us!" John Stam wrote. "Workmen only spend time and trouble on materials they can make something out of."

◆ *Sacrifice is a source of joy and fulfillment.* When the apostles faced persecution in the early days of the church, they rejoiced because they had been counted worthy to suffer for the name of Christ. Peter later told believers, "Rejoice that you participate in the sufferings of Christ, so that you may be overjoyed when his glory is revealed" (1 Pet. 4:13).

We *need* to be expended. The boredom and depression of modern life often result from lack of purpose. Just as surely as we need food, clothing, and shelter, we need a supreme reason for living. We need something and someone to give our lives for. There is the heart of the Stams' fulfillment. Preoccupation with discovering, preserving, and enriching self may cost us more than we ever suspected. It's just possible that spending ourselves in loving service to God and others would produce more lasting pleasure than anything else in the world. Think about it: Who smiles more and sleeps better at night, Mother Teresa or Donald Trump?

In Dr. Lloyd Ahlem's *Do I Have to Be Me?* an exploration of the dimensions of human need, he describes the mystery of fulfillment through loving expendability. He notes that this is the dominant theme of every life permeated by God's love. Rather than centering in self, we are set free in a secure orbit around him. As we transfer ownership of our lives to the Lord, we are increasingly released from worry, competition, and possessiveness. How do we develop this life-style? Dr. Ahlem says, "We learn selflessness only through revelation, and it is best explained by the life of Jesus."

Sacrificial living goes against the flow of our culture. Those who walk this road will not be considered normal. But then neither was Jesus.

Bible scholar A. W. Tozer summed it up well: "While Christ was the perfect example of the healthy, normal man, He did not live a normal life. He sacrificed many pure enjoyments to give Himself to the holy work of moral rescue. His conduct was determined not by what was legitimate or innocent, but by human need. He pleased not Himself but lived for the emergency; and as He was, so are we in this world!"

As we consider Jesus and his suffering, it's important to remember that he was no masochist bent on self-destruction. He endured the cross because of the joy he knew waited on the other side of suffering. Because of the perfect trust that bound him to the Father, he remained convinced in the midst of what appeared to be crushing defeat that victory would result. He knew that his willingness to share human pain and grief would purchase happy endings to the life stories of millions. His hope held him steady, helping him resist every temptation to compromise eternal joy for temporary relief.

That same hope in God's loving justice has the power to anchor us in the storms of life. It can purify our dreams and challenge us to new achievements. It can whisper comfort to us in our darkest moments. Looking to Jesus and a future secure in his victory, we can joyfully pay the hidden price of greatness.

Steps to Spiritual Greatness
- Dedicate. Give all that you are and have to the Master.
- Dare. Trust the Lord to display his glory in you as he chooses.
- Deny. Learn to say no to yourself and yes to God.
- Delight. Experience the pleasure of life in the center of his will.

Therefore, I urge you, brothers, in view of God's mercy, to offer your bodies as living sacrifices, holy and pleasing to God—this is your spiritual act of worship. (Rom. 12:1)

APPENDIX
Biographical Timelines

Aurelius Augustine of Hippo, 354–430

354, November 13 —Augustine was born in Tagaste, Numidia, North Africa (now Algeria), 150 miles from Carthage. His father, Patricius, a burgess, was a pagan, and his mother, Monica, was a Christian.

370—(Age 16) Augustine chose a group of wicked friends and followed them in a life of crime and excess. He took a mistress, to whom he was faithful for fifteen years.

371—(Age 17) Augustine became a student at the University of Carthage. His first intention was to study law, but he soon decided on philosophical and literary pursuits instead.

372—Augustine's father died shortly after his deathbed conversion.

372—(Age 18) Augustine fathered a son, Adeodatus, by his mistress.

373—After reading Cicero's "Hortensius," Augustine became deeply interested in philosophy and attracted to the Manichaean sect (a Persian blend of Christianity and Zoroastrianism, religious dualism teaching the coexistence of good and evil). He remained part of this cult for nine years. He also developed a deep interest in astrology.

375—(Age 21) Augustine began his teaching career by conducting a school of rhetoric in Tagaste.

376—Augustine returned to Carthage to seek a more brilliant career. There he became professor of rhetoric and was recognized in literary circles for his poetry.

383—(Nearing 30) Augustine lost faith in the Manichaean religion. Though he retained his friendships within the cult, his beliefs were decidedly agnostic. Augustine and his mistress and son moved to Rome, a great city of 1.25 million residents. He taught a school of rhetoric there, suffered ill health, and became increasingly unhappy.

384—Augustine left Rome for a professorship in Milan. There he was appointed as public orator for the court. His mother, Monica, followed in hopes of winning him to Christ. While in Milan, he was greatly influenced by Bishop Ambrose. During this period he became a Neoplatonist. Augustine sent his mistress back to North Africa and took another.

386, summer—(Age 32) Augustine converted to Christianity. He spent some time in the desert in prayer and study.

387, Easter Eve—Augustine and his son, Adeodatus, were baptized by Bishop Ambrose. Soon after, on the way back to Tagaste with her son and friends, Monica died. She was fifty-six.

388—Augustine returned to Africa and established a Christian community devoted to study and prayer at Tagaste.

390—Augustine's son, Adeodatus, died.

391—Augustine became a priest at Hippo and quickly acquired great influence in the African church.

395—Augustine was consecrated coadjutor bishop to Valerius, bishop of Hippo.

396—(Age 42) Augustine succeeded Valerius as bishop of Hippo. In this capacity he fought hard and successfully against Donatism (which made good works the basis for receiving sacraments) and Pelagianism (which denied original sin, teaching man is free to do right or wrong), major heresies of that time. He also preached almost daily and wrote seventy theological books.

ca. 397–401—Augustine wrote his best-loved book, *Confessions*.

410, August 24—Rome fell to Alaric, king of the Visigoths.

411, June—Augustine confronted Donatist bishops in debate at a conference (Synod of Carthage) ordered by the emperor to settle the doctrinal controversy. The Donatists lost.

413–427—Augustine wrote his greatest theological work, *The City of God*.

430, August 28—(Age 76) Augustine died during the Vandal siege of Hippo.

Susanna Annesley Wesley, 1669–1742

1662, November—Samuel Wesley (future husband) was born in Whitchurch; he was fathered by poor Nonconformist minister John Wesley.

1669, January 20—Susanna was born in London; she was the twenty-fifth and final child of Puritan minister Dr. Samuel Annesley.

1682—(Age 13) Susanna disagreed with her father's Nonconformist doctrines and allied herself with the Church of England.

1683—Samuel ran away from home to attend Oxford University; he became an Anglican (Church of England) priest.

1688—Samuel graduated from Oxford with a B.A. degree; he was ordained as an Anglican deacon seven weeks later. A steadfast and devout academic, he earned a M.A. degree from Cambridge.

1689, February—Samuel was ordained as an Anglican church

priest; he was appointed to naval chaplaincy, from which he earned a good salary.

1689, late—(Age 27) Samuel left his naval chaplaincy to marry Susanna (age 20). He became curate of Holborn (London) parish, earning a meager salary, but supplemented his income by writing.

1690, February 10—First child, Samuel, born.

1690, June—The Wesleys moved to South Ormsby, Lincolnshire.

1691—First daughter, Susanna, born.

1692—Emilia born.

1693—Baby Susanna died.

1694—Twins, Annesley and Jedediah, born.

1695—Second namesake, Susanna (Ellison), born.

1695—Twins died.

1696—Mary (Whitelamb) born.

1697—The Wesleys moved to Epworth. Mehetabel "Hetty" born.

1698—Child born; soon died.

1699—John born; soon died.

1700—Benjamin born; soon died.

1701, May 17—Unnamed twins born; soon died.

1702—Samuel Wesley, Sr., left for a protracted stay in London. This followed a major dispute with his wife over political views.

1702—Anne (Lambert) born.

1703, June 17—John (founder of Methodism) born.

1704—Oldest son, Samuel (age 14), left home to attend Westminster Academy.

1705, May—Son born May 8; he was smothered by a careless nurse on May 30. These were especially difficult times due to extreme persecution by people in Epworth. Samuel Wesley, Sr., was put in debtors prison for several months.

1706, May 8—Martha "Patty" (Hall) born.

1707, December 18—Charles (famous hymn writer and Methodist minister) born.

1709, February 9—Epworth rectory burned down; young John was barely saved. The family was separated over the next year, living with various relatives who were able to offer aid until the house was rebuilt.

1709, March—Kezziah born.

1711—Five children had smallpox while their father was away from home for the winter attending the London Convocation. Susanna held services in her home (often attended by up to 200) in addition to family duties.

1714—John (age 11) attended a London academy.

1720—John (age 17) enrolled at Oxford University.

1724—The Wesley family moved to Wroot, a neighboring parish that Samuel added to his Epworth pastorate. Never a good businessman, Samuel was more than 350 pounds in debt.

1725, spring—Samuel Wesley, Sr., (age 63) had a light stroke and lost use of his right hand. Hetty (age 28) eloped with a lawyer her parents disapproved of. After one night together (which resulted in her becoming pregnant), the man deserted her before their marriage. An unwed mother and outcast from her parents' home, she was forced to accept the first proposal offered, a choice resulting in much suffering.

1725—Another smallpox epidemic took a heavy toll on the family's health.

1725, September 19—John was ordained as a deacon at Oxford.

1726, March 17—John (age 23) became a Fellow of Lincoln at Oxford, freeing his father of his support. John remained there until his marriage twenty-six years later.

1726—Charles (age 19) became a student at Oxford.

1727—Samuel and Susanna were in poor health. John came

home to substitute for his father as curate for a year.

1728, September 22—John was ordained as a priest in the Church of England at Oxford.

1731, July 21—Samuel Wesley, Sr., was thrown from a wagon and gravely injured. Though he resumed his duties, he never recovered.

1731—The Wesleys returned to Epworth rectory in such dire poverty that when Samuel's brother visited, he was horrified and took Patty home to live with him until her marriage several years later.

1732, February—Susanna was often ill and bedridden. (The strain of heavy responsibilities aged her far beyond her sixty-three years.)

1734, November—Daughter Mary (Whitelamb, age 38) died in childbirth after one year of a happy marriage.

1735, April 25—Samuel Wesley, Sr., (age 73) died. He left no provision for Susanna, who lived with her children the rest of her life.

1735, October 14—John and Charles Wesley accompanied Oglethorpe's second expedition to the new colony of Georgia in America.

1736, December—Charles returned from America.

1737—John returned from America.

1738, May 21—Charles experienced conversion.

1738, May 24—John experienced conversion at a meeting in Aldersgate Street.

1739—John and Charles began an itinerant evangelistic ministry, often preaching in fields because churches were closed to them.

1739, November 6—Samuel (age 49), favorite son of Susanna, died. He had spent his life as an Anglican priest.

1740—Susanna came to live with John at the Foundry (the London center of the rapidly growing Methodist movement). She became active in Methodist meetings and formation and was largely responsible for the acceptance of lay preachers in the movement—the key to its flexible structure and rapid growth.

1741, March 9—Kezziah (age 32) died.

1742, July 23—Susanna (age 73) died while living with son John at Moorfields Foundry. She was buried in Dissenters' cemetery (burial place of John Bunyan and Isaac Watts).

Francis August Schaeffer, 1912–1984

1912, January 30—Francis was born in Germantown, Pennsylvania.

1930—(Age 18) He committed his life publicly to Christ at a tent meeting held by Anthony Zeoli.

1935, June—He graduated from Hampden-Sydney College (second in his class).

1935, June 26—(Age 23) Francis married Edith Seville (age 20).

1935, September—Schaeffer began studies at Westminster Theological Seminary, Philadelphia, Pennsylvania, a split-off of Princeton Seminary; it was founded by J. Gresham Machen, Cornelius Van Til, and other Presbyterian professors and students who advocated total biblical inerrancy.

1937, January 1—J. Gresham Machen died, creating a leadership crisis among the separatist Presbyterians.

1937—Schaeffer became a student at the newly formed Faith Seminary, a split-off of Westminster Seminary; it was founded by Carl McIntire and J. Oliver Buswell. Central issues were premillenialism and abstinence from alcoholic drinks. Group formed the Bible Presbyterian Church, a new denomination.

1938—(Age 26) He graduated from Faith Seminary and

moved to Grove City, Pennsylvania, where he became the first ordained pastor of Bible Presbyterian Church.

1941—He became pastor in Chester, Pennsylvania.

1941—He was active in Carl McIntire's new organization, the American Council of Christian Churches (ACCC), which was an attempt at cooperation among churches who found the Federal Council of Churches too liberal. (Members in its churches were estimated at fifty thousand.)

1942—The National Association of Evangelicals (NAE) was formed in St. Louis, Missouri, under Dr. Harold Ockenga. (It opposed McIntires's methods of militant attack on the Federal Council of Churches and endorsed an "evangelical" rather than a "fundamentalist" position. It received the backing of notables such as Billy Graham and Carl F. H. Henry, editor of *Christianity Today*. McIntire condemned the NAE as a group of compromisers.)

1943—Schaeffer became pastor in St. Louis, Missouri.

Between 1943 and 1947—He resigned from the St. Louis board of Child Evangelism Fellowship because of its fellowship with "liberal" pastors and churches and formed Children for Christ, Inc.

1947—He was asked to be a missionary to Europe by the Independent Board for Presbyterian Foreign Missions, headed by J. Gresham Machen.

1948—The family moved to Lausanne, Switzerland, where Francis became secretary of the new International Council of Christian Churches (ICCC), of which Carl McIntire was president and founder. (His close relationship with McIntire lasted many years. He continued his own organization, Children for Christ, Inc.)

1949—The Schaeffer family moved to Champrey, Switzerland.

1951, early—(Age 39) Francis struggled with Christianity in

both a deeply personal and a corporate sense. He was terribly hurt and disillusioned with the "separatist movement," of which he had been an integral part. This period resulted in the book *True Spirituality* and led to the establishment of L'Abri.

1951, Easter—Francis spoke at Hugh E. Alexander's Conference in Geneva. (Alexander was a Scot and strongly influenced by the Welsh revival.) During the conference, which was marked by a deep emphasis on spiritual warfare but under the control of the Holy Spirit and through identifying with Christ's sufferings and resurrection, he felt the burden he'd been struggling with lift away.

1951—He countered the "transcendental theology" of Karl Barth and was an outspoken opponent of secularism, Catholicism, and "theological liberalism."

1953—Schaeffer returned to the United States for an eighteen-month fund-raising tour, lecturing on deeper spiritual life and lessons learned during his recent spiritual crisis. He was prominent in a break from the Bible Presbyterian church that eventually led to the formation of the Reformed Presbyterian Church, Evangelical synod. This resulted in a permanent break with McIntire.

1954, May—He received an honorary Doctor of Divinity degree from Highland College, Long Beach, California.

1954, September—The family returned to Champrey, Switzerland. His two-year-old son, Franky, contracted polio on the voyage and one daughter became ill with rheumatic fever.

1955, April—The family moved to Huemoz, Switzerland; a chalet home was purchased for L'Abri Fellowship. (This ministry was the central focus of his life, other than writing.)

1968—*The God Who Is There*, the first of twenty-three books, was published.

1971, June—Schaeffer received an honorary Doctor of Letters degree from Gordon College, Wenham, Massachusetts.

1975–1977—Schaeffer worked on the book and film *How Should We Then Live?*

1977—He helped found International Council on Biblical Inerrancy.

1977—He began work on the film series *Whatever Happened to the Human Race?*

1978, October—(Age 66) Francis was diagnosed with lymphoma cancer at Mayo Clinic, Rochester, Minnesota. He and his wife moved near Mayo Clinic so he could undergo treatment.

1979—He conducted national tour for latest film series.

1983—He received honorary Doctor of Law degree from Simon Greenleaf School of Law, Anaheim, California.

1984, May 15—(Age 72) Francis Schaeffer died at his home in Rochester, Minnesota.

Alexander Cruden, 1699–1770

1699, May 31—Alexander was born in Aberdeen, Scotland, the second child of William and Isabel (Pyper) Cruden. His father was a successful merchant and bailie (municipal magistrate), a Presbyterian church elder, and a staunch Calvinist.

1707—(Age 8) Alexander began Latin study at Town Grammar School (already a master of basic reading, writing, and arithmetic).

1712—He enrolled in Marischal College, an extreme Presbyterian school in Aberdeen, where he became engulfed in major religious and political controversies regarding the Houses of Hanover and Stuart.

1718—(Age 19) Having earned his M.A. degree, he began a tutoring career.

1719—He fell in love with an Aberdeen minister's daughter who refused his affection. Later he discovered she was sexually involved with and pregnant by her own brother.

1720, November—He was confined two weeks in the Tolbooth (Aberdeen's substitute asylum) due to shock over scandal involving his beloved. He quickly recovered mental control but fled Aberdeen in shame.

1721, April—He held several private tutoring jobs in England.

1726—He worked in London as proofreader of classical and academic books.

1729, June—Cruden was appointed "Reader in French" to Lord Derby and moved to Sussex.

1729, July 7—He was dismissed from Lord Derby's service when it was learned he could only read French silently. (He was unskilled in proper pronunciations.) Crushed, he desperately attempted to become fluent, but could not persuade Derby to restore his job.

1729, September—He escaped to Lancashire due to humiliation but pursued Lord Derby further. He is thought to have obtained a tutorial appointment in the Isle of Man on Lord Derby's recommendation.

1732—Cruden returned to proofreading in London. He took employment as a bookseller.

1735—He received the Royal Warrant of Bookseller to Queen Caroline of Anspach (wife of King George II and a highly cultured and intelligent lady).

1736—(Age 37) He began his *Complete Concordance of the Old and New Testaments*.

1737, November 3—*Concordance* was published; Cruden dedicated it to his patroness, Queen Caroline. He received about twenty pounds for his exhaustive accomplishment.

1737, November 20—Queen Caroline died, leaving Cruden

without a promised 100-pound grant and his title of Queen's Bookseller.

1737, late to 1738, spring—He tried unsuccessfully and quite obsessively to win the affections of the Widow Pain.

1738, March—Cruden was tricked into entering a coach that took him to a private madhouse in Bethnal Green, where he endured terrible captivity for ten weeks.

1738, May 31—Escaped from the madhouse on his thirty-ninth birthday.

1738, winter—Alexander resumed full-time work in London after a long recuperation from confinement.

1739, June—His father died in Aberdeen.

1739, July 17—He sued those who had assaulted and imprisoned him, but he lost the case.

1740—His mother died in Aberdeen; his spinster sister, Isabella, lived with him in London until her marriage in August 1753. Cruden worked as a proofreader of academic books and Latin and Greek classics.

ca. 1753—(Age 54) Cruden began calling himself "Alexander the Corrector"; he began what he considered a divine mission of trying to correct England's morals.

1753—He prepared index of new edition of Milton's works (similar to his biblical concordance); proofread a new edition of Spenser's "Fairie Queen."

1753, September—His sister (Mrs. Wild) committed him to a private asylum in Chelsea for two weeks following a street brawl that resulted from his moral police work.

1753, September 29—Cruden was released from the asylum.

1753, October—Romantically pursued Elizabeth Abney of Newington, daughter of London's former mayor. He inundated her with letters for over a year but never met her.

1754, February 20—He sued his sister for his illegal imprisonment, asking damages of ten thousand pounds; he lost the case.

1754—Continued work as national corrector, seeking official appointment to the office. Sought knighthood in recognition of his *Concordance*; tried to gain seat in House of Commons.

1755—Toured England as the Corrector (never an official title).

1761—Second edition of *Concordance* was released; Cruden received approximately six hundred pounds.

1763—He was involved in securing pardon for an unfortunate sailor; this resulted in his gradually becoming active in ministry at Newgate Prison.

1769—He visited his family home in Aberdeen for several months—his only return since leaving as a youth.

1769—Third edition of *Concordance* printed; received approximately three hundred pounds. Cruden made revisions and improvements on both the second and third editions.

1770, autumn—He returned to Islington, England.

1770, November 1—(Age 71) Cruden was found dead on his knees at bedside prayer by his maid, a woman he rescued from prostitution. He was buried in a Dissenters' cemetery in Southwark—now thought to be underneath a brewery.

Charles Haddon Spurgeon, 1834–1892

1834, June 19—Charles was born in Kelvedon, Essex, England. His father, John Spurgeon, was an independent minister and coal yard clerk.

1835—(10 months old) The family moved to Colchester.

1836—Charles lived with minister grandfather and absorbed his rich spiritual influence for the next six years.

1850, January 6—(Age 15) Charles became a Christian after

entering a Methodist chapel to warm himself during a snowstorm. (Less than fifteen people were present, excluding the minister. A layman preached on Isaiah 45:22: "Look unto me, and be ye saved.")

1850, May—He made his public profession of faith in Jesus Christ in the Artillery Street Primitive Methodist Chapel, Colchester, England.

1851—Spurgeon began his preaching career; he became pastor of Waterbeach Baptist Church, Cambridgeshire.

1854, April 19—(Age 19) He was called to pastor the New Park Street Baptist Chapel in London—one of the three largest of 113 Baptist churches in London at that time—membership of 232.

1854, summer—He spent long, weary hours visiting the sick, comforting the dying, and preaching funerals during a terrible outbreak of Asiatic cholera. At the breaking point, a passage from Psalm 91 stuck in a shoemaker's window lightened his spirit and gave him faith to withstand the epidemic.

1855—Having outgrown New Park Street Chapel, the congregation met in Exeter Hall.

1856, January 7—(Age 22) Charles married parishioner Susannah Thompson (age 24).

1856, September 10—The Spurgeons moved to Helensburg House.

1856, September 20—Twin sons, Charles and Thomas, were born.

1856, October 19—(Age 23) He preached the Sunday evening service in Surrey Music Hall in the Royal Surrey Gardens—the only building in London large enough to accommodate the crowds. That evening ten thousand attended and another ten thousand stood outside, unable to enter. A false cry of fire led to panic, seven deaths, and twenty-eight seriously injured people.

1856, November 2—Back in the pulpit speaking at New Park Street Chapel, he declared his determination to preach at the music hall.

1856, November 23—Preached the Sunday morning service at the music hall; services continued to be held there until December 1859.

1861, March 18—The Metropolitan Tabernacle opened in London with six thousand members; Spurgeon pastored. (During his son Thomas's pastorate at the same church 38 years later, on the night of April 20, 1899, it burned to the ground.)

1864—Stopped using the title *Reverend;* harshly criticized evangelical clergymen who remained in the Church of England.

1865—Helped form the London Baptist Association.

1868—His wife (age 36) became an invalid. Though housebound, she started a charitable book ministry, supplying Christian workers with free books.

1869—Spurgeon established an orphanage.

1870—He began a six-volume commentary on the Psalms, *The Treasury of David;* he completed it in 1885.

1887—He left the Baptist Union due to belief that many of its younger ministers no longer believed in or taught salvation through the atonement, the inspiration of the Bible, and justification by faith.

1891, June 7—Spurgeon preached his last sermon at London Metropolitan Tabernacle. During his thirty-eight-year ministry there, over fourteen thousand new members were added to the original congregation of six thousand. Many of his sermons were delivered from a couch due to his severe gout and Bright's disease.

1892, January 31—(Age 57) Charles Haddon Spurgeon died in Mentone, France, a favorite retreat during times of illness. Had pastored the Metropolitan Tabernacle in

London from 1861 to his death and had written the forty-nine-volume *Metropolitan Pulpit*.

1903, October 22—His wife, Susannah, died after thirty-five years as an invalid.

Helen Roseveare, 1925–present

1925—Helen was born in Hertfordshire, England, into the home of a mathematics schoolteacher and his wife.

1937–1944—Attended Howell's School, a girls' boarding school in Denbigh, North Wales; she excelled academically.

1944–1947—Became a medical student at Newnham College, Cambridge. (She packed her life full with studies and sports. Feeling empty still, she began attending Christian prayer meetings and Bible studies.)

1944, Christmas—Became a Christian while attending a house party at Mount Hermon Bible College, Ealing.

1946–1953—Helen taught a Saturday and Sunday girls' Bible class with the Girl Crusaders' Union.

1947–1950—Helen studied at West London Hospital, London.

1953—(Age 28) She arrived in Ibambi in the Congo (Zaire) as a missionary doctor with World Evangelization Crusade (WEC).

1954—Helen suffered from malaria and jaundice.

1955, October—After attending Imbambi Bible School for eighteen months and learning Swahili, Helen moved seven miles deeper into the forest to her appointment at Nebobongo. In the next three years, she turned the deserted leper colony there into an efficient hospital.

1957—Dr. John Harris and wife came to supervise the hospital work in Nebobongo, enabling Helen to spend most of each month establishing village clinics—forty-eight in all. She visited the clinics monthly, averaging six per day. After a severe bout with the flu, she developed meningitis.

1958, early—After five years in the Congo, Helen became convinced she was a failure as a missionary, possibly due to overwork, illness, and malnutrition.

1958, summer—Returned to London on early leave at WEC's request to facilitate a rotation of furlough and because of her ill health.

1959, February—Took houseman and Casualty Officer positions at Mildmay Mission Hospital in Shoreditch, East London. (Desperate to find a husband to return to the Congo with, she requested a year's extension on her leave.)

1959, late—Helen became House Surgeon at Newport Hospital, Monmouthshire, after a failed romance in London. She decided to return to the Congo and requested permission to try mission work again.

1960, May—She returned to the Congo alone in spite of warnings of approaching violence due to Congo's recent independence from Belgium. A week later, most medical missionaries decided to leave. Helen stayed for four years in continuing great danger.

1961—Helen was severely stricken with cerebral malaria.

1964, June—Unsuccessful United Nations troops left the Congo, opening the way for increased violent rebellion and political upheaval.

1964, August—Helen learned that rebel soldiers (Simbas) had taken over Stanleyville, but Helen remained. Soon Simba soldiers took over her area.

1964, October 28—She was beaten and raped by a Simba officer. Her native medical assistant was beaten almost to death. Two days later the Simbas arrested Bill McChesney, one of the few remaining American missionaries. He came with Helen to the Congo in 1960 on his first tour of duty.

1964, November 24—Simbas massacred Belgian planters, Catholic priests, and white missionaries (including McChesney)—an act of retaliation against white mercenaries hired by the Congo government to fight the Simbas. Two days later, Simba soldiers took Helen and six other mission workers prisoner and confined them to a Catholic convent at Wamba.

1964, December—Five wives and several children of murdered Belgian planters were brought to the convent. The women and many of the nuns were frequently raped.

1964, December 31—Mercenaries rescued Helen and the others imprisoned at the convent. She flew home to London.

1966, January—Civil war ended in Congo; the government invited missionaries to return.

1966, March—Helen returned to Congo to establish a nursing school and continue her medical ministry—in partnership with Dr. Carl Becker, senior veteran missionary with the African Inland Mission.

1966, October—Three nursing school dormitories and homes for twenty-one married students were ready for occupation. Instruction began in a borrowed mission hall.

1971—Helen was debilitated by tick-typhus fever.

1973 to present—Resigned her position as director due to strike of nursing students protesting her strict discipline. She returned to England and later moved to Ireland. She is active in speaking and writing ministry, primarily directed toward preparing missionaries to face the harsh realities of total commitment to service.

Blaise Pascal, 1623–1662

1623, June 19—Blaise was born in Clermont-en-Auvergne to French aristocrats Etienne and Antoinette Pascal. (1619—Sister, Gilberte, born.)

1625, October 5—Blaise's sister, Jacqueline Pascal, was born.

1626—Blaise's mother died.

1631, November—Etienne Pascal moved family to Paris due to his attraction to the city's intellectual advantages. (As the children grew, he increasingly dedicated himself to their education.)

1636—Blaise mastered the fundamentals of Euclidian geometry without instruction and became a recognized mathematical prodigy.

1640—(Age 16) He published his first essay, a result of his study of the cone and formulation of a basic theorem of projective geometry. He left Paris soon after to live with his father who was sent on a mission to Rouen by Richelieu.

1641, June—Gilberte married Florin Perier and moved to Clermont.

1643—Pascal perfected a calculating machine (the basis of today's computer) to aid his father in tax accounting.

1646, January—Blaise was converted to Jansenism by two men who attended his ailing father. Soon he converted his family to the Jansenist belief in grace and election.

1646—Pascal applied his mind to study of the vacuum.

1647, early—He entered the arena of theological debate with a Capuchin friar, Sieur de Saint-Ange, who taught that divine mysteries may be comprehended through human reason. Pascal destroyed Saint-Ange's religious career by his ruthless and effective arguments.

1647, Spring—Never healthy, he became seriously ill from overexertion. (He suffered terrible headaches, intestinal disorders, and temporary paralysis.)

1647, Summer—Blaise returned to Paris with his sister Jacqueline for diversion and relaxation as prescribed by his doctors.

1647, September—Unable to give up his research, he exchanged ideas with Rene Descartes on the problem of the vacuum.

1647, October—Pascal became involved in a volatile controversy with a Jesuit priest over principles of physics.

1647, late—He and his sister Jacqueline frequently visited the Jansenist abbey, Port Royal of Paris. There they received teaching; Jacqueline decided to become a nun, but her father prevented it until his death.

1651—Pascal completed his research on the equilibrium of fluids.

1651, September 24—His father died.

1652, January 4—Jacqueline Pascal entered the Port Royal convent against her brother's objection.

1652—Pascal devoted his energies to lectures on the vacuum and his calculating machine, which he was trying to market. He was active in Paris social life and was at war with sister Jacqueline.

1652, October—He left Paris to live with married sister, Gilberte Perier, in Clermont.

1653, June 5—Jacqueline Pascal took her vows at Port Royal after terrible conflict with Blaise over releasing her inheritance to the convent as a dowry.

1653, summer—Blaise returned to Parisian social life.

1654, January–June—Pascal was involved again in serious scientific and mathematical studies. Paris gambling led him to delve into statistical analysis and the theory of probability.

1654, September—He confessed to his sister Jacqueline that he was becoming disenchanted with his worldly life-style.

1654, October—He moved to Rue des Francs-Bourgeois in Saint-Michel, near Port Royal.

1654, November 23—Pascal experienced his "second conversion," an emotionally charged, supernatural visitation from God.

1655, January—He retreated to Port Royal des Champs to deepen his Jansenist faith and practice. Pascal continued dialoguing with the "gentlemen hermits."

1655, December—The Roman Catholic Church applied strict measures to correct apparent heresies in the Jansenist movement. The Jesuits opposed it the strongest.

1656, January–1657, April—Pascal anonymously wrote series of eighteen brilliant letters (*Lettres Provinciales*) in defense of Jansenism and attacking the Jesuits' mixture of sixteenth-century naturalism with Roman Catholicism. (France was captivated by his effective prose and use of irony and logic.)

1656, March 24—Pascal inspired to begin notes for a massive apologetic work on the Christian faith after niece, Marguerite Perier, was miraculously healed of an incurable lachrymal fistula in the Port Royal chapel.

1657–1658—He devoted himself to work on his Christian apologetic and his letters defending Jansenism.

1659—He published his findings on the cycloid after conducting a questionable contest with other mathematicians.

1659, February—His health collapsed, forcing him to cease all activities for over a year.

1660—Pascal moved to Clermont, near his sister Gilberte.

1661, spring—Port Royal community was crushed—result of the Roman Catholic church demand that all members of Port Royal sign a formulary condemning Jansenist doctrine.

1661, October 4—Jacqueline died (her health was destroyed by grief over the Jansenist persecution).

1662, January—Pascal sharply disagreed with Port Royal leaders over their perceived timidity in defending Jansenism; he completely separated from the controversy.

1662, March—His idea of omnibus transportation is first implemented.

1662, June 29—He stayed at Gilberte's home in Paris because of his critical illness.

1662, August 19—Blaise died after twenty-four hours of convulsions due to brain hemorrhage. (He revived long enough to receive Communion and last rites and to pray, "May God never forsake me.")

1663—Research on fluids was published.

1665—Research on triangular arithmetic was published.

1670—The *Pensées*—extensive notes for his planned apologetic of the Christian faith—was published.

Fanny J. Crosby, 1820–1915

1820, March 24—Frances Jane "Fanny" was the first child born to John and Mercy Crosby, Presbyterian farmers of Southeast Putnam County, New York.

1820, April—She developed a serious eye infection and was blinded by hot compresses applied by a quack doctor.

1820, November—Her father died of overexposure to cold, rainy weather; her widowed mother (age 21) took employment as a housemaid.

1825, spring—Fanny's mother saved enough money to take her to specialists in New York City who diagnosed her as irreversibly blind.

1825—The Crosbys moved to North Salem, a Quaker community, due to her mother's employment.

1828—Already interested in the life of the mind and the music of language, she wrote her first poem.

ca. 1829—She moved to Ridgefield, Connecticut, with her mother.

1831—Fanny grew increasingly depressed because of her blindness, mostly because she felt restricted from learning. In spite of her blindness, she developed her musical ability, became an excellent horsewoman, memorized many long Bible passages, and dictated numerous poems.

1835, March 3—(Age 14) Fanny left home to attend the New York Institution for the Blind in Manhattan—an answer to prayer that she receive an education.

1838, February 4—Her mother married Thomas Morris; Fanny acquired a stepfather, a stepsister, and two stepbrothers.

1839—She became the Institution's resident poet and most outstanding student. There she met William Cullen Bryant, Horace Greeley, and other notables, including the young Grover Cleveland. She was an accomplished musician (sang, and played several instruments) and stayed on as a teachers' assistant after completing her studies.

1839, May—Her mother bore Wilhelmina, but the baby died before the year's end.

1840s, early—Fanny's poetry was published in many papers and magazines.

1840, August 9—Her mother bore Julia, affectionately called "Jule."

1842—Fanny was one of twenty Institution pupils who traveled down the Hudson by canalboat to promote education for the blind.

1843, fall—(Age 23) She became an English and history teacher at the Institution.

1843, December 25—Her mother bore Carolyn, better known as "Carrie."

1844, January—Fanny appeared before joint sessions of Congress with other blind students, seeking funding of education for the blind.

1844, April—Her father and two stepsisters joined the Mormons, leaving her mother and stepbrother William, who refused to go with them to Nauvoo, Illinois.

1844—Her first book of poems was published.

1846, April—Fanny appeared before Congress; she had dinner at the White House and sang for President Polk. (She was part of a delegation to Congress seeking government support of free institutions for the blind.)

1849–1850—She suffered depression regarding her spiritual condition following a New York City cholera epidemic.

1850, November 20—She received a deep spiritual experience that brought her peace while attending a revival at the Methodist Broadway Tabernacle. Though she was extremely nonsectarian, she remained loyal to the Methodist church.

1854—Fanny began writing lyrics for popular songs; several became hits. She only received one or two dollars payment for these and most of the other lyrics she wrote.

1855—Alexander "Van" VanAlstine became a music teacher at the Institution for the Blind from which he graduated. (He was the first student from the Institution to attend college—Union College in Schenectady, New York.)

1857, fall—Van left the Institution to become a private music teacher in Maspeth, Long Island (now Queens). He and Fanny were in love and, because of poor administration at the school, eager to build a new life together elsewhere.

1858, March 2—Fanny resigned her teaching position.

1858, March 5—(Age 38) She married Van (age 27) and settled in Maspeth, a rural farming community.

1858—She compiled third volume of poetry. Fanny enjoyed her private role as homemaker.

1859—First (and only) child born, who died in infancy.

1860—She and Van moved back to Manhattan, not far from the Institution. (New York City was in the midst of a major revival often referred to as the Second Great Awakening.)

1861—She was an ardent and vitriolic Union supporter when the Civil War broke out.

1864, January—She met William B. Bradbury, the foremost hymn writer of that day. Through a vision she was convinced to become a hymn writer. She agreed to be Bradbury's lyricist and collaborated with several other hymn writers. Most of her work was published by Bigelow & Main; she used several pseudonyms to disguise it because of the huge amount.

1865—Met and developed a strong friendship with Phoebe Palmer Knapp (daughter of a lady holiness preacher and wife of the founder of Metropolitan Life Insurance Company). The two collaborated on many songs.

1867—She lived in a tenement on Manhattan's Lower West Side in one-half of a third-floor garret. She gave most of her small income to the poor.

1868, January 7—Songwriting partner, William Bradbury, died of consumption (age 51).

1868—Howard Doane, a successful hymn writer and business tycoon, became her new writing partner.

1876—She met Dwight Moody and Ira Sankey. She and Sankey collaborated on hymns for Moody's revival meetings. (Through these famous evangelists, her songs became more popular than ever.) She worked extensively with the poor and prisoners and became a sought after speaker.

1877—By her late fifties, Fanny had written almost all of her most famous hymns. Most of her later work paraphrased what she had written earlier. Her home missions work in New York's Bowery district increasingly claimed more of her time.

1880s—She and husband, Van, separated, probably due to growing apart in their interests and friendships.

1883 or 1884—Fanny joined a church for the first time (Cornell Memorial Church).

1890, September 1—Mother (age 91) died. Fanny's sisters applied to the court for and were awarded all their mother's estate. Fanny did not contest the ruling.

1890s—Fanny wrote several hymns each week, still worked in the Bowery missions, and traveled alone, as she always had, to her numerous speaking engagements.

1896—She moved to an apartment in a poor section of Brooklyn near her prosperous friends Ira Sankey and Phoebe Knapp, who watched out for her welfare. (Van lived nearby and she visited him often.) Fanny became a foreign missions intercessor.

1896—Her book of poems, *Bells at Evening*, was released by Bigelow & Main. The company gave her 100 percent of the royalties (50 cents per copy) to provide for her in old age.

1900, June—(Age 80) After a serious illness, she agreed to return to Bridgeport, Connecticut, with her sisters. She and Carrie set up housekeeping, and Carrie spent the rest of her life caring for Fanny and working as her secretary. Ira Sankey paid their rent and sent them a stipend each month. Fanny became involved in Methodist missions to the poor of Bridgeport and continued her traveling and speaking ministry.

1902, July 18—Van died at the home of friends, the Underhills of publishing fame. Fanny arranged for his burial in Maspeth where they had lived as newlyweds.

1903—*Fanny Crosby's Life-Story*, a book of autobiographical sketches written by Will Carleton from interviews with Fanny, was published.

1904, winter—Fanny wrote a more extensive autobiography, *Memories of Eighty Years*, assisted by Adelbert White. It was released in 1906 with an endorsement by Fanny's long-time friend Grover Cleveland.

1905, March 24—Fanny Crosby day in churches across America.

1906—Reduced her hymn writing from about two hundred to fifty songs per year.

1906, June 25—Sister Carrie died. Fanny spent the rest of her life with her niece Florence Booth.

1915, February 12—(Almost age 95) Fanny died, leaving a legacy of an estimated nine thousand hymns.

Charles Elmer Cowman, 1868–1924
Lettie Burd Cowman, 1870–1960

1868, March 13—Charles born on farm near Toulon, Illinois, to devout Methodists David and Mary Cowman.

1870, March 3—Lettie born to Issac, a highly successful farmer and bank president, and Margaret Burd near Thayer, Union County, Iowa.

1870, May—The Cowman family moved to Clarke County, Iowa, near the Burd family.

1881—(Age 13) Charles gave his heart to Christ in the Methodist Episcopal church.

1883—The Cowmans moved to Osceola, the county seat, so Charles could attend high school. Charles became a telegraph operator and train dispatcher. The Chicago, Burlington & Quincy Railroad hired and stationed him in Lettie's home town.

1883, June 22—Charles escorted thirteen-year-old Lettie to her piano recital. The two became devoted

sweethearts, and Lettie pledged to wait for him when
he was transferred away.

1886—Charles transferred to Chicago where he experienced
rapid career advancement; he forsook his Christian
commitment during this time. He left the railroad to
become manager of the Western Union Office in
Glenwood Springs, Colorado.

1889, June 8—Charles (age 21) and Lettie (age 19) were
married in the Methodist Episcopal Church in Afton,
Iowa. They lived briefly in Glenwood Springs and then
moved to Chicago where Charles became the Western
Union traffic chief and, later, wire chief of the New
York division.

1893, December—Lettie gave her heart to Christ while at a
musical program at Grace Methodist Episcopal
Church.

1894, January—The couple attended a revival service at Grace
Church. Unable to respond to the altar call, Charles
rededicated his life to Christ that night at home; soon
he led a fellow telegraph operator, Ernest A. Kilbourne
(his future missions partner), to Christ.

1894, September 3—The Cowmans attended the missionary
convention of Dr. A. B. Simpson, founder of the
Christian and Missionary Alliance. Charles consecrated
himself to missions.

1896, April—Charles studied at Moody Bible Institute in
Chicago while continuing to work at night.

1897, early—The Cowmans met Juji Nakada, a young
Japanese preacher studying at the Institute. Through
him they began to feel the tug toward Japan.

1897, September 1—Charles heard God's call to preach. For
the next three years, he and Lettie struggled with
where and how to fulfill their missionary call.

1900, August 11—Charles received divine direction to go to

Japan and contacted the Methodist Mission Board for sponsorship.

1900, September 22—The Cowmans went to Cincinnati, Ohio, to attend and assist in God's Bible School, College and Missionary Training Home.

1900, December—Charles felt directed to go to Japan without mission board support, relying completely on divine provision. The couple was ordained to the ministry in Chicago by several Wesleyan holiness ministers.

1901, February 1—They sailed from San Francisco on the *China Maru* bound for Japan.

1901, February 22—They arrived in Tokyo and were met by Juji Nakada. Plans were under way for an independent mission and Bible school in downtown Tokyo. Oriental Missionary Society (OMS) founded.

1901, March 11—Moved into large two-story building God provided for their new missionary work in Tokyo. By early April, Central Gospel Mission was operating.

1902, July 21—Cowman and Nakada secured a larger building for gospel services. Between 1902 and 1912 fifteen thousand conversions occurred in the hall.

1902, August—Ernest and Julia Kilbourne and their three children joined the Cowmans in Japan.

1902, November—The Cowmans and Kilbournes began publishing a magazine, *Electric Messages* (renamed *The Oriental Missionary Standard* in 1914).

1904, June–1905, January—The Cowmans left Japan to itinerate in England and the United States, sharing the OMS vision and raising funds.

1904, October 31—Bible Institute moved to a new two-acre site adequate for the rapidly expanding enrollment.

1905, September–1906, November—Journeyed to raise funds.

1907, Late–1908, April—The Cowmans traveled to England and possibly the United States.

1907—Central Gospel Mission, directed by Charles Cowman and E. A. Kilbourne, had twelve branch missions with twenty-two gospel workers. Both men became convinced the way to reach Japan was through training Japanese evangelists.

1909, October–1911, May—The Cowmans left Japan to raise funds.

1912—OMS mission school was founded in Korea.

1912–1918—The Cowmans conducted the Great Village Campaign of Japan: over 10 million gospel literature pieces went to homes throughout Japan at a cost of approximately $100,000, and more than seven thousand Japanese were reported saved.

1912, May–1914, March—The Cowmans visited the United States and England several times to appeal for funds on behalf of the Great Village Campaign. Furlough was needed to allow Charles to recover from nervous exhaustion and overwork.

1915, May–1917, spring—They traveled to the United States to recruit urgently needed workers for the Great Village Campaign.

1917, October—Nakada and others formed the Japan Holiness Church, comprising 400 congregations born out of the original Tokyo mission.

1917, November 3—The Cowmans left Japan due to Charles's (age 49) broken health.

1918, early–1918, September—They traveled across the United States on behalf of OMS. Charles's severe heart attack on the trip forced their permanent return to Los Angeles. During the next six years he constantly neared death.

1924, spring—Ernest A. Kilbourne returned from Japan to assume leadership of OMS.

1924, July 17—Charles suffered a stroke that paralyzed his left side.

1924, September 25—(Age 56) Charles died at his home in Los Angeles.

1924—Lettie wrote *Missionary Warrior*, a biography of her husband, and *Streams in the Desert*, one of the world's most popular Christian devotional books. She also became first vice-president of OMS under president Kilbourne.

1925, October 4—Cowman Memorial Bible Institute was opened by OMS in Shanghai, China.

1928, April—Kilbourne (age 63) died of a cerebral hemorrhage. Lettie (age 56) became president of OMS.

1932—OMS launched the Kilbourne Memorial Bible Institute in Peking, China.

1932—Lettie's devotional *Consolation* published.

1936, August—She became consumed with massive literature distribution campaigns. Joined forces with Rees Howells of Wales in an Every Creature Crusade of global proportions which remained her central focus for the rest of her ministry. Her vision carried her to Finland, Estonia, Poland, Lithuania, Sweden, Belgium, Luxembourg, Switzerland, France, Egypt, Syria, Israel, and Cuba.

1939–1940—Visited the OMS work in the Orient for the last time. Second devotional book, *Springs in the Valley*, published.

1941, July —Lettie received the vision for a literature campaign to reach all of Mexico. The number of Protestants in Mexico doubled during the five-year campaign.

1942, July—OMS opened the Allahabad Bible Institute in North India.

1944, February—OMS Bible Seminary of Colombia opened in Bogotá.

1945, April—OMS dedicated a seminary in Medellín, Colombia.

1947, February—Lettie kicked off the literature campaign in Greece.

1947—Lettie's book *Mountain Trailways for Youth* published.

1949, October 25—Lettie (age 79) resigned as president of OMS. She became head of a new organization, World Gospel Crusades, which concentrated on literature campaigns.

1949—OMS established Cowman Publications (now merged with Zondervan), proceeds from which went to World Gospel Crusades.

1950—Lettie's book *Handfuls of Purpose* published.

1951, March 4—Fiftieth anniversary of OMS.

1951—OMS missionaries forced out of China by the communist regime.

1957—Lettie entered a convalescent home due to failing vision and health; over the next three years she suffered almost total disability.

1960, April 17, Easter—(Age 90) Lettie died in San Pasqual Sanitorium, Pasadena, California.

1966—OMS moved from Los Angeles to Indianapolis, Indiana.

Richard Allen, 1760–1831

1760, February 14—Richard was born into slavery in Philadelphia. His family was owned by Benjamin Chew, a prominent attorney.

1767—The Allen family (father, mother, and four children) was sold to Mr. Stokely, a plantation owner near Dover, Delaware.

1777—Richard converted in a Methodist meeting. He joined a black Methodist class that met in the woods and influenced his mother, older brother, and sister to become Christians. He attempted self-education. Before the year's end, he had established a Methodist meeting in Stokely's home, saw his master come to Christ, and purchased his freedom. Afterward, he made a living by farm labor, chopping wood, working in a brick yard, and driving a freight wagon.

1783—(Close of the American Revolution) Allen began itinerant preaching in Delaware, New Jersey, and Pennsylvania.

1784, December 24–1785, January 2—He attended the first American conference of the Methodist Episcopal Church held in Baltimore, Maryland.

1785—He stayed in Baltimore and received training from circuit preacher Richard Whatcoat. Bishop Francis Asbury requested that Allen become his assistant. Allen declined because it would require going to the Carolinas and Georgia, where he feared slavery.

1785, late—Allen returned to Pennsylvania and became assistant on the Lancaster Circuit.

1786, February—He came to Philadelphia and began regular preaching at St. George's Methodist Episcopal Church. He also preached in as many other churches as possible—sometimes up to five sermons per day. When over forty blacks began looking to him as their leader, he requested a separate meeting place but was denied.

1787, April 12—Free African Society was organized. The social aid group was administrated by Jones and Allen. Both men became increasingly successful in the community. Allen's business enterprises included a shoe shop and a chimney sweep service.

1787, November—Conflict with white dominance of St. George's led to a permanent rift with Negro believers. Allen (age 27) and Absalom Jones (age 41) became leaders of the black group.

1788, June 20—Allen was officially dropped from membership in the Free African Society on charges of sowing division. (His Methodist evangelistic zeal was resented by Episcopal and Quaker elements.)

1790, September—Free African Society began work to establish regular religious services. Allen cooperated, especially in fund raising, until it became evident the church would be Episcopal.

1793—Allen and Jones led blacks in a citywide aid program during a severe yellow fever epidemic.

1794, May 5—Allen and others began organizing a black Methodist church. Funds were raised to purchase a large frame blacksmith shop, which was moved onto a lot owned by Allen.

1794, July 17—St. Thomas African Church was dedicated; Absalom Jones became pastor.

1794, July 29—Bethel African Methodist Church was dedicated; Bishop Asbury preached the dedicatory sermon.

1794, November 3—Bethel Church declared its property free of Methodist control while agreeing to remain under the bishop's ecclesiastical rule. White preachers were supplied to its pulpit by St. George's elders.

1795—Bethel Church started a day school with approximately sixty students.

1796, September 12—Bethel Church became an incorporated body under Pennsylvania law.

1796, October—Bethel Church trustees started a Sunday school and night school to better educate Philadelphia blacks.

1797—Allen and Jones became leaders of a Negro Freemason lodge.

1798, spring—Allen reported to Bishop Asbury that a revival was occurring at Bethel Church in which four to eight were converted each night and many "backsliders" were reclaimed.

1799, June 11—Allen ordained a deacon by Bishop Asbury.

1799, December 29—The New York *Gazette & General Advertiser* and the Philadelphia newspapers carried reports of Allen's sermon eulogizing George Washington.

1801—Allen published a hymnal for use at Bethel Church.

1803—Bethel Church numbered 456 communicants.

1804—Allen organized an education society.

1814—During the War of 1812, Philadelphia secured Allen's assistance in organizing a Negro defense force. Approximately twenty-five hundred black men were recruited to help protect the city from possible British attack.

1816, January 21—Bishop Daniel Coker preached a victory sermon at Bethel Church, celebrating the Pennsylvania State Supreme Court ruling in favor of Bethel's freedom from outside interference. Birth of the African Methodist Episcopal Church as a denomination; Allen elected as first bishop.

1817, January—Convention for the aid and protection of Negroes held at Bethel Church by wealthy black businessman James Forten. The purpose was to oppose deportation of United States blacks to Africa.

1817—First annual conference of the African Methodist Episcopal churches was held in Baltimore and Philadelphia. A 228-page statement of the AME doctrine and discipline was formulated followed by publication of an AME hymnal.

1818—Absalom Jones, lifelong friend, died.

1818–1820—Allen served as AME general book steward.

1820—AME discipline was revised to exclude slave-holding blacks from membership.

1822—AME church expanded into New York.

1824—AME Church included three conferences, seventeen

itinerant ministers, ten circuits, three stations, three missionaries, and 7,937 members, with church property valued at $75,000.

1826—AME Church sent a missionary to Haiti, where many free United States blacks were emigrating.

1829–1830—AME Church did extensive mission work in the South.

1830—AME Church organized in Ohio.

1831, March 26—(Age 72) Allen died. His personal property was valued at almost three thousand dollars, a large sum for a black American of his day. Additionally, he owned considerable real estate. During his years as minister of Bethel Church, he received the sum of only eighty dollars.

Charles Thomas "C. T." Studd, 1862–1931
Norman Grubb, 1895–present

1862, December 5—Charles born to a wealthy British family in Wiltshire, England.

1883—He studied at Cambridge University and fully surrendered his life to Christ under the ministry of Dwight L. Moody. He and six other university men formed the Cambridge Seven who committed their lives and wealth to missions. Studd gave away about $150,000 (approximately half a million dollars by today's standards) plus his fame as England's best cricket player.

1885—Cambridge Seven went to China as missionaries with China Inland Mission. There Studd met and married Priscilla Steward, a Salvation Army worker.

1894—Studd returned to England because of poor health. He spent next six years speaking for missions in the Student Volunteer Movement.

1895, August 2—Norman Grubb (future son-in-law and associate of C. T.) born in London to a scholarly Irish clergyman and his wife.

1900–1906—The Studd family served as missionaries to India.

1910—Studd visited Africa to investigate the possibility of starting a mission in the interior. Returning to England, he set up the Heart of Africa Mission (later enlarged to World Evangelization Crusade).

ca. 1912—Grubb attended Trinity College, Cambridge, where he helped found Inter-Varsity Christian Fellowship.

1913—Studd and Alfred Buxton left England for Africa's Belgian Congo. Studd's family remained because of his wife's severe heart problem. Concurrently, Grubb fully surrendered his life to God and Christian service.

1916—Studd took his only furlough back to England. His wife's health had improved enough to run the mission's home office. A small group returned with him, including daughter Edith, who was to marry Alfred Buxton.

1917—Grubb received the Military Cross for World War I service as a lieutenant of Gloucester Regiment. Active in France, he became romantically involved with C. T.'s youngest daughter, Pauline, while recovering from a war wound.

1918—Alfred and Edith Buxton left the Congo mission for a much needed furlough.

1919, November 24—Pauline Studd married Norman Grubb.

1919, December 24—The newlyweds went to the Congo to work with C.T.

1921—Norman and Pauline Grubb lost their first baby, Noel Palmer, on his first birthday.

1921—Alfred Buxton returned to the Congo and took over the work at Nala so Studd could go deeper into the forest to set up a mission at Imbambi.

1923—Norman and Pauline Grubb returned to England on furlough. A second son, Paul, and a daughter, Priscilla, were born to them there. Norman frequently visited the Congo as Studd's assistant and representative to the home office. Studd decided that leadership of the home office was the call for Norman and Pauline Grubb.

1920s—Studd's health rapidly worsened: he suffered from asthma, severe malarial fevers, dysentery, chills, digestive disorders, gallstones, and had several heart attacks.

1925—Studd rallied his remaining "troops" to the cry of "D.C.D." (Don't Care a Damn—but that Christ's work is accomplished and his name glorified) following a period of severe conflict in the mission over his relentless demands for holiness and hard work.

1928—Mrs. Studd visited her husband in the Congo for two weeks (their only visit since 1916, and their last). C. T. looked so old and haggard from illness that the natives thought his wife was his daughter. Studd was so sick that for a week he was expected to die momentarily. A Belgian Red Cross doctor treated him and began Studd's use of morphine, which continued until his death.

1929—Mrs. Studd died while visiting Spain. From this time on, the mission committee in England intensified its opposition to Studd's leadership. The Grubbs were forced into positions of little power.

1930—The Grubbs went to the Congo to alert Studd regarding the mission committee's plan to radically change the nature of the mission at his death. Through Studd's forceful rule and the Grubbs intervention, the Committee conceded defeat and started another mission organization.

1931, July 16—C. T. Studd died. His faithful Congo partner

Jack Harrison continued the Congo work, while the Grubbs reorganized and ran the home office.

1965—Norman Grubb resigned his position as General Secretary of World Evangelization Crusade, having filled that post since Studd's death. Since that time, he has engaged in an active ministry of writing and speaking.

1966—Norman and Pauline Grubb took up residence with their daughter, Priscilla, in a home on the WEC head-quarters' grounds in Fort Washington, Pennsylvania. Norman continues his writing and speaking minisry from that base.

1981, September 16—Pauline Grubb passed from this life into the presence of her Lord.

Gladys May Aylward, 1902–1970

1902, May 24—Gladys was born, the first child of an Edmonton, London, postman and his wife.

1916—(Age 14) She quit school and landed first job as assistant in the Penny Bazaar (variety store) and progressed to a grocer's shop.

1919—Post–World War I job shortage forced her into domestic service as a parlormaid in London homes. Long hours and small wages were offset by her enjoyment of trips to the theater, where she dreamed of being an actress.

1920—Gladys became a Christian and regularly participated in youth and street meetings. She talked about going to China as a missionary.

1930—Just before her twenty-eighth birthday, she enrolled in London's China Inland Mission Center but was dismissed after three months of unsuccessful study.

1930—She became a "Rescue Sister" on the docks at Swansea,

New South Wales and saved young girls from prostitution by taking them to the mission hostel.

1931—Gladys became parlormaid in the home of Sir Francis Younghusband, a famous soldier, author, and explorer, in order to raise her fare to go to China.

1932, October 15—She began journeying on the Trans-Siberian Railroad to China.

1932, November 16—She arrived in Tsechow, Shansi Province, China. Then she went to Yangcheng and became assistant to seventy-three-year-old veteran missionary Jeannie Lawson. The two converted their mission compound into an inn as a means for evangelizing local travelers. Mrs. Lawson soon died and so did the support for the Yangcheng Mission.

ca. 1935—Gladys chosen by local mandarin to educate area women against binding their baby daughters' feet. This gave her the weight of government backing for her missionary work.

1939—A naturalized Chinese citizen, she became increasingly involved in the Chinese Nationalist movement. Through her missionary work, she gathered sensitive information regarding the Japanese occupation forces to pass on to the Nationalists. Grew to love a young Nationalist colonel named Linnan.

1940, spring—Led one hundred children from the orphanage in Yangcheng across the Shansi Mountains to Sian in Free China—a journey of several weeks—in order to escape death during the Japanese occupation. Sian already overflowing with refugees, she took the children on to Fufeng, where she collapsed with typhus.

1940—Gladys hospitalized in a Baptist mission. She recuperated in missionaries' home in Meihsien for six months; she suffered extreme mental disorientation and physical weakness from the fever and often felt she might die.

ca. 1941—She regained her health enough to begin working with refugees of Sian.

1947—She returned to England for surgery on serious injuries incurred in a beating by the Japanese. Following her recovery, she spoke throughout England, started a hostel in Liverpool for Chinese seamen, and became mother to many relocated Chinese students.

1957—Gladys established orphanages in Hong Kong and Taipei, Formosa (Taiwan).

1957—British Broadcasting Company (BBC) reporter Alan Burgess's story of her life, *The Small Woman*, was released.

1958—Twentieth Century-Fox purchased *The Small Woman* for the filmmaking of *The Inn of the Sixth Happiness*. Ingrid Bergman quickly agreed to play Gladys. Gladys supported herself in Formosa on her half of the book and film proceeds. Because of a serious dispute between the Formosan government and the movie producer, the story was filmed in Wales rather than Formosa as originally planned. This was a hardship for Gladys with the Formosan people; she refused to see the movie and regretted ever agreeing to it.

1959—She visited America in route to England on a fund-raising tour for the orphanage. World Vision, Inc., took her under its wings. She gained considerable fame as she spoke in U.S. and Canadian churches. Numerous speaking tours resulted, including trips to Australia and New Zealand.

1959—Acquired a new ministry partner, Kathleen Langton-Smith, a Nottingham postmistress of twenty years whose skill was accounting.

1963, March—She arrived in London at the invitation of the BBC. Surprisingly, she discovered the purpose was a "This Is Your Life" program. This resulted in a visit with the Queen.

1963 or 1964—Upon returning to Taipei and the orphanage with a trustee, it was discovered that the superintendent (a young man married to one of Gladys's orphanage daughters) had embezzled over one million Taiwan dollars. Consequently, a painful two-year scandal and court case rocked Gladys's faith to its foundation.

1966—She returned to England and was well received by the press and the BBC. She spent several months speaking in schools and churches.

1967, early—Gladys returned to work in Formosa (Taiwan).

1970, January 1—(Age 68) Gladys died in Formosa, working until her final day. Kathleen Langton-Smith carried on the orphanage work.

1970, January 10—Ingrid Bergman visited Formosa hoping to meet Gladys, whose life had impacted her greatly as she portrayed her. In spite of Gladys's total disdain and criticism of *The Inn of the Sixth Happiness*, Miss Bergman played a prominent role in securing ongoing financial support for the orphanage from then on.

George Whitefield, 1714–1770

1714, December 16—George born in Gloucester, England. He was a self-indulgent youth who experienced bouts of conviction, during one of which he felt the call to preach.

1732—He met the Wesley brothers while a student at Oxford. He actively sought assurance of salvation for the next three years.

1735, March—Whitefield experienced spiritual rebirth and began evangelistic work.

1736—He graduated from Oxford and began preaching mostly at open-air meetings. Because of his tremendous vocal ability, thousands of listeners could hear him.

1738, May 3–August 28—Whitefield arrived in America; he preached throughout the Colonies. (First of seven visits to America.)

1740, March 25—Construction began on the Bethesda Orphanage in Savannah, Georgia—the oldest orphanage in America. It was built and paid for from contributions raised by Whitefield through his ministry in England and America.

1740, November 23—In Pennsylvania, he received word by mail that the family of Elizabeth Delamotte, whom he had been in love with for three years, would not grant them permission to marry.

1740, December 24—He wrote a letter publicizing his conflict with John Wesley, one of his closest friends, over the doctrines of predestination and sanctification.

1741, January 24—Renounced his love—a difficult decision—for Elizabeth, accepting that evidently she was not God's choice for him.

1741, fall—First of fifteen trips to Scotland.

1741, November 14—(Age 27) He married a childless widow, Elizabeth James Burwell (about age 36), in Wales. She was employed as a housekeeper. Six days after the wedding, he set off on a preaching tour, leaving Elizabeth behind as he would during most of their marriage.

1741-1743—He broke ties with the Wesleys over doctrines of free grace and predestination. Whitefield established a ministry base in a large wooden tabernacle in Moorfields.

1743—He formed the Calvinist Methodist Society.

1743, September—In her last month of pregnancy, Elizabeth was taken riding in an open chaise by her husband. He absentmindedly drove off into a fourteen-foot-deep ditch. The narrow escape from death convinced Whitefield that his baby was destined to be the greatest evangelist the world had ever known.

1743, October—Elizabeth bore a son, John. George was away preaching when the news reached him. He hurried back to London and baptized the baby, declaring the mighty works God would do through him.

1743, late November—Returned from a preaching tour. Baby John appeared in excellent health, so George arranged for Elizabeth and the child to travel to Gloucester slowly. He would go on ahead, meet them there, and accompany them to Elizabeth's house in Abergavenny.

1744, February 8—George arrived at the Bell Inn in Gloucester to be met by his brother with bad news. His child, scarcely four months old, had just died suddenly of a stroke or seizure. The Whitefields had no other children.

1744, October—The Whitefields arrived in Portsmouth, New Hampshire, after a harrowing twelve weeks at sea. It was Elizabeth's first trip to America. Shortly afterward, Whitefield almost died of angina.

1745, fall—The couple visited the orphanage in Savannah, Georgia, which was flourishing and the pride of the struggling colony. Whitefield (age 31) presented his plan to introduce slavery to the colony. He threw his influence behind mounting agitation for repeal of the act that excluded Negroes from Georgia and prevented colonists from owning slaves, claiming that converted owners could best bring Negroes to saving knowledge of Christ.

1748—He resigned his position as leader and moderator of the Calvinist Methodist Association because of his obligations in America and to facilitate reconciliation with the Wesleys.

1748—He began preaching to British aristocrats who gathered to hear him in the home of the Countess of Huntingdon.

1749—Founded a large church on Tottenham Court Road, London.

1750—Georgia obtained parliamentary sanction for slavery, and Whitefield converted Bethesda Orphan House into a slave plantation. His slaves were the best treated in the South, but the damage to American history was irreparable.

1768—Whitefield founded Trevecca College.

1768, August 9—Elizabeth (about age 63) died of a fever.

1770, September 30—George died in Newburyport, Massachusetts. His last words were, "I had rather wear out than rust out." His will left Bethesda Orphanage to Lady Huntingdon, but in three years it burned down and was never rebuilt.

Dwight Lyman Moody, 1837–1899

1837, February 5—Dwight was born in Northfield, Massachusetts, the sixth child of Edwin and Betsy Moody.

1841, May 28—His father died, leaving nine children.

1854, spring—Dwight left home to work in a Boston shoe store owned by his mother's brother. At his uncle's insistence, he began regular church attendance at Mount Vernon Congregational Church. He joined the Young Men's Christian Association (YMCA), then an evangelistic organization.

1855, April 21—(Age 18) He was led to Christ by his Sunday school teacher, Edward Kimball.

1855, May—Moody was denied church membership because he could not answer basic questions concerning his new faith.

1856, March 12—He was granted church membership following several months of Bible study.

1856, autumn—(Age 19) He moved to Chicago, intent on a business career. (His goal was to make $100,000.) He

joined Plymouth Church and taught a Sunday school
class at North Wells Street Mission every Sunday
afternoon. He again joined the local YMCA and
participated in noon prayer meetings.

1958, autumn—Began a Sunday school in the North Market
Hall, which became so famous for reaching Chicago's
"hoodlums" that President Lincoln stopped to visit on
his way to Washington for his first term.

1860—(Age 23) A burning desire to see souls saved led to his
leaving his successful career as a shoe salesman. His
income at that time was over five thousand dollars a
year, a large sum for a young man. Met Emma C.
Revell (age 17); they became engaged. His
commitment to work with the YMCA increased.

1861—He began evangelistic work in Chicago. Much of his
ministry was to soldiers at Fort Douglas, where over
fifteen hundred services were held and many attendees
converted. Because of his success, Moody traveled to
other camps to minister throughout the Civil War.

1862—(Age 25) Dwight married Emma.

1863—First child, Emma, born.

1864—Illinois Street Church formed from the North Market
Hall Sunday School. Moody served as a deacon.

1865—Civil War ending, Moody returned to his work in
Chicago. He became head of the Chicago YMCA, a
position he held until 1871. Through the Illinois Sunday
School Convention and the YMCA, he began traveling
and teaching others how to conduct similar ministries.

1867, September 29—Due to Moody's work on behalf of the
YMCA, its first hall in America—Farwell Hall—was
dedicated. Four months later the hall burned down.

1867—First trip to England to study British Sunday Schools
and to meet Charles Spurgeon and George Müller.
There his speaking greatly endeared him to the British.

1869—Son, William, born.

1870—The second Farwell Hall, superior to the first, was erected. Moody resigned as president of the Chicago YMCA.

1870—Ira D. Sankey became song evangelist for all of Moody's revival meetings.

1870—Moody returned to the British Isles for meetings.

1871, October—Great Chicago Fire occurred. Moody's church and home burned down. Moody (age 34) suffered from weariness and exhaustion with his life and ministry.

1871, December 24—Moody dedicated his new church, Northside Tabernacle, in Chicago. The Moody and Sankey families lived in the makeshift building through winter. Continuous revival services were held for months.

1872, June—Moody returned to England to further his studies of Sunday school and evangelism methods. After unwillingly preaching in London, revival broke out and he continued on for ten days. Several hundred were added to the church.

1873, June—He returned to England for extended evangelistic meetings. He also preached in Ireland and Scotland.

1873, September—*Sacred Songs and Solos* was released, often referred to as the "Moody and Sankey Hymnbook." Subsequent versions of the song book were released; royalties from all sales went to a committee that dispersed them to various Christian works.

1875, August—Moody returned to America to begin large evangelistic campaigns in major cities.

1875, October—First American campaign was held in Brooklyn, New York. From there he went to Philadelphia, followed by a large crusade in New York City. These extremely successful meetings established him as a great American evangelist.

1876—Moody became president of the Illinois State Sunday School Union.

1879—Third and final child, Paul, born.

1879, November 3—Northfield Seminary for Young Women, a project of Moody's in his birthplace, was formally opened. By 1899 the school had acquired 500 acres, nine dormitories, full college facilities, and 400 students.

1880, September 1—Began the Northfield Christian Workers' Conference in Northfield, Massachusetts. Over three hundred clergy and laity attended.

1880, winter— He preached in California.

1881, May—Mount Hermon School for Young Men was opened by Moody near the Northfield girls' school. (Tuition at both schools was very low; students worked on campus to supplement it.)

1881, October—Moody returned to work in the British Isles; he was so successful, he stayed into 1884. He came home for a "rest" in the summer of 1883 and held a three-day convention in Chicago.

1884–1886—He preached in cities throughout America.

1886—Moody founded the Chicago Bible Institute (now Moody Bible Institute).

1891—He visited the British Isles.

1892, April—He took time off from revival campaigns to visit the Holy Land.

1893—He conducted a large campaign in Chicago during the World's Fair.

1895—During the Spanish-American War, Moody became chairman of the Evangelistic Department of the Army and Navy Christian Commission, which provided soldiers with preaching by well-known ministers, YMCA tents for relaxation, free Christian literature, and hospital visitation.

1895, autumn—He spent several weeks preaching in Atlanta during the Atlanta Exposition.

1896, autumn—He held a huge crusade in New York City in the Cooper Union.

1897, January—(Age 60) He preached two services each day for two months in Boston—his energy and enthusiasm unabated.

1899, November 12—Last evangelistic campaign was held in Kansas City, Missouri. He became too ill to finish the sermon on the closing night.

1899, December 22—(Age 62) Moody died.

Catherine Marshall, 1914–1983

1914, September 27—Sarah Catherine Wood born in Johnson City, Tennessee, into a Presbyterian minister's family.

1932—An aspiring young writer, she enrolled in Agnes Scott College in Decatur, Georgia. She attended Westminster Presbyterian Church in Atlanta and was attracted to its young Scottish pastor, Peter Marshall.

1936, November 4—(Age 22) She married Peter Marshall (age 34).

1937, November—Husband became pastor of New York Avenue Presbyterian Church in Washington, D.C. She faced huge demands as young and inexperienced "first lady" of the twelve-hundred-member congregation.

1940—Son, Peter John, born.

1943, March—Catherine contracted tuberculosis; she was confined to bed for two years. She began what was to become a lifelong search for a deep, Spirit-filled walk with God.

1946—Her husband suffered first heart attack. He refused doctor's orders to reduce his activities.

1947, January—Peter elected chaplain of the United States Senate.

1949, January 25—Husband (age 46) died of a massive coronary. Catherine (age 34) was left with her young son and no experience in managing financial affairs.

1949, November—*Mr. Jones, Meet the Master,* a book of Peter Marshall's sermons edited by Catherine, was released; it became an immediate best-seller.

1951, October—Her husband's biography, authored by Catherine and entitled *A Man Called Peter,* became a national best-seller for three years.

1953—Catherine received the Woman of the Year Award in Literature from the Women's Press Club.

1955—*A Man Called Peter* became a motion picture by 20th Century-Fox.

1957—Catherine authored *To Live Again.*

1958–1960—She was women's editor for *Christian Herald* magazine.

1959, November 14—(Age 49) Married Guideposts editor Leonard LeSourd (age 40); became stepmother to his children--Linda (10), Chester (6), and Jeffrey (3). She left her custom-made home in Washington, D.C., to move to his home in Chappaqua, New York.

1960—She joined Guideposts publishers as a roving editor. The couple became best friends to John and Elizabeth (Tibby) Sherrill, also Guideposts editors and neighbors.

1961, spring—Son Peter graduated from Yale University with a history degree and no faith or life direction.

1961, summer—Peter gave his life to Christ at a Fellowship of Christian Athletes conference in Colorado Springs, Colorado. He immediately enrolled in Princeton Seminary to prepare for full-time Christian ministry.

1961—Catherine's book *Beyond Our Selves* was released. Len edited it and all her subsequent books.

1962—The couple became increasingly involved in the charismatic renewal movement.

1964, spring—The family moved to Boynton Beach, Florida, for the sake of Catherine's health. Len continued to work at Guideposts, alternating weeks between New York and Florida. Daughter Linda attended boarding school in New York; Catherine cared for their boys in Florida.

1965—Peter John married Edith Wallis, a fellow student at Princeton, and moved to West Hartford, Connecticut, where Peter became assistant pastor of a Presbyterian Church.

1966, December 3—First grandchild, Peter Christopher Marshall, born; he died two weeks later due to birth defects.

1967—First novel, *Christy*, hit the best-seller list. Catherine became increasingly troubled about whether her marriage to Len, a divorced man, had been an act of spiritual disobedience.

1969, March 1—Edith and Peter's daughter, Mary Elizabeth, was born. The Marshalls were by then pastoring their own congregation on Cape Cod.

1969, spring—Catherine decided her next book project would be a novel tentatively entitled *Gloria*. It was to be based on the life of a mystical friend and prayer partner in Florida. Len and Catherine's editor friend, Tib Sherrill, advised against the project.

1971, May—Her marriage became temporarily strained due to Len's six years of commuting to New York, her difficulties with raising stepchildren, and her anxiety about his previous divorce.

1971, June—Catherine's world seemed to be tumbling in on her. The movie version of *Christy* planned by MGM was shelved. Her editor at McGraw-Hill was fired. Tib Sherrill tried to dissuade Catherine from writing

Gloria, and, without her editorial help, the book was not developing well. Linda's graduation from Ohio Wesleyan was a particularly unhappy time. Catherine felt Peter and Edith rejected all her advice. She could not resolve her difficulties with Len or with stepparenting. She agonized over the internal conflict produced by United States military involvement in Southeast Asia.

1971, July 22—Amy Catherine was born to Peter and Edith. From the moment of birth, her life hung by a fragile thread because of a rare genetic disease. Catherine and Len came to Cape Cod immediately.

1971, August 8—The LeSourds organized an intercessory prayer vigil for the baby's healing. Sixteen carefully chosen people joined them at Cape Cod for four days of intense prayer. Many amazing healings and miracles occurred, but baby Amy remained in critical condition.

1971, September 4—Amy died after over six weeks of fighting for her life. Catherine had stayed by her side almost the entire time. Upon the baby's death, she plunged into deep depression that lasted over six months.

1972, spring—Her depression finally began to lift as God directed her to study the suffering of Christ. Recovery was slow but steady, and as she neared her sixtieth birthday a new book idea was born to replace *Gloria*.

1974—*Something More* was released, followed by *Adventures in Prayer* (1975), *The Helper* (1978), *Meeting God at Every Turn* (1980), *Catherine Marshall's Story Bible* (1982), *The Best of Peter Marshall* (1983), and *My Personal Prayer Diary* (1983).

1974, May 4—Peter Jonathan was born to Edith and Peter.

1974—Len resigned his position at Guideposts. The LeSourds and the Sherrills founded a small publishing company named Chosen Books.

1980—The LeSourds established "The Intercessors," a prayer ministry. It now has over two thousand members.

Linda LeSourd married Philip Lader, who became president of Winthrop College, Rock Hill, South Carolina, in 1983.

1980, August—Chester LeSourd married Susan Scott. He credited his stepmother for giving him the best launching into adult life he could have had through her tough, prayer-centered discipline.

1980, September 24—David Christopher was born to Peter and Edith.

1983, March 18—(Age 68) Catherine died of a lung ailment after completing her novel *Julie*.

1984—*Julie* was published, thanks to Len's polishing of Catherine's manuscript.

1985, February 2—Linda and Philip Lader bore a daughter and namesake to Catherine. The birth was credited to Catherine's strong intercession for the couple's childlessness.

1985, June—Len married Sandra Simpson, a Christian writer and divorced mother of three adult children.

1986—*A Closer Walk*, Len's gleanings from the legacy of Catherine's journals, was published.

1986, October—Jeffrey LeSourd married Nancy Oliver, a graduate of Agnes Scott College (Catherine's alma mater).

1987, June 17—The Laders had a second daughter named Linda Whitaker Lader.

1989, February 19—Leonora Whitaker Wood, Catherine's mother and heroine of the novel *Christy*, died at age ninety-seven.

1989—*Light in My Darkest Night*, the story of Catherine's "dark night of the soul" experience, was published.

David Brainerd, 1718–1747

1718, April 20—David was born to Hezekiah and Dorothy (Hobart) Brainerd in Haddam, Connecticut. His father was a member of His Majesty's Council; his mother was a daughter and granddaughter of Church of England ministers. He had four brothers and four sisters. The family owned a beautiful estate.

1726—Hezekiah died when David was eight years old.

1732—David's mother died, leaving him an orphan at age fourteen. He received a sizeable inheritance, which he eventually used to educate himself and several other young men. From that time on, he suffered acute depression.

1732–1738—He lived with a sister and worked on a farm.

1738—Brainerd returned to Haddam to study under an elderly minister.

1739, July 12—After many years of spiritual struggle, he at last believed himself truly converted.

1739, September—He became a theological student at Yale University.

ca. 1740—He returned to Haddam from Yale to recover from a severe case of measles. During this time, he was particularly distressed emotionally.

1742—Brainerd was caught up in the Whitefield revival to which Yale authorities were opposed. He was expelled after criticizing a Yale tutor's lack of spirituality and other alleged improprieties.

1742—Brother, Nehemiah, died of tuberculosis.

1742, July 29—Brainerd was licensed to preach by the Association of Ministers at Danbury, Connecticut, following a period of study under the Reverend Jedediah Mills of Ripton, Connecticut.

1742, November—He went to New York City for an interview with the Society in Scotland for the Propagation of

Christian Knowledge, regarding missions work among the American Indians.

1743, April—He was appointed missionary to the Indians by the Correspondents of the Society in Scotland for the Propagation of Christian Knowledge. Immediately he began his work among the Indians in Kaunaumeek, New York, a settlement between Stockbridge and Albany, and he continued there a year.

1743—He appealed to Yale University governors to allow him to make a public apology in order to receive his degree. The school refused in spite of Brainerd's endorsements from several prominent ministers, including Jonathan Edwards.

1743–1744, winter—Brainerd unsuccessfully studied the Indian language under John Sergeant, who had already done extensive missionary work among the Stockbridge area Indians.

1744, spring—He convinced the Indians to move to Stockbridge so Sergeant could take over their care. He saw virtually no success in his missions work but still turned down a call to pastor in East Hampton.

1744, May—He began a summer of ministry to Indians at the Forks of the Delaware (near current Easton, Pennsylvania) with the help of an interpreter. He next went to Crosswecksung (near present Freehold, New Jersey).

1744, June 12—Brainerd was ordained by the Presbytery of New York at Newark, New Jersey.

1744, October—He traveled west to the Susquehanna River, preaching to Indians in various places through an interpreter. The trip brought little result, so he returned to the Forks of the Delaware to complete his second year of missionary work.

1745, May—He completed a 350-mile evangelization trip that brought so little response that he decided to resign his position with his sponsoring missions society if things didn't improve significantly by year's end.

1745, summer—Revival broke out among the Indians in Crossweeksung, New Jersey. Brainerd baptized twenty-five converts.

1745, November—In the preceding nine months, he traveled over three thousand miles in an attempt to reach the Indians while the revival lingered. His health suffered seriously from constant exposure to the elements. He wrote to his brother John, "I am in one continued, perpetual and uninterrupted hurry."

1745, winter—He started a school for the Crossweeksung converts.

1746, May—Brainerd gathered the Indians scattered about the area of Crossweeksung together in a community at Cranbury, about a fifteen-mile relocation, and established an Indian congregation there. In a year and a half, there were almost 150 converts.

1746, August 12—He set out on his fourth trip to the Susquehanna River area with six Indian converts. He was very ill on most of this journey but had more success than previously.

1746, November—Left Cranbury to visit friends in New England. On reaching Elizabethtown, New Jersey (near Newark), he became too ill to continue. He spent the winter with Jonathan Dickinson, president of the College of New Jersey, attempting to improve his health.

1747, March 18—His health deteriorated rapidly, forcing him to say good-bye to his work and beloved Indians in Cranbury. He returned to Elizabethtown the next day.

1747, April 10—His brother John took over as pastor of the Indian congregation at Cranbury.

1747, April 21—(Age 29) Brainerd set out again for New England from Elizabethtown. He hoped to recover his health by riding (a treatment approach often recommended at that time).

1747, early May—He visited among old friends in Haddam, Connecticut.

1747, May 28—Arrived at Jonathan Edwards's parsonage in Northampton, Massachusetts. Edwards summoned the famed Dr. Mather to examine him. The diagnosis was consumption (tuberculosis); little hope of recovery was offered.

1747, June 9—Journeyed to Boston with Jonathan Edwards's daughter, Jerusha, who acted as his nurse.

1747, June 12—The two arrived in Boston. Within a week he became so ill he was expected to die at any moment; however, he managed to write a large number of important letters as well as the introduction to a theological work by Thomas Shepard. He conversed with area ministers at length on the major theological concerns of the time. He was visited by his youngest brother, Israel, who was a student at Yale; he received news of his sister Spencer's death.

1747, July 25—David and Israel Brainerd and Jerusha Edwards arrived back in Northampton. Israel stayed until July 29 and then went back to Yale, expecting never to see his brother again.

1747, September 5—John Brainerd visited his dying brother; he brought news of the Indian congregation and David's diary and other writings. John left on September 14 for important business in New Jersey.

1747, September 17—Israel Brainerd came to stay with David until his death. Throughout this final period of illness, David continued important correspondence through dictation. He also corrected a small volume of his writings on qualifications of ministers for publication.

1747, September 28—David grew so ill in the evening that his friends and family gathered about him to await the end.

1747, September 29—Conducted an important interview of two candidates for mission service to the Indians. It was the last time he was able to sit up.

1747, October 7—John returned to Northampton after being delayed in New Jersey due to serious illness among the Christian Indians.

1747, October 9—David died in the home of Jonathan Edwards.

1747, October 12—Jonathan Edwards conducted Brainerd's funeral, an event attended by a large congregation.

1748, January 6—Israel Brainerd died at New Haven of a fever after a two-week illness.

1748, February 14—Jerusha Edwards died of tuberculosis contracted during her care of Brainerd. She had cared for Brainerd constantly for nineteen weeks.

1748, May 6—Sarah Edwards (wife of Jonathan) bore her tenth child. Baby Elizabeth was the Edwardses' only frail child, possibly a result of the stress and grief Sarah experienced during the pregnancy.

1749—Jonathan Edwards's meticulous edition of the diaries of David Brainerd was released, the first complete missionary biography ever published. It was over three hundred pages in length and quickly gained international recognition.

Peter Yakovlevich Vins, 1898–1942
Lydia Mikhailovna Vins, 1907–1985

1898—Peter Vins born to devout Russian Christian parents. He grew up in Samara (now Kuibyshev).

1907, March 30—Lydia born in Blagoveschensk, Siberia, on the Russian-Chinese border.

ca. 1916—Peter Vins came to the U.S. for theological training at Weston Memorial Baptist Church in Philadelphia, Colgate-Rochester Divinity School in Rochester, New York, and the Southern Theological Seminary in Louisville, Kentucky.

1919—Lydia (age 12) gave her life to Christ during a period of great revival.

1922—Lydia (age 15) began teaching Sunday school. She became increasingly certain that God had chosen her for special service and suffering.

1926—Peter Vins came to pastor the thriving Baptist church in Blagoveschensk. He served there through 1930.

1927—Peter Vins proposed to Lydia Mikhailovna. All he offered her was a life of hardship and danger. Soon after his proposal they were married.

1928—Peter relinquished his United States citizenship in order to remain in Russia.

1928, August 4—Son, Georgi, born.

1929—Persecution of the Russian church intensified. The Vinses decided to go to America until it abated, but God challenged them to stay in Russia. Their willingness to stay and suffer strengthened thousands of believers for the purge that followed. Before it was over, twenty-two thousand Christians had given their lives.

1930—Peter was arrested for preaching the gospel and opposing government intrusion into church affairs. He was sentenced to three years in Svetlaya Bay labor camp. Lydia and two-year-old Georgi were evicted from their house.

1933—Peter was exiled to Biisk, Siberia. Lydia and Georgi were allowed to join him there.

1934, January—The USSR granted Peter a passport and permission to move with his family to Novosibirsk.

1935—The Vins family moved to Omsk. Peter worked at a

government-approved job all day and ministered to
believers every night.

1936—Due largely to the Vinses' ministry, Omsk numbered
1,000 born-again believers. Peter was arrested and
spent ten months in prison.

1937—Peter was arrested a third time. He received a ten-year
sentence. Lydia was denied the right to visit or
correspond with him.

1941—Georgi (age 13) became a Christian.

1943, December 27—(Age 45) Peter died in prison. Lydia and
Georgi were not informed of his death.

ca. 1944-1960—Lydia and Georgi lived in Kiev. Georgi
attended an electromechanical institute and then a
polytechnical school. He earned degrees in
engineering and economics. He married Nadezhda
("Nadia") Ivanovna, a graduate in Romance and
German languages.

1960—Georgi, now an electrical engineer, helped form a new
Baptist church in Kiev, which started with sixty
members. He soon became a prominent leader of the
Reformed Baptists and an outspoken critic of the
government-sponsored church organization.

1962—Georgi ordained and chosen as pastor of Kiev Baptist
Church.

1963—Georgi left his job in a design institute to become a
full-time minister.

1963, December 24—Finally learning of her husband's death,
Lydia succeeded in having him posthumously declared
rehabilitated.

1964—Lydia, Georgi, and others organized the All-Union
conference of Baptist Prisoners' Relatives, the first
organized movement to crusade for human rights in
the communist world. The organization provided

information to Christians regarding the charges, sentences, and places of imprisonment of believers. It aided families of Christian prisoners. Lydia was the leading voice in this movement. She frequently traveled to court- rooms to offer moral support during trials, visited families of prisoners to offer comfort and relief, and spoke in many churches. She wrote a book about women in the Bible to encourage Christian women in Russia and helped start women's Bible study groups in churches.

1965, September 18—Georgi became secretary of the Council of Churches of the Evangelical Christians and Baptists (CEBC). Hundreds of Russian churches broke away from the state-controlled church union to join the new alliance, resulting in a fresh wave of persecution.

1966, May 16—Georgi and others organized a demonstration before the Communist Central Committee in Moscow. Five hundred Baptist representatives from 130 towns came. Most of them were bused to various Moscow jails.

1966, May 19—Georgi was arrested when he went to inquire what had been done with the Baptist demonstrators who had been bused away from the demonstration. He received a three-year sentence to a prison in the Ural Mountains. His wife, Nadia, lost her job as a translator, leaving her without visible means of support for herself and their four children.

1968, January—Georgi's health rapidly failed. He suffered an infection that led to heart disease, running sores, high blood pressure, and a double inguinal hernia. In spite of his condition, he was subjected to hard physical labor.

1969, May—Georgi was released from prison; he returned to Kiev where the church had grown to four hundred members.

1970, January—Georgi arrested and sentenced to one year monitored labor in a Kiev factory where his wages were docked as further punishment. He did not complete the sentence because it was clear he would be sent back to prison soon, and he wanted to devote all his time to ministry. For over three years he lived in hiding to escape arrest.

1970, December—(Age 63) Lydia was arrested and sentenced to three years in a labor camp for her Christian work. She had serious heart disease, diabetes, and stomach trouble.

1973—Lydia was released from prison; she resumed her work with the Prisoners' Council.

1974, January—Natasha, oldest daughter of Georgi, lost her hospital job because of her Christian faith. His son, Petya, also could not get employment.

1974, March 30—Georgi was imprisoned a second time. This time the charge was for printing Bibles. He received a ten-year sentence to a concentration-type camp in Siberia.

1974, September—Andre Sakharov of the unofficial Human Rights Committee appealed to the World Council of Churches on Georgi's behalf. Georgi had been on a four-month hunger strike at that time.

1975, January 25—Georgi was tried and sentenced to five years in a concentration-type camp and five years' exile in Siberia.

1977—Peter, son of Georgi and namesake of his martyred grandfather, was arrested and tried for "parasitism," the communists' term for those refusing atheism. He was sentenced to a year in labor camp.

1978, January 6—Young Peter was released from prison following a brutal beating; he was certified as "physically unfit for work." He went to visit his father, Georgi, at a labor camp in Siberia. Shortly thereafter, he was rearrested on the same charge.

1978, June 10—Georgi was beaten and placed in an underground isolation cell.

1979, May—Georgi exiled to America through a prisoner exchange agreement arranged by President Jimmy Carter. Six weeks later his family, including Lydia, joined him. In America, the Vinses began working immediately to aid the believers left behind in Russia. Lydia traveled across the States and Europe, telling Westerners of the tremendous suffering of Russian Christians. Her work to aid Christians in the USSR kept her busy visiting government officials, organizing meetings, and writing letters.

1979, July—Georgi chosen to represent CEBC and all persecuted Christians through speaking and writing in the free world.

1980—International Representation for the Council of EBC of the Soviet Union was established by Georgi Vins in Elkhart, Indiana. (The Vins' ministry is now known as Russian Gospel Ministries International.)

1985, May 19—(Age 78) Lydia died.

1988, December—All Evangelical Baptist prisoners were released. Soviet Union began allowing Bibles to enter the country freely. Russian Gospel Ministries began supplying Bibles and Christian literature free of charge in Russian, Ukranian, Moldavian, Georgian, and other languages.

1990, June—Georgi underwent successful heart bypass surgery after suffering several heart attacks.

1990, August 15—Mikhail Gorbachev restored Georgi's Soviet citizenship.

1990, November 15—Georgi and wife returned to USSR, able to preach and witness freely. He plans to divide ministry time between U.S. (where he will keep home base) and USSR.

Elizabeth Alden Scott Stam, 1906–1934
John Stam, 1907–1934

1906—Elizabeth ("Betty," first child) born to missionary parents Dr. and Mrs. Charles Ernest Scott in Albion, Michigan. Soon afterwards, the family went to Tsingtao, Shantung Province, China. Two sisters and two brothers were eventually added to the family.

1907—John (fifth of nine children) born to Dutch immigrants Mr. and Mrs. Peter Stam in Paterson, New Jersey. Father was a successful builder whose business grew to include real estate, insurance, and a lumberyard. A devout Christian family, they spent much time in home missions work.

1920—John completed Christian grammar school education then went on to business college for two years since he had no interest in higher education.

1922, spring—John (age 15) became a Christian; this awakened a great love of learning and beauty that he had never known.

1922–1928—He worked as stenographer and bookkeeper in various business offices in Paterson and New York City. He became increasingly involved in the mission his parents ran, particularly in street witnessing.

1923—The Scott family returned to the United States after six months of travel and study in Egypt, Israel, Greece, Switzerland, France, and England.

1924, fall—Betty entered Wilson College, Chambersburg,

Pennsylvania. She had been seriously ill with inflammatory rheumatism and resulting heart weakness in the previous year, during which she began writing poetry.

1925—Betty attended a "deeper life" conference in Keswick, New Jersey, and fully consecrated her life to Christ. Though already a committed Christian, she determined from this time on to abandon herself to God and his will at any cost. To fortify her resolve, she began a consistent practice of daily quiet time.

1928—Betty graduated from college and enrolled in Moody Bible Institute to gain practical skill in evangelism before returning to China.

1929—John enrolled in Moody Bible Institute. His father's dream was that this training would enable John to return to Paterson and take over the mission there. John's vision for missions lay far from Paterson. He met Betty at a weekly prayer meeting for the China Inland Mission.

1931, January—John began service as supply pastor in Elida, Ohio, two hundred miles from Chicago; he served there for nineteen months.

1931, May 24—from John Stam's diary: "Betty is in Philadelphia now [at the CIM Home in Germantown as a missionary candidate], but I have not been able to write her a letter. . . . While Betty and I are looking forward to the same field, I cannot move one step in her direction until I am sure that it is the Lord's directive will. I don't want to wreck her life and mine too."

1931, fall—Betty sailed for China. She and John, by now deeply in love, determined not to become engaged until they were certain John's call would also be to China. They resolved never to let their personal feelings or desires overrule their usefulness and obedience to God.

1932, spring—John completed his studies at Moody. In his speech to the graduating class, he challenged them to expend their lives for Christ and in winning the lost.

1932, July—John was accepted for service with the China Inland Mission. He immediately proposed to Betty by mail. He returned home to briefly visit his family and have necessary surgery on August 1.

1932, September 24—John sailed from Vancouver on the *Empress of Japan*, at last bound for China. Betty's reply didn't reach him before he left the United States.

1932, October—Betty was in Shanghai recovering from tonsillitis when John's boat docked there. They became officially engaged, with CIM approval for their marriage in a year. They parted, John going to Anking and CIM language school and Betty to her post at Fowyang.

1932, December—John wrote to his parents about the brief occupation by communist soldiers of the school where Betty worked in Fowyang.

1933, March 25—John completed basic language training and led morning worship in Chinese for the first time.

1933, summer—John went to Suancheng, the central mission station for that region and his assigned post for extended training. He began work immediately, filling in for the vacationing mission director, George A. Birch.

1933, October—John and Betty met at her parents' home in Tsinan and made final wedding preparations after their year-long separation.

1933, October 25—John and Betty were married. (Of their 200 guests, 140 of them were Chinese Christians.) Their two-week honeymoon was in Betty's childhood home of Tsingtao.

1934, February—The Stams did a twenty-four-day preaching and walking tour through rugged terrain. A primary stop was Tsingteh (60 miles from Suancheng), which was to be their parish at the end of their training period. They met Evangelist Lo who would be John's Chinese assistant.

1934, September 11—Helen Priscilla was born in the Methodist Hospital at Wuhu. Her Chinese name, Ai-lien, means Love Link.

1934, October—While Betty and baby Helen waited in Wuhu, John scouted out southern Anhwei Province, especially Tsingteh, to determine its safety for his family. The district magistrate assured him it was perfectly safe and free of communist threat.

1934, Late November—Stams arrived in Tsingteh and started their pioneer work.

1934, December 6—A communist army of two thousand staged a surprise attack on Tsingteh and quickly gained control of the city. The Stamses' home was raided and the couple arrested. John wrote the CIM office in Shanghai, relaying their captors' demands for $20,000 for their release. Evangelist Lo, his wife, and his son miraculously escaped arrest.

1934, December 7—Stams were marched with the communist forces to Miaosheo, twelve miles from Tsingteh, for imprisonment.

1934, December 8—John and Betty were paraded down the street of Miaosheo in their underwear. On reaching Eagle Hill outside the city, they were executed by decapitation.

1934, December 9—Helen Stam (almost three months old) was rescued by Evangelist Lo after being abandoned for thirty hours in the vacant house where her parents had been imprisoned. Lo also buried John and Betty before taking Helen and his own family to safety.

1934, December 14—Evangelist Lo, his wife, their son, and
Helen Stam arrived in Suancheng at the home of
George A. Birch, director of the central station, after a
difficult and dangerous journey. Helen was in excellent
health and was nicknamed the "Miracle Baby." She
soon went to live with her grandparents, Dr. and Mrs.
Scott, in Tsinan.

BIBLIOGRAPHY

SECTION ONE
Chapter 1 From Prodigal to Pillar—Augustine
F. L. Cross & Elizabeth A. Livingstone, eds., *Oxford Dictionary of the Christian Church* (Oxford: Oxford University Press, 1974), 108–109.

Edith Deen, *Great Women of the Christian Faith* (New York: Harper & Brothers, 1959), 21–27.

James Dobson, "With Love to Parents Who Hurt," *Christian Parenting*, Sept./Oct. 1989, 70–72. Excerpted from *Parenting Isn't for Cowards* (Waco, Tex.: Word Books, 1987).

J. D. Douglas & Earle E. Cairns, eds., *New International Dictionary of the Christian Church* (Grand Rapids: Zondervan, 1978), 86–88.

Richard Foster, "The Good Life," *Christianity Today*, 11 Dec. 1987, 20–24.

Michael Marshall, *Restless Heart* (Grand Rapids: William B. Eerdmans, 1987), 42, 59–63, 67–68.

Malcolm Muggeridge, *A Third Testament* (Boston: Little, Brown & Co., 1976), 29–53.

John D. Woodbridge, ed., *Great Leaders of the Christian Church* (Chicago: Moody Press, 1988), 85–90.

Chapter 2 A House Divided—Wesley
Deen, *Great Women*, 141–149.

Rebecca Lamar Harmon, *Susanna: Mother of the Wesleys* (Nashville: Abingdon Press, 1968), 43–53, 78–80, 144–145, 158–161.

Ruth Tucker & Walter Liefeld, *Daughters of the Church* (Grand Rapids: Academie Books, Zondervan, 1987), 236–242.

Ruth A. Tucker, *First Ladies of the Parish* (Grand Rapids: Ministries Resources Library, Zondervan, 1988), 51–59.

Chapter 3 A Sea with No Shore—Schaeffer

Stephen Board, "An Evangelical Thinker Who Left His Mark," *Christianity Today*, 15 June 1984, 60–61.

Vernon C. Grounds, "A Friend Remembers Francis Schaeffer," *Christianity Today*, 15 June 1984, 61–62.

Lane T. Dennis, ed., *The Letters of Francis Schaeffer* (Westchester, Ill.: Crossway Books, 1986), 7–19, 25–28, 31–68.

James Morris, *The Preachers* (New York: St. Martins, 1973), 192–199.

Ronald W. Ruegsegger, ed., *Reflections on Francis Schaeffer* (Grand Rapids: Academie Books, Zondervan, 1986), 7–17, 45–65, 269–301.

Francis A. Schaeffer, *True Spirituality* (Wheaton: Tyndale House, 1971), preface, 153.

Woodbridge, *Great Leaders*, 361–366.

SECTION TWO
Chapter 4 In Search of Sanity—Cruden

S. Elgin Moyer, *Who Was Who in Church History* (Chicago: Moody Press, 1962), 107–108.

Edith Oliver, *The Eccentric Life of Alexander Cruden* (London: Faber & Faber Limited, 1934), 22–25, 56–67, 82–142, 217–228.

Warren Wiersbe, *Walking with the Giants* (Grand Rapids: Baker, 1976), 247–253.

Philip Yancey, "Good News about Loneliness," *Charisma*, Mar. 1980, 51–57. Excerpted from *Unhappy Secrets of the Christian Life* (Grand Rapids: Zondervan, 1978).

Chapter 5 Fainthearted Soldiers—Spurgeon

Arnold Dallimore, *C. H. Spurgeon* (Chicago: Moody Press, 1984), 69–72, 186–187.

Richard E. Day, *The Shadow of the Broad Brim* (Philadelphia, Judson Press, 1934), 96.

W. Y. Fullerton, *Charles H. Spurgeon* (Chicago: Moody Press, 1966), 80–89.

Charles H. Spurgeon, *Spurgeon at His Best*, compiled by Tom Carter (Grand Rapids: Baker, 1988).

———, "Songs in the Night," *Decision*, July 1973, 10, 13.

Elmer L. Towns, *The Christian Hall of Fame* (Grand Rapids: Baker, 1971), 126–128.

Sherwood E. Wirt, ed., *Great Reading from Decision* (Minneapolis: World Wide, 1960), 143–150.

Woodbridge, *Great Leaders*, 334–338.

Chapter 6 The Ultimate Shame—Roseveare

Morton Bard & Dawn Sangrey, *The Crime Victim's Book* (New York: Basic Books, Inc., 1979), 47, 89–99.

Linda Braswell, *Quest for Respect* (Ventura, Calif.: Pathfinder Press, 1989), 3–13, 42–59.

Alan Burgess, *Daylight Must Come* (New York: Delacorte Press, 1974), 3–56, 243–251.

Helen Roseveare, *He Gave Us a Valley* (Downers Grove, Ill: InterVarsity Press, 1976), 24–41.

———, *Living Faith* (Chicago: Moody Press, 1981).

———, *Living Sacrifice* (Chicago: Moody Press, 1979), 20–26.

———, "The Cost of Loving Jesus," *Christianity Today*, 12 May 1989, 45.

———, "Seeds of Bitterness," *World Christian*, May/June 1984, 20–21. Excerpted from *Give Me This Mountain* (Downers Grove, Ill.: InterVarsity Press, 1966).

———, "Counting the Cost," *World Christian*, Nov./Dec. 1986, 36–39. Excerpted from *Declare His Glory among the Nations,* ed. David M. Howard (Downers Grove, Ill.: InterVarsity Press, 1977).

Ruth A. Tucker, *Guardians of the Great Commission* (Grand Rapids: Academie Books, Zondervan, 1988), 232–235.

SECTION THREE
Chapter 7 Crucified with Christ—Pascal

Morris Bishop, *Pascal, The Life of Genius* (Westport, Conn.: Greenwood Press, 1968), 40–47, 135–141, 166–182, 307–349.

Emile Cailliet, *Pascal* (New York: Harper & Brothers, 1961), 149–151, 340–345.

Douglas & Cairns, *New International Dictionary,* 76–77, 524.

Roger Hazelton, *Blaise Pascal, The Genius of His Thought* (Philadelphia: Westminster Press, 1974), 46–50, 140–145, 172–175.

Jean Mesnard, *Pascal* (Tuscaloosa, Ala.: University of Alabama Press, 1969), 11–20.

Malcolm Muggeridge, *A Third Testament* (Boston: Little, Brown & Co., 1976), 55–83.

Woodbridge, *Great Leaders,* 257–260.

Elliot Wright, *Holy Company* (New York: Macmillan, 1980), 183–187.

Chapter 8 Eyes of the Heart—Crosby

Deen, *Great Women,* 306–307.

Edward T. James, ed., *Notable American Women 1607–1950,* vol. 1 (Cambridge: Belknap Press of Harvard University Press, 1971), 411–412.

Bernard Ruffin, *Fanny Crosby* (Westwood, N.J.: Barbour & Co., Inc., 1976).

Diana Schneider, "Songs in the Night," *Christian Herald,* Sept. 1984, 37–39.

Leslie K. Tarr, "Fanny Crosby," *Decision,* Mar. 1990, 23–24.

Tucker & Liefeld, *Daughters,* 257.

Chapter 9 Streams in the Desert—Cowman

Bruce Barron, *The Health & Wealth Gospel: A Fresh Look at Healing, Prosperity & Positive Confession* (Downers Grove: InterVarsity Press, 1987).

Lettie B. Cowman, *Charles E. Cowman, Missionary Warrior* (Los Angeles: Oriental Missionary Society, 1928), 180–181, 242–243, 327–359, 376–385.

Edward & Esther Erny, *No Guarantee But God* (Greenwood, Ind.: OMS International, Inc., 1969), 1–22, 63–97.

B.H. Pearson, *The Vision Lives* (Greenwood, Ind.: OMS International, Inc., 1972), 55–72.

Lewis B. Smedes, ed., *Ministry and the Miraculous* (Pasadena: Fuller Theological Seminary, 1987), 11, 22, 28, 37–38, 51–53, 76, 78–79, 80–81.

Robert D. Wood, *In These Mortal Hands* (Greenwood, Ind.: OMS International, Inc., 1983), 30–33, 109–123, 317–327, 332–333 (note: entire book used for chronology).

SECTION FOUR
Chapter 10 Bound in Chains—Allen

Anne B. Allen, "A Voice Counter to Public Opinion," *The Living Church*, 11 Feb. 1990, 8–9.

Richard Allen, *The Life, Experience, and Gospel Labors of the Rt. Rev. Richard Allen* (Philadelphia: Lee & Yeocum, 1887).

Charles W. Ferguson, *Organizing to Beat the Devil* (Garden City, N.J.: Doubleday & Co., Inc., 1971), 210–217.

Clarence Walker, *A Rock in a Weary Land* (Baton Rouge: Louisiana State University Press, 1982), 4–21.

Joseph R. Washington, Jr., *Black Sects and Cults* (Garden City, N.J.: Doubleday & Co., Inc., 1972), 44–55.

Charles H. Wesley, *Richard Allen: Apostle of Freedom* (Washington, D.C.: The Associated Publishers, 1969), 36–54.

Henry J. Young, *Major Black Religious Leaders, 1755–1940* (Nashville: Abingdon, 1977), 25–40.

Chapter 11 Missionary Shipwreck—Studd/Grubb

Norman P. Grubb, *C. T. Studd* (Fort Washington, Pa.:
Christian Literature Crusade, 1985), 3–4, 150–154,
170–173, 196–211, 227–228.

———, *C. T. Studd, Cricketer & Pioneer* (Fort Washington, Pa.:
Christian Literature Crusade, 1933), 228–236.

———, *Once Caught, No Escape* (Fort Washington, Pa.:
Christian Literature Crusade, 1969), 76–87, 90–100,
109–121.

Ruth A. Tucker, *From Jerusalem to Irian Jaya* (Grand Rapids:
Academie Books, Zondervan, 1983), 263–268.

Chapter 12 Sentenced to Scrub—Aylward

Gladys Aylward as told to Christine Hunger, *Gladys Aylward,
The Little Woman* (Chicago: Moody Press, 1970), 81–102.

Ingrid Bergman & Alan Burgess, *My Story* (New York:
Delacorte, 1980), 362–363, 369, 380.

Alan Burgess, *The Small Woman* (New York: E. P. Dutton &
Co., 1957), 16–25, 198–207.

Phyllis Thompson, *A Transparent Woman* (Grand Rapids:
Zondervan, 1971), 17–24, 41–43, 68–89,186–187.

Tucker & Liefeld, *Daughters*, 327.

Tucker, *Guardians*, 179–183.

SECTION FIVE
Chapter 13 Running Ahead of the Spirit—Whitefield

Arnold Dallimore, *George Whitefield*, vol. 2 (Westchester, Ill.:
Crossway Books, 1980), 166–169, 471–473, 520–523,
534–535.

John Pollock, *George Whitefield and the Great Awakening*
(Tring, Herts, England: Lion, 1972), 187–189,
204–208, 256.

Herman H. Riffel, *Voice of God* (Wheaton, Ill.: Tyndale House,
1971), 103–114, 125–137, 139–148.

John White, *The Fight* (Downers Grove, Ill.: InterVarsity
    Press, 1976), 153–177.
Woodbridge, *Great Leaders*, 295–300.

Chapter 14 Out of the Ashes—Moody
John Ellsworth Day, *Bush Aglow* (Philadelphia: Judson Press,
    1936), 105–117, 128–139, 143–148.
Deen, *Great Women*, 403–404.
V. Raymond Edman, *They Found the Secret* (Grand Rapids:
    Zondervan, 1960), 73–78.
James F. Findlay, Jr., *Dwight L. Moody, American Evangelist*
    (Chicago: University of Chicago Press, 1969), 92–99,
    128–135, 175, 218–220.
D. G. Kehl, "Burnout: The Risk of Reaching Too High,"
    Christianity Today, 20 Nov. 1980, 26–28.
William R. Moody, *The Life of Dwight L. Moody* (New York:
    Fleming H. Revell, 1900), 40–47, 146–151.
J. C. Pollock, *Moody* (New York: Macmillan, 1963), 81–101,
    212–213.
Tucker, *First Ladies*, 121–129.
Warren Wiersbe, *Listening to the Giants* (Grand Rapids: Baker,
    1980), 311–316.
Woodbridge, *Great Leaders*, 339–342.

Chapter 15 Night without Morning—Marshall
Garrett J. DeWeese, "The Silence of God," *Discipleship
    Journal*, no. 27, 1985, 12–16.
William Gurnall, *The Christian in Complete Armor*, vol. 1
    (Edinburgh: Banner of Truth Trust, 1986).
Janet Wilson James, ed., *Women in American Religion*
    (Philadelphia: University of Pennsylvania Press, 1980),
    253–271.
C. S. Lewis, *The Problem of Pain* (New York: Macmillan, 1962).
H. Charles Lippy, *Twentieth Century Shaper of American*

Popular Religion (Westport, Conn.: Greenwood Press, 1989), 283–291.

Catherine Marshall, *Something More* (New York: McGraw-Hill, 1974), 1–18, 44–51, 133–136.

Martha Thatcher, "Hearing God's Voice," *Discipleship Journal*, no. 37, 1987, 43–46.

Tucker, *First Ladies*, 147–157.

SECTION SIX
Chapter 16 A Grain of Wheat—Brainerd

David Brainerd, *Life and Diary of David Brainerd*, ed. Jonathan Edwards (Grand Rapids: Baker, 1981).

Elisabeth D. Dodds, *Marriage to a Difficult Man* (Philadelphia: Westminster Press, 1971), 114–129.

Russell T. Hitt, ed., *Heroic Colonial Christians* (Philadelphia: J. B. Lippincott Co., 1966), 151–203.

Moyer, *Who Was Who*, 55.

Iain H. Murray, *Jonathan Edwards: A New Biography* (Edinburgh: The Banner of Truth Trust, 1987), 300–310.

Paul Tournier, *Creative Suffering* (San Francisco: Harper & Row, 1981), 1–38.

Tucker, *From Jerusalem*, 91–93.

Chapter 17 The Fellowship of Suffering—Vins

"An Interview with Georgi Vins," *Eternity*, Aug. 1979, 21–23.

James & Marti Hefley, *By Their Blood* (Milford, Mich.: Mott Media, 1979), 243–257.

Barbara Hitching, "Valiant in Life and Death," *Moody Monthly*, Nov. 1985, 62–64.

Ellen Santilli Vaughn, "In Solitary Cells on Winter Nights," *Christianity Today*, 15 Dec. 1989, 26–29.

Georgi Vins, "Babushka, Friend of the Prisoners," *Prisoners Bulletin*, Summer 1985, 4–6.

———, "Seven Years of Freedom," *Prisoners Bulletin*, Summer 1986, 2–3.

———, *Testament from Prison*, trans. Jane Ellis, ed. Michael Bourdeaux (Elgin, Ill.: David C. Cook, 1975).

Correspondence with Natasha & Georgi Vins, Russian Gospel Ministries International, Inc., P.O. Box 1188, Elkhart, IN 46515.

Chapter 18 To Die Is Gain—Stam

Lloyd H. Ahlem, *Do I Have to Be Me?* (Glendale, Calif.: Regal Books, 1973), 93–105.

Chuck Colson, "Is Nothing Worth Dying For?" *Good News*, Mar./Apr. 1989, 22–25.

E. Schuyler English, *By Life and By Death* (Grand Rapids: Zondervan, 1938): 14, 20, 26, 34, 36, 46, 54, 56–61.

L. Mary Hammack, *A Dictionary of Women in Church History* (Chicago: Moody Bible Institute, 1984), 138.

Hefley & Hefley, *By Their Blood*, 55–59.

"Martyrdom: the Most Potent Factor in World Evangelization," *World Pulse*, 7 July 1989, 5.

Mrs. Howard Taylor, *The Triumph of John and Betty Stam* (Philadelphia: China Inland Mission, 1936), 35, 46–47, 51–52, 54–56, 60, 70–71, 92–94, 97–129 (note: also used for chronology).

CPSIA information can be obtained
at www.ICGtesting.com
Printed in the USA
BVHW041257231122
652652BV00004B/188